Photography and the Law

Photographers and publishers of photographs enjoy a wide range of legal rights including freedom of expression and of publication. They have a right to create and publish photographs. They may invoke their intellectual, moral and property rights to protect and enforce their rights in their created and/or published works. These rights are not absolute. This book analyses the various legal restrictions and prohibitions which may affect these rights.

Photography and the Law investigates the legal limitations faced by professional and amateur photographers and photograph publishers under Irish, UK and EU law. Through an in-depth discussion of the personal rights of the public, including the right not to be harassed, the book gives a clear analysis of the current legal standpoint on the relationship between privacy and freedom of expression. Additionally, the book looks at the reconciliation of photographers' rights with the state's interest in public security and defence, alongside the enforcement of ethical and moral codes. Comparative legal standing in the European Union is used as a springboard to further analyse Irish and UK statutes and case law, including recent reforms and current proposals for future change. The book ends with pertinent suggestions for the necessary reforms and enactments required to rebalance the relationship between the personal rights of individuals, the state's duties and the protection of photographers' and photograph publishers' rights.

By clearly explaining the theoretical and conceptual reasoning behind the current law, alongside proposed reforms, the book will be a useful tool for any student or academic interested in photography law, privacy and media law, alongside professional and amateur photographers and photograph publishers.

Michael O'Flanagan was awarded a Ph.D. in Law by the National University of Ireland Galway for his doctoral research on the topic 'Taking and Publishing Photographs: The Legal Rights and Restrictions'. His research work was funded by the University's School of Law's R.D.J. Glynn Doctoral Research Fellowship. Prior to undertaking his Ph.D., he graduated from the University of Limerick with a Bachelor of Laws (Hons.), a Bachelor of Business Studies (specialising in Marketing Management) and a Diploma in Business Studies (specialising in Personnel Management). He was also awarded a Graduateship of the Marketing Institute of Ireland. A Licentiate of the Irish Professional Photographers' & Videographers' Association and a freelance photographer member of the National Union of Journalists, to-date he has won 71 awards (5 Gold, 45 Silver and 21 Bronze Awards) for his photographic work at the Irish Professional Photographers' & Videographers' Association's Annual Photographer of the Year Awards. The creation and implementation of national and international advertising, promotional and public relations campaigns featuring high-quality photographs has formed an integral element of his marketing management experience over the past four decades.

Routledge Research in Media Law

Available titles in this series include

Public Service Broadcasting 3.0
Legal Design for the Digital Present
Mira Burri

Forthcoming titles

Journalists, Anonymous Sources and the Law
A Comparative, Theoretical and Critical Analysis
Damian Carney

Public Service Media and the Law
Theory and Practice in Europe
Karen Donders

Photography and the Law
Rights and Restrictions
Michael O'Flanagan

Photography and the Law

Rights and Restrictions

Michael O'Flanagan

Routledge
Taylor & Francis Group
LONDON AND NEW YORK

First published 2019
by Routledge
2 Park Square, Milton Park, Abingdon, Oxon OX14 4RN

and by Routledge
52 Vanderbilt Avenue, New York, NY 10017

First issued in paperback 2020

Routledge is an imprint of the Taylor & Francis Group, an informa business

British Library Cataloguing-in-Publication Data
A catalogue record for this book is available from the British Library

Library of Congress Cataloging-in-Publication Data
Names: O'Flanagan, Michael (Photographer)
Title: Photography and the law : rights and restrictions / Michael O'Flanagan.
Description: New York, NY : Routledge, 2019. | Series: Routledge research in media law
Identifiers: LCCN 2018033981 | ISBN 9781138604773 (hbk)
Subjects: LCSH: Photography—Law and legislation.
Classification: LCC K3778 .O35 2019 | DDC 344/.097—dc23
LC record available at https://lccn.loc.gov/2018033981

ISBN 13: 978-0-367-58411-5 (pbk)
ISBN 13: 978-1-138-60477-3 (hbk)

Typeset in Galliard
by Apex CoVantage, LLC

Contents

Table of cases

Ireland

United Kingdom

Court of Justice of the European Union

European Court of Human Rights

Table of legislation

Ireland

Constitution of Ireland

Acts of the Oireachtas

Bills of the Oireachtas

Statutory instruments

Bye-laws

Rules of Court

United Kingdom

Acts of Parliament

Statutory instruments

Miscellaneous legal agreements

European Union

International conventions and treaties

1 Introduction

This book offers an original perspective on the legal rights of still photographers and photograph publishers in Ireland to take and/or publish still photographs and on the legal restrictions and/or prohibitions, which either are or may be imposed on such rights. For comparative purposes, an analysis of the applicable law in the United Kingdom is also offered by the author. Particular attention has been paid to developments in law and policy occurring at EU and Council of Europe levels.

The creation and publication of a still photograph are two separate, but related, activities. A still photograph may be published either by the individual who created the photograph (the photographer) or by a third party, such as a newspaper publisher. The book focuses exclusively on the law relating to still photography and the publication of still photographs. It does not extend to encompass movie photography. Although this book discusses the law as applicable to professional still photographers and still photograph publishers, the same legal rules and principles apply equally to amateur photographers and photograph publishers.

The book investigates the legal rights of photographers and photograph publishers to take and publish photographs. Photographers and photograph publishers enjoy a wide range of legal rights including fundamental rights. They have the right of freedom of expression (particularly artistic and commercial expression) and the freedom of publication. Specifically, they have the right to create and publish photographs. They also have intellectual, moral and property rights including the right to protect their rights in their created and/or published works. These rights are guaranteed through constitutional provisions; statutory law; European Union Law and the Charter of Fundamental Rights; as a consequence of court judgements; and through international treaties and conventions.

The over-arching right of photographers and photograph publishers to freedom of expression and the main vehicle for the implementation in practice of that right by them, namely through copyright law, is examined. The book identifies and examines photographers' rights under copyright law, how copyright law protects those rights and the remedies available under copyright law to the owners of the copyright in photographs against the infringement of those rights. It investigates whether, how and the extent, if any, to which photographers and publishers' rights under copyright law are being eroded and whether those rights should be further protected and enforced.

The legal rights of photographers and photograph publishers are not absolute. They may compete with the legal personal rights of others, such as one's right to privacy, the right to one's good name, the right to a fair trial and property rights. This book identifies and investigates these competing legal rights and how the courts balance such rights. Legal restrictions and/or prohibitions may be placed upon photographers' and photograph publishers' rights, as a consequence of, for example, the protection and enforcement of the legal, personal rights of others, and of the state's duty to maintain public order; to protect the security and defence of the state; to prevent and/or to investigate crime, and to protect public morals. The book investigates such various restrictions and prohibitions. In addition, ethical codes of behaviour, which may result in restrictions being imposed on photographers' and photograph publishers' legal rights, are also explored.

The book investigates the nature and scope of the legal interplay between photographers' and photograph publishers' rights, responsibilities and restrictions, the extent of this interplay and how such might be categorised. It also investigates how the legal rights enjoyed by photographers and publishers of photographs in Ireland and the responsibilities and restrictions placed upon them compare to the situation in other selected legal jurisdictions and in particular in the United Kingdom. The author questions how and the extent to which opportunities arising from developments in communication technologies pose challenges and threats to existing legal rights of photographers (including e-privacy – one's right to privacy online), their clients, the public and the traditional media and how such competing interests currently are and should be regulated and balanced.

A number of recommendations are offered by the author which would strengthen the protection and enforcement of photographers' and photograph publishers' existing legal rights – particularly their rights under copyright law. The author also recommends the enactment of statutory provisions concerning some specific personal rights of individuals, including, for example, the right to privacy and the right not to be harassed by photographers and photograph publishers.

Moving on from Chapter 1, Chapter 2 examines the theoretical and conceptual basis of the legal rules, principles and doctrines from and upon which the various types of rights and restrictions applicable to photographers and photograph publishers has been developed. Having considered rights as a concept and the origin and types of rights that exist, it identifies and examines the foundation of the legal right to take and publish photographs. Central to this examination is the right of freedom of expression and particularly the rights of artistic and commercial expression. The chapter goes on to investigate photographers' and photograph publishers' rights granted under the Constitution of Ireland, statutory provisions, international conventions and treaties and as recognised by the common law.

Having discussed the over-arching right of photographers and photograph publishers to freedom of expression in Chapter 2, Chapter 3 focuses on the main vehicle for the implementation, in practice, of that right by photographers' and photograph publishers', namely through copyright law. It identifies and examines photographers' and publishers' rights under copyright law. It also examines how copyright law protects those rights and the remedies available under copyright law to the owners of the copyright in photographs against infringers of their rights under copyright. It investigates the legal exceptions to those rights. The chapter examines whether, how and the extent, if any, to which photographers' and publishers' rights under copyright law are either being eroded and whether those rights should be further protected and enforced.

Photographers' and publishers' legal rights to take and publish photographs are not absolute rights. Such rights may be legally restricted in order to protect the guaranteed, legal rights of others. Chapter 4 examines the range of legal personal rights, which frequently come into contention with the rights of photographers and photograph publishers, including the individual's right to privacy, the right not to be harassed, the right to one's good name, the right to be forgotten and private property rights. The chapter also examines the concept of individuals having a legal right over their personal images and a right of publicity.

In addition to the legal restrictions that may be imposed on the legal rights of photographers as a consequence of the protection and enforcement of the rights of other individuals, restrictions may also be placed on photographers' and photograph publishers' rights as a result of the state undertaking its legally required duties. The state has a duty to maintain public order, to protect the security and defence of the state and its citizens; to prevent, investigate and prosecute criminal activity and to protect the administration of justice. Its duties also extend to the protection of public morality. Chapter 5 investigates how and the extent to which these various duties, as placed upon and exercised by the state, may restrict the rights of photographers and photograph publishers. Other restrictions on the activities of photographers may result from a variety of statutory provisions, such as those designed to protect wildlife, or due to the terms of contracts or accreditation schemes. In addition, the rights of photographers and photograph publishers to take and/or publish photographs may also be restricted on ethical grounds. Ethical standards or codes of behaviour as implemented by a range of organisations, such as the Press Council of Ireland, may result in the restriction of photographers' and photograph publishers' rights. Chapter 5 examines the various codes of practice, which have a direct relevance to, and impact on, the activities and work practices of photographers and photograph publishers.

In Chapter 6, the author offers his overall conclusions and makes a number of recommendations for legislative changes relating to the legal protection and enforcement of photographers' and photograph publishers' rights and also the rights of third-party individuals.

2 The legal rights of photographers and photograph publishers

2.1) Introduction

The creation and publication of still photographs are two distinct, but related activities. Photographers and photograph publishers enjoy a range of legal rights which are derived both directly and indirectly from a number of sources at the global, European, European Union and national levels, international treaties and conventions, the Constitution of Ireland, statutory legislation and the common law. Through their application of constitutional, statutory or common law, the courts have recognised the legal right of individuals to both take and publish photographs. However, these legally recognised rights are not absolute and they may be restricted either by legislative provisions or by the courts when they are balancing the rights of photographers and photograph publishers with the competing rights of others. Underlying the rights of photographers and photograph publishers to take and/or publish photographs is the right of freedom of expression, including its sub-sets – the right of artistic expression and the right of commercial expression.

Chapter 2 examines how the right of freedom of expression and the rights of photographers and photograph publishers have developed in Ireland and how such development has been both influenced and contributed to by Ireland's participation in international affairs at global, European and European Union levels. Prior to doing so, it is firstly of benefit to briefly consider the origin, types of and justification for rights and how this relates to the rights of photographers and photograph publishers in practice.

2.2) Rights: their origin and types

A right is a power or an authority possessed by one person with a correlating duty placed upon other person(s) to respect that power or authority. Some duties, but not all, have correlating rights. Rights are generally viewed as having two distinct origins, namely those which exist under natural law (natural rights) and those which have been created under positive law (man-made rights). The status of natural law has been recognised by positive law – for example through the Constitution of Ireland, which states: 'The State acknowledges that man, in virtue of his rational being, has the natural right, antecedent to positive law, to the private ownership of personal goods.'[1] People possess numerous rights across a broad range of issues and rights may be grouped under a number of headings, namely civil; political; social, economic and cultural; personal, human rights and fundamental rights. The importance of the status of fundamental or basis rights is recognised by the Constitution of Ireland, which guarantees a variety of fundamental rights.[2] Fundamental rights are protected by the courts. As will be shown later in this and the subsequent chapters of the book, a number of these categories of rights could apply to photographers' rights. For example, the central right of photographers – freedom of expression – can be categorised as both a fundamental right (it is necessary in a democracy), a personal right (it belongs to everyone) and a public/political right (it contributes to public debate). Also, copyright, which is an important safeguard for photographers' artistic and commercial ventures, can be categorised as both an intellectual property and a private property right; a personal right (the right to artistic expression and the right to a livelihood), an economic right (to be recompensed for one's artistic creations) and a socio-political or cultural right (to enable the public to enjoy a created artistic work). Together with the property and economic rights under copyright law, photographers also have moral rights in their works.

2.3) Right of freedom of expression

The term "freedom of expression" embraces the right to ask or search for, to receive and/or to communicate to others ideas, opinions or information through any medium of communication without restriction. Speech is one of the many methods of communication and the term 'freedom of speech'[3] is frequently used as a synonym for freedom of expression. Publishing is an enabler of the right of free speech, as are the creation and publication of photographs. If freedom of expression is not permitted within a society, then its members will be prevented from discovering and/or communicating to others information and opinions relating to any particular issue without being hindered. While the permitting of free speech will not guarantee that the truth about a particular matter will be discovered and/or communicated, neither will its restriction. However, the unrestricted exercise of the rights of freedom of speech and of expression on the premise that such rights are being exercised may result in harm being caused to others. Examples of such harm could include the infringement of a photographer's copyright in his/her created works; the creation and/or publication of photographs, which infringe the privacy or property rights of

1 Constitution of Ireland *(Art. 43.1.1°)* (on Private Property)
2 Constitution of Ireland, *Arts. 40–44* (on Fundamental Rights)
3 For a discussion of theories on freedom of speech, see Eric Barendt, *Freedom of Speech* (2nd edn, Oxford University Press 2005)

others, the incitement of hatred towards individuals or groups within society and the undue influencing of individuals through false or misrepresentative advertising.

2.4) Development of photographers' and photograph publishers' rights

Ireland's participation in international affairs at the global, European and European Union levels and its ratification of international conventions and treaties has both influenced and contributed to the development of rights in general in Ireland and specifically the right of freedom of expression. The right of freedom of expression is the core right upon which photographers' and photograph publishers' rights are founded. It is therefore the focus of the following sections, which briefly trace its origin and development and identify the key principles that have emerged in relation to freedom of expression.

2.4.1) Universal Declaration of Human Rights, the International Covenant on Civil and Political Rights and the International Covenant on Economic, Social and Cultural Rights

The Universal Declaration of Human Rights details a wide range of rights of individuals, which the United Nations has classified as being fundamental rights. Included among these are the right to freedom of opinion and expression and the right of authors to the protection of their moral and material interests in their scientific, literary or artistic creations.[4] The Declaration is not binding on member states of the United Nations. It is purely a declaration – an announcement. It sets out the fundamental or basic rights, which should be enjoyed by people and how, in an ideal world, states should treat people while they enjoy those rights. However, subsequent to the adoption of the Declaration, two covenants, namely the International Covenant on Civil and Political Rights (hereinafter "ICCPR")[5] and its two optional protocols[6] and the International

4 United Nations, *The Universal Declaration of Human Rights*, arts 19 and 27 <www.un.org/en/universal-declaration-human-rights/index.html> accessed 28 March 2018

5 United Nations, Office of the High Commissioner for Human Rights, *International Covenant on Civil and Political Rights* <www.ohchr.org/en/professionalinterest/pages/ccpr.aspx> accessed 28 March 2018

6 United Nations, Office of the High Commissioner for Human Rights, *Optional Protocol to the International Covenant on Civil and Political Rights* <www.ohchr.org/EN/ProfessionalInterest/Pages/OPCCPR1.aspx> accessed 28 March 2018 and United Nations, Office of the High Commissioner for Human Rights, *Second Optional Protocol to the International Covenant on Civil and Political Rights, Aiming at the Abolition of the Death Penalty* <www.ohchr.org/EN/ProfessionalInterest/Pages/2ndOPCCPR.aspx> accessed 28 March 2018

Covenant on Economic, Social and Cultural Rights (hereinafter "the ICESCR")[7] and its Optional Protocol[8] were adopted by the General Assembly of the United Nations. These two covenants and the optional protocols are legally binding on member states, which have signed and ratified them. The individual articles of the Universal Declaration are the foundation stones and guiding principles of the articles contained within these two covenants. In essence, these two covenants give legal effect to the contents of the articles of the Declaration. For one to freely enjoy the rights enshrined in the ICCPR and the ICESCR, two essential requirements are the right to hold opinions and beliefs and the right of freedom of expression. If one may not freely hold and express opinions and beliefs, then one's ability to enjoy or enforce one's other fundamental rights or to have them upheld is completely restricted and is virtually an impossible task. Also, without the right of freedom of expression it would not be possible to freely promote an awareness and understanding of the existence of the other fundamental rights available under the Universal Declaration, the ICCPR and the ICESCR. The importance of the right of freedom of information was highlighted during the first session of the General Assembly of the United Nations in December 1946, when it passed Resolution 59(1).[9] The view that freedom of information is the "cornerstone" of the international human rights legal system was advanced in the preamble to Resolution 59(1). That assertion has been re-affirmed and given international legal effect through both the ICCPR and the ICESCR. Freedom of expression is the indispensable enabling element of freedom of information and the positioning of the right of freedom of expression as the cornerstone or touchstone of all human rights has gained currency. References to such are frequently made at both an international[10] and an Irish national level[11] in comments and discussions on freedom of the media. The right of freedom of information or the right to have access to records held by public bodies as a corollary to the right of freedom of expression has been given

7 United Nations, Office of the High Commissioner for Human Rights, *International Covenant on Economic, Social and Cultural Rights* <www.ohchr.org/en/professionalinterest/pages/cescr.aspx> accessed 28 March 2018

8 United Nations, Office of the High Commissioner for Human Rights, *Optional Protocol to the International Covenant on Civil and Political Rights* <www.ohchr.org/EN/Professional Interest/Pages/OPCCPR1.aspx> accessed 28 March 2018

9 United Nations, General Assembly, Resolutions Adopted by the General Assembly During its First Session, *Calling of an International Conference on Freedom of Information* Res 59(1) <www.un.org/documents/ga/res/1/ares1.htm> accessed 28 March 2018

10 For example, see United Nations Human Rights Committee, *General Comment No. 34 on Article 19 of the International Covenant on Civil and Political Rights* (on Freedom of Expression) CCPR/C/GC/34, para 13 (Geneva, 12 September 2011) <www2.ohchr.org/english/bodies/hrc/docs/gc34.pdf> accessed 28 March 2018

11 For example, see Dáil Éireann, Debate on Human Rights Issues: Dáil Deb 10 November 2011, vol 746 col 318 <http://oireachtasdebates.oireachtas.ie/debates%20authoring/DebatesWebPack.nsf/takes/dail2011111000046?opendocument> accessed 28 March 2018

legal effect in numerous countries. For example, in Ireland this right has been legally granted through the Freedom of Information Act 1997,[12] as amended. However, this right is not an absolute right and is subject to restrictions permitted by the Act in support of other interests, primarily privacy-related.

In relation to the ICCPR and the ICESCR, Art. 19 of the ICCPR, which deals with the right of freedom of expression, and Art. 15 of the ICESCR, which concerns both one's right to participate in cultural life and the right to the protection of one's moral and material interests in one's authored works, are of primary importance. Under Art. 19 of the ICCPR,[13] the right of freedom of expression encompasses the right to freely look for, to obtain and/or to communicate information and ideas through any medium. The Art. 19 right of freedom of expression is not absolute. But, under Art. 19, it may only be subject to restrictions, which are provided for in law and which are necessary for a number of stated purposes including the protection of the rights of others and for maintenance and protection of national security and public order. The United Nations' Office of the High Commissioner for Human Rights' Human Rights Committee[14] comprises independent experts, who perform a number of functions in relation to the operation of the ICCPR. Such functions include the monitoring of the implementation of the ICCPR by States Parties that have ratified it; the examination of States Parties' reports on their implementation of the ICCPR and the production of recommendation comments on such reports and the examination of both inter-state complaints under Art. 41 of the ICCPR and individual complaints under the First Protocol to the ICCPR. Under Art. 1 of the First Protocol, States Parties to it recognise the Committee's authority to consider complaints from individuals, who claim that their rights enumerated in the ICCPR have been violated by a States Party.[15] The Protocol permits individuals who claim that any of their ICCPR-enumerated rights have been violated by a States Party and who have exhausted all available domestic remedies, to lodge a written complaint for consideration by the Human Rights Committee.[16] In relation to the ICESCR, similar provisions exist under Articles 1

12 Freedom of Information Act 1997, s 6
Note: The Freedom of Information Act 1997 and its amending Act (Freedom of Information (Amendment) Act 2003) were both entirely repealed by the Freedom of Information Act 2014. The previously mentioned right of access to records held by public bodies persists under Section 11 of the 2014 Act.

13 United Nations, Office of the High Commissioner for Human Rights, *International Covenant on Civil and Political Rights*, art 19 <www.ohchr.org/en/professionalinterest/pages/ccpr.aspx> accessed 28 March 2018

14 United Nations, Office of the High Commissioner for Human Rights, *Human Rights Committee* <www.ohchr.org/EN/HRBodies/CCPR/Pages/CCPRIntro.aspx> accessed 28 March 2018

15 United Nations, Office of the High Commissioner for Human Rights, *Optional Protocol to the International Covenant on Civil and Political Rights*, art 1 <www.ohchr.org/EN/ProfessionalInterest/Pages/OPCCPR1.aspx> accessed 28 March 2018

16 ibid art 2

and 2 of the Optional Protocol to the ICESCR, which permit the Committee on Social, Cultural and Economic Rights to consider complaints made by individuals or groups claiming a violation of their rights under the ICESCR by a States Party to the Protocol.[17]

Under General Comment No. 34 of the Human Rights Committee on Art. 19 of the ICCPR (on Freedom of Expression), any restrictions imposed on the right of freedom of expression by States Parties must be provided for by law. Also, restrictions must have a necessary legitimate purpose and they must be proportionate to the aims for which they are introduced.[18] Furthermore, there is a duty on States Parties to ensure that any imposed restrictions are proportionate not only in the laws providing for their introduction and implementation, but also in how they are applied both administratively and judicially.[19] The drafters of the General Comment comprehended that in certain circumstances it may be necessary to restrict the freedom of journalists to report on certain events or from certain places as a consequence of the implementation of journalist accreditation systems by event organisers. However, the General Comment stated that any systems for the licensing of journalists by States Parties are not in keeping with the provisions of Art. 19(3) of the ICCPR.[20] In view of the fact that communications technologies have substantially developed and expanded since the time of the adoption of the ICCPR, it is interesting to note that subsequent to the publication of General Comment No. 34 in 2011, the United Nations Human Rights Council, in July 2012, adopted Resolution No. 20/8, which deals with the promotion, protection and enjoyment of human rights on the Internet. Article 1 of the Resolution, concerning freedom of expression online, provides that individuals have the right to enjoy the same rights online as those which they enjoy offline.[21]

Closely linked to the right of freedom of expression are the rights granted through Art. 15 of the ICESCR, which deals with socio-economic rights. These rights have a clear significance to photographers. Among the rights granted under Art. 15 is the right of everyone to take part in cultural life. From a

17 United Nations, Office of the High Commissioner for Human Rights, *Optional Protocol to the International Covenant on Economic, Cultural and Social Rights*, arts 1–2 <www.ohchr.org/EN/ProfessionalInterest/Pages/OPCESCR.aspx> accessed 28 March 2018

18 United Nations, Office of the High Commissioner for Human Rights, Human Rights Committee, *General Comment No. 34 on Article 19 of the International Covenant on Civil and Political Rights* (on Freedom of Expression) CCPR/C/GC/34, paras 33–34 (Geneva, 12 September 2011) <www2.ohchr.org/english/bodies/hrc/docs/gc34.pdf> accessed 28 March 2018

19 ibid para 34

20 ibid para 44

21 United Nations, Office of the High Commissioner for Human Rights, Human Rights Council Resolutions, *Resolution 20/8: The promotion, protection and enjoyment of human rights on the Internet*, art 1 (A/HRC/RES/20/8) (Geneva, 16 July 2012) <http://ap.ohchr.org/documents/dpage_e.aspx?si=A/HRC/RES/20/8> accessed 28 March 2018

photographer's perspective, participation in cultural life could embrace a wide range of activities varying from educating one's self on the various aspects of one's culture to the creation, display and/or publication of photographs of the cultural life of one's society. For one to freely perform any or all of these types of activities requires that one has a right of freedom of expression. Article 15 also states that the authors of scientific, literary and artistic works have the right to the protection of their moral and material interests in their works.[22] General Comment No. 17 of the Committee on Economic, Social and Cultural Rights on Art. 15(1)(c) of the ICESCR concerned the right of everyone to benefit from the protection of the moral and material interests resulting from any scientific, literary or artistic production of which he or she is the author. In this General Comment, in 2005, the Committee differentiated between the right granted under Art. 15(1)(c) and intellectual property rights granted under other international intellectual property treaties and national intellectual property legal regimes by categorising the right granted under Art. 15 as a *human right.*[23] The Committee regarded this human right as being timeless. Yes, a human right could be said to be timeless and this distinction is important both in theory and in the realisation of human rights in general. However, the time-limited intellectual property rights available to photographers and photograph publishers are of immense practical importance to them to on a day-to-day basis.

2.4.2) Council of Europe Convention for the Protection of Human Rights and Fundamental Freedoms

The provisions of the Council of Europe Convention for the Protection of Human Rights and Fundamental Freedoms (sometimes referred to as the European Convention on Human Rights) (hereinafter "ECHR") have been incorporated into Irish law, at a sub-constitutional level, through the European Convention on Human Rights Act 2003, as amended.[24] The right of freedom of expression is guaranteed by Art. 10(1) of the ECHR states:

22 United Nations, Office of the High Commissioner for Human Rights, *International Covenant on Economic, Social and Cultural Rights*, art 15 <www.ohchr.org/EN/ProfessionalInterest/Pages/CESCR.aspx> accessed 28 March 2018

23 United Nations, Office of the High Commissioner for Human Rights, Committee on Economic, Social and Cultural Rights, *General Comment No. 17: Article 15(1)(c) – Right of Everyone to Benefit From the Protection of the Moral and Material Interests Resulting From Any Scientific, Literary or Artistic Production of Which He or She Is the Author*, para 2, introduction and basic principles para 2 (E/C.12/GC/17) (Geneva, 12 January 2006) <http://tbinternet.ohchr.org/_layouts/treatybodyexternal/TBSearch.aspx?Lang=en&TreatyID=9&DocTypeID=11> accessed 28 March 2018

24 European Convention on Human Rights Act 2003, sch 1
Note: In the United Kingdom, the provisions of the Convention were given statutory legal effect through their incorporation in the Human Rights Act 1998.

> Everyone has the right to freedom of expression. This right shall include freedom to hold opinions and to receive and impart information and ideas without interference by public authority and regardless of frontiers. This Article shall not prevent States from requiring the licensing of broadcasting, television or cinema enterprises.[25]

It is noticeable, that while the latter part of Art. 10(1) makes provision for the licensing of specified forms of media, it does not do so in respect of the print media, which in 1950s Europe would have been the dominant sector of communications media, but mainly in private hands rather than the responsibility of, and subject to, licensing by the state. Freedom of expression through the print and other organs of the media may be subject to restrictions, which States Parties may impose in accordance with Art. 10(2) of the ECHR.[26] The exercise of the legal restrictions permitted under Art. 10(2) and their implications for photographers and photograph publishers will be discussed in Chapter 4 and Chapter 5.

Article 19 of the ECHR provided for the establishment of a European Court of Human Rights (hereinafter "ECtHR"), whose function is to ensure through its judgements in the cases that come before it that the contracting parties observe their duties and responsibilities under the terms of the ECHR.[27] There is an onus on the Irish courts while they are interpreting Irish law to take cognisance of the provisions of the ECHR and to aim to be compatible with them.[28] Decisions of the ECtHR are highly persuasive, but non-binding on the Irish courts. However, under S.4 of the 2003 Act, the Irish courts must take due cognisance of, among other matters, the decisions of the ECtHR.[29] The ECtHR frequently considers the Art. 10 right of freedom of expression in cases before it and three seminal cases, namely *Handyside v The United Kingdom*,[30] *The Sunday Times v The United Kingdom*[31] and *Müller et al. v Switzerland*,[32] are worthy of mention at this juncture, as they raised important issues relating to this right. In *Handyside*, the ECtHR held that the scope of the right to exercise the right of freedom of expression, subject to the previously mentioned, permitted restriction under Art. 10(2), extends to cover expressions which are not favourably received either by a state or a section of the general public. The

25 European Convention on Human Rights Act 2003, sch 1, art 10(1)
26 ibid sch 1, s 1, art 10(2)
27 ibid sch 1, s 1, art 19
28 ibid s 2(1)
Note: Under Section 2(1) of the Act: 'In interpreting and applying any statutory provision or rule of law, a court shall, in so far as is possible, subject to the rules of law relating to such interpretation and application, do so in a manner compatible with the State's obligations under the Convention provisions.'
29 ibid s 4
30 *Handyside v The United Kingdom* 1 EHRR 737, para 49
31 *The Sunday Times v The United Kingdom* [1979] ECHR 1
32 *Müller et al. v Switzerland* App no 10737/84 (ECtHR, 24 May 1988)

Court also determined, that any restriction imposed under Art. 10(2) must be proportionate to any lawful aim of an imposed restriction.[33]

In *The Sunday Times*, the Court held that, in addition to exercising its duty to ensure that a state interference with the right of freedom of expression comes within the types permitted under Art. 10(2), it must also be satisfied, having taken into consideration all of the facts and the circumstances of the particular case being determined by it, that the state's interference is necessary.[34]

In *Müller*, the Court dismissed the applicants' claim that the Swiss court in ordering the confiscation of Müller's paintings and the imposition of a conviction and fine on the applicants for publishing obscene materials at their public exhibition had breached their Art. 10 right.[35] The Court held that Art. 10 neither stated what specific forms of expression come within the meaning of Art. 10 nor did it expressly exclude artistic expression from the Article's scope. It also held that the activities of the types of media enterprises specifically mentioned in Art. 10 encompass art. Holding that artistic expression comes within the right of freedom of expression, the Court noted that Art. 19(2) of the ICCPR makes specific reference to art as being a medium through which the right of freedom of expression may be expressed.[36] But, the Court also stated that artists and art promoters were not immune from the restrictions that may be imposed on the right of freedom of expression in accordance with Art. 10(2) of the Convention.[37] From the previous example cases, it is clear that photography (an art form) comes within the scope of Art. 10 of the ECHR and that it enjoys the same rights and is subject to the same limitations as other forms of expression.

2.4.3) Charter of Fundamental Rights of the European Union

As a result of Ireland becoming a member of the European Union (formerly known as the European Economic Community), a large body of EU law has become part of Irish law. Directives, regulations and decisions of the European Union have legal effect in Ireland. This has resulted in additional EU-related rights being made available to Irish citizens, such as the right to freedom of movement. The Lisbon Treaty of the European Union came into force in December 2009 and as a result the Charter of Fundamental Rights of the European Union 'was given binding legal effect equal to the Treaties of the European Union'.[38] The preamble to the Charter states that it 'reaffirms with

33 *Handyside v The United Kingdom* 1 EHRR 737, para 49
34 *The Sunday Times v The United Kingdom* [1979] ECHR 1, para 65
35 *Müller et al. v Switzerland* App no 10737/84 (ECHR, 24 May 1988), para 44
36 ibid para 27
37 ibid para 34
38 Official Journal of the European Union, *Charter of Fundamental Rights of the European Union* (2010/C 83/391) <www.eur-lex.europa.eu/LexUriServ/LexUriServ.do?uri=OJ:C:2010:083:0389:0403:EN:PDF> accessed 31 March 2018

due regard for the powers and tasks of the Union and for the principle of subsidiarity, the rights as they result from the constitutional traditions and international obligations common to the Member States, the European Convention for the Protection of Human Rights and Fundamental Freedoms, the Social Charters as adopted by the Union and by the Council of Europe and the case-law of the Court of Justice of the European Union and of the European Court of Human Rights'.[39] On freedom of expression, Art. 11 of the Charter states:

> (1) Everyone has the right to freedom of expression. This right shall include freedom to hold opinions and to receive and impart information and ideas without interference by public authority and regardless of frontiers.
> (2) The freedom and pluralism of the media shall be respected.[40]

Article 11 of the Charter does not itself place any restrictions on the right of freedom of expression. However, this right is not absolute and it may be subject to limitation, as Art. 52 of the Charter provides for the limitation of rights granted by the Charter. But, any limitations implemented must meet the criteria specified in Art. 52(1):

> Any limitation on the exercise of the rights and freedoms recognised by this Charter must be provided for by law and respect the essence of those rights and freedoms. Subject to the principle of proportionality, limits may be made only if they are necessary and genuinely meet objectives of general interest recognised by the Union or the need to protect the rights and freedoms of others.[41]

39 ibid preamble
Note: In respect of the impending withdrawal of the United Kingdom from the European Union, under Section 2 of the European Union (Withdrawal) Act 2018 EU-derived domestic legislation in force before the exit day will continue to have effect. Subject to savings and incorporations, under S.5 of the Act the supremacy of EU law will not apply to any enactment or rule of law passed or made by the EU on or after the exit day and the Charter of Fundamental Rights of the European Union will not be part of domestic law on or after exit day. Section 6 of the Act states that a court or tribunal will not be bound by any decisions made by the Court of Justice of the European Union on or after the exit day and that the Supreme Court and the High Court of Judiciary (when sitting in specified circumstances) will not be bound by any retained EU case law.

40 Official Journal of the European Union, *Charter of Fundamental Rights of the European Union* (2010/C 83/391) art 11(1) <www.eur-lex.europa.eu/LexUriServ/LexUriServ.do?uri=OJ:C:2010:083:0389:0403:EN:PDF> accessed 31 March 2018

41 ibid art 52(1)

The Council of the European Union in its 2014 *EU Human Rights Guidelines on Freedom of Expression Online and Offline*[42] highlighted the significance of the right of freedom of expression:

> Freedom of opinion and expression are essential for the fulfilment and enjoyment of a wide range of other human rights, including freedom of association and assembly, freedom of thought, religion or belief, the right to education, the right to take part in cultural life, the right to vote and all other political rights related to participation in public affairs. Democracy cannot exist without them.[43]

The Guidelines make specific mention of freedom of artistic expression and state:

> Freedom of expression, including artistic expression, is essential for the development and manifestation of individuals' identities in society.[44]

Attention is drawn by the Guidelines to both the need for, and the importance of, a free and independent media so as to protect the right of freedom of opinion and expression.[45] While recognising that the right to freedom of opinion and expression is not an absolute right and may be subject to restriction, Annex (1) to the Guidelines[46] highlight a range of actions and activities that would undermine the enjoyment of the right of freedom of opinion and expression and the use of which the Council opposes. For example, the Council opposes any attacks on people, particularly journalists, solely because of their practising their right of freedom of expression. The Council states that any restrictions imposed on the right must be provided for in law; they must be necessary and proportional to their aims. In relation to defamation legislation, such should not be used for the purpose of restricting criticism or debate on public issues. Similarly, national security laws and particularly those relating to anti-terrorism must conform to international human rights law. The Guidelines also state that legislation concerning "hate speech" – a term, which according to the Guidelines, does not have a universally accepted definition under international law – should not be misused to prevent debate on topics of public interest. In relation to the right of freedom of expression "online", the Guidelines make specific mention of the restriction of access to the Internet by operators and that such should only be undertaken in limited circumstances and in conformity with legislation (for

42 Council of the European Union, *EU Human Rights Guidelines on Freedom of Expression Online and Offline* (Brussels, 12 May 2014) <www.consilium.europa.eu/uedocs/cms_data/docs/pressdata/EN/foraff/142549.pdf> accessed 31 March 2018

43 ibid para 2

44 ibid para 3

45 ibid para 4

46 ibid annex 1

example, legislative provisions concerning child pornography) or court orders.[47] According to the Guidelines, the restriction of access to websites for the purpose of the protection of intellectual property rights, and specifically copyright protected materials, could amount to a 'disproportionate restriction' and that any such restriction imposed must be in keeping with the Guideline's specified three-part cumulative test.[48] In line with the principles of legal certainty, predictability and transparency; legitimacy, and necessity and proportionality, this three-part cumulative test holds that any restrictions imposed must:

> (1) be provided for by law, which is clear and accessible to everyone . . .
> (2) pursue one of the purposes set out in article 19.3 ICCPR, i.e. to protect the rights or reputations of others; to protect national security, public order or public health or morals . . .
> (3) be proven necessary and as the least restrictive means required and commensurate with the proposed aim.[49]

On the relationship of the right to privacy and data protection with the right of freedom of expression, the Guidelines stated:

> Illegal surveillance of communications, their interception, as well as the illegal collection of personal data violates the right to privacy and the freedom to hold opinions without interference and can lead to restrictions on freedom of expression.[50]

It is evident from these Guidelines that freedom of expression is legally recognised by the EU as being a necessity for members of society to enjoy their other human rights. Freedom of expression includes the sub-set of artistic expression, which includes photography. Photographers enjoying their rights of freedom expression and of artistic expression may be subject to limitations being placed on those rights. Any limitations placed on photographers' enjoyment of these rights must be in compliance with the previously mentioned three-part test.

47 ibid
48 ibid
49 Council of the European Union, Foreign Affairs Council *EU Human Rights Guidelines on Freedom of Expression Online and Offline* (Brussels, 12 May 2014), para 20 <www.consilium.europa.eu/uedocs/cms_data/docs/pressdata/EN/foraff/142549.pdf> accessed 31 March 2018
50 ibid annex 1

2.4.4) Rights under intellectual property conventions and treaties

Ireland has ratified a number of intellectual property conventions and treaties, namely the Berne Convention for the Protection of Literary and Artistic Works,[51] the World Intellectual Property Organisation (WIPO) Copyright Treaty,[52] the World Trade Organisation (WTO) Agreement on Trade-related Aspects of Intellectual Property Rights (TRIPS)[53] and the WIPO Marrakesh Treaty.[54] As the rights granted under these conventions and treaties, as they pertain to photographers and photograph publishers, concern rights under copyright law, they are discussed in Chapter 3, which exclusively examines photographers' and photograph publishers' rights under copyright law and the legally permitted exemptions to such rights.

2.4.5) Rights under the Constitution of Ireland

2.4.5.1) Freedom of expression

In 1937, the people of Ireland enacted the current Constitution of Ireland. It is the fundamental law of the land and is superior to any laws enacted by the Oireachtas (the Irish Legislature).[55] Articles 40–44 of the Constitution deal with fundamental rights. Some, but not all, fundamental rights are specifically mentioned in the Constitution. Those that are specified are grouped under the following categories: Personal Rights, The Family, Education, Children, Private Property and Religion.[56] The right of freedom of expression is one of the specified personal rights. The Constitution does not explicitly include a legal right to either take or publish a photograph. These rights are, however, provided through the constitutional right of freedom of expression contained in Art. 40.6.1°. The rights guaranteed under Art. 40.6.1° are not unqualified and they may be restricted.[57] Article 40.6.1°(i) of the Constitution states:

51 *Berne Convention for the Protection of Literary and Artistic Works* <www.wipo.int/treaties/en/ip/berne/trtdocs_wo001.html> accessed 31 March 2018

52 World Intellectual Property Organisation, *WIPO Copyright Treaty* <www.wipo.int/treaties/en/ip/wct/trtdocs_wo033.html> accessed 31 March 2018

53 World Trade Organisation, *Agreement on Trade-Related Aspects of Intellectual Property Rights (TRIPS)* <www.wto.org/english/docs_e/legal_e/31bis_trips_01_e.htm> accessed 31 March 2018

54 World Intellectual Property Organisation, *Marrakesh Treaty to Facilitate Access to Published Works for Persons Who Are Blind, Visually Impaired or Otherwise Print Disabled* <www.wipo.int/treaties/en/ip/marrakesh/> accessed 31 March 2018

55 Note: The Oireachtas comprises two house, namely Dáil Éireann (Lower House) and Seanad Éireann (Senate).

56 Constitution of Ireland (*Arts. 40–44*) (on Fundamental Rights)

57 Constitution of Ireland *(Art. 40.6.1° (i))* (on Personal Rights)

> The State guarantees liberty for the exercise of the following rights, subject to public order and morality:
>
> > (i) The right of the citizen to express freely their convictions and opinions.
> >
> > The education of public opinion being, however, a matter of such grave import to the common good, the State shall endeavour to ensure that organs of public opinion, such as the radio, the press, the cinema, while preserving their rightful liberty of expression, including criticism of Government policy, shall not be used to undermine public order or morality or the authority of the State.[58]

In relation to organs of public opinion, Art. 40.6.1°(i)'s inclusion of the words "such as" means that it is open-ended rather than being exclusive by expressly referring to the radio, the press and the cinema – the means of mass communication at the time of the Constitution's writing (1937). Thus, more modern means of mass communication, such as television, the Internet and its social media sub-platforms, would all come within the Article's meaning of organs of public opinion. The constitutional right of freedom of expression is not an absolute right and it may be restricted either by laws or by the courts. The Irish Superior Courts have held that the rights of freedom of expression and of the press under Art. 40.6.1°(i) apply not only to the expression of opinions, but also to the expression and communication of facts and information. One should note that opinions, facts and information may be expressed or communicated through photographs. The Irish Supreme Court case of *The State (at the prosecution of Seán Lynch) v Cooney and The Attorney General*[59] was the first case in which the constitutional right to free speech was deliberated upon by the superior courts. In *Lynch*, O'Higgins CJ held that Art. 40.6.1°(i) placed an obligation upon the state to ensure that organs of public opinion are not used to undermine the authority of the state.[60] The decision of the Court to restrict the right of freedom of expression in the case of *Lynch* was made in support of the authority of the state during a period of political violence in Northern Ireland. Under the Broadcasting Authority Act 1960, as amended,[61] the publication of a photograph through a broadcast during that period could also be restricted if it was deemed to be likely to promote or incite crime or to undermine the authority of the state. Since then, decisions of the courts have gradually given more recognition to the positive role of freedom of expression and of the media

58 Constitution of Ireland *(Art. 40.6.1° (i))* (on Freedom of Expression)

59 *The State (at the Prosecution of Seán Lynch) v Cooney and The Attorney General* [1982] 1 IR 337

60 ibid 360

61 Broadcasting Authority Act 1960, s 31 as amended by Section 16 of the Broadcasting Authority (Amendment) Act 1976

in a democratic society and have been increasingly influenced by Art. 10 of the ECHR.

2.4.5.2) *The right to communicate*

The creation and publication of photographs is one of many methods through which one may communicate personal ideas and beliefs or information to other members of society. But, does one have a legal right to communicate? Is the right to communicate an integral element of the right of freedom of expression or is it a separate right? The personal right to communicate was one of the issues raised in 1983 in the Irish High Court case of *A.G. v Paperlink Ltd.*[62] In *Paperlink*, Costello J differentiated the right of freedom of expression from the right to communicate and he concluded that the latter right was an unspecified personal right guaranteed by Art. 40.3.1° of the Constitution.[63] However, Costello J went on to hold that although the Court recognised the right to communicate as an unenumerated constitutional right under Art. 40.3.1°, it is not an absolute right and that it may be restricted by the state.[64] The right to communicate was raised in the later Irish Supreme Court case of *The Irish Times v Ireland*.[65] In *The Irish Times*, in contrast to Costello J's previously mentioned differentiation between the right of freedom of expression and the right of communication, Barrington J held that Art. 40.6.1(i) guaranteed citizens the right to express opinions and also the right to communicate facts and information.[66] These two constitutional rights may come into contention with other constitutionally guaranteed personal rights.

2.4.5.3) *Freedom of expression, the right to communicate and the public interest*

While Chapter 4 and Chapter 5 will examine in detail how the courts have or may restrict the right of freedom of expression and specifically the legal rights of photographers and photograph publishers, the following sample cases highlight a number of specific issues in respect of the right of freedom of expression and the right of communication, which are relevant to photographers. First of all, the courts must take the public interest into account, when they are balancing competing rights. The Irish Supreme Court case of *National Irish Bank*

62 *A.G. v Paperlink Ltd.* [1983] ILRM 373
63 ibid para 31
Note: Article 40.3.1° of the Constitution states: 'The State guarantees by its laws to respect, and as far as practicable, by its laws to defend and vindicate the personal rights of the citizen.'
64 *A.G. v Paperlink Ltd.* [1983] ILRM 373, para 32
65 *The Irish Times v Ireland* [1998] 1 IR 359
66 ibid 404

Ltd. v Radio Telefís Éireann[67] involved a balancing of the right of freedom of information with the right to maintain information confidential. The Court held that in instances where the public interest in preventing illegal or dishonest behaviour could be facilitated by the publication of confidential information, then that need could out-balance the public interest in keeping the information confidential.[68]

A hierarchy of constitutionally guaranteed personal rights is not favoured by the courts as a means of balancing conflicting rights.[69] However, the courts place a strong emphasis on the right of freedom of expression. The Irish High Court of *M.M. v Drury*[70] concerned, among other matters, the photographing and publication of children without parental consent. In *M.M.*, the plaintiff had sought an interlocutory injunction against a proposed publication of material relating to her marriage, the veracity of which was not disputed. O'Hanlon J drew attention to the strength of the explicit guarantee of freedom of expression in the Constitution and he refused to grant the injunction, which had been sought by the plaintiff on the basis that the publication of the material would cause distress to her children.[71]

Whether the media is required to prove a public interest justification for the publication of a news story or a photograph in order to invoke its right of freedom of expression and whether the media's right to exercise that right is confined to stories of worth were issues raised in the Irish Supreme Court case of *Mahon v Post Publications.*[72] Regarding the public interest justification, Fennelly J stated:

> The media are not required to justify publication by reference to any public interest other than that of freedom of expression itself. They are free to publish material which is not in the public interest.
>
> . . . So far as the facts of the present case are concerned, the decision of Mr. O'Kelly to publish the names of three T.Ds in direct defiance of the

67 *National Irish Bank v Radio Telefís Éireann* [1998] 2 IR 465

68 ibid 494

69 Note: In the 2017 Irish Supreme Court case of *Sunday Newspapers Limited and Others V Gilchrist and Rogers* [2017] IESC 18, O'Donnell J, at para 36, stated 'The Constitution does not itself rank the rights and obligations it provides for, nor does it tell us how to divine any hierarchy. The obligation of a court is to uphold all the provisions of the Constitution . . . In truth the Constitution should not be too readily interpreted to require any hierarchical ranking of rights with the consequent possibility of subordination of one right to another. The Constitution was intended to function harmoniously, and where there were points of potential conflict between the rights and obligations provided for, that should be sought to be resolved without the subordination or nullification of one provision.'

70 *M.M. v Drury* [1994] 2 IR 8

71 ibid

72 *Mahon v Post Publications* [2007] IESC 15

> wishes of the tribunal was disgraceful and served no identifiable public interest. On the other hand, that does not mean that it was unlawful.[73]

On whether or not the right of freedom of expression is limited to publications of worth, Fennelly J stated:

> The right of freedom of expression extends the same protection to worthless, prurient and meretricious publication as it does to worthy, serious and socially valuable works. The undoubted fact that news media frequently and implausibly invoke the public interest to cloak worthless and even offensive material does not affect the principle.[74]

Prior to *Mahon*, in the 2003 Irish Court of Criminal Appeal case of *The People v Catherine Nevin*,[75] Geoghegan J held that the trial judge had correctly ruled that the applicant's right to a fair trial out-balanced the media's right to comment on the applicant's in-court dress and hair styles and general appearance.[76]

The right to publish photographs that were taken in a public street and the right to privacy featured in the Irish High Court of *Hickey v Sunday Newspapers Ltd.*[77] In finding for the defendant newspaper, Kearns P held that there is 'an inherent illogicality in asserting rights to privacy over material which is already in public circulation and which was, I would add in this case, notoriously so'.[78] Having not been provided with any convincing evidence which would tilt the balancing of the competing rights in favour of the plaintiff, Kearns P stated:

> Were I to hold otherwise, it would represent a radical ratcheting up of the right to privacy at the expense of the right of freedom of expression to a degree which, in my view, should more properly be the subject matter of legislation.[79]

73 ibid para 86
74 ibid para 43
75 *The People (at the Suit of the Director of Public Prosecutions) v Catherine Nevin* [2003] 3 IR 321
76 ibid para 326
77 *Hickey v Sunday Newspapers Ltd.* [2010] IEHC 349
78 ibid
79 ibid
Note: On the taking of photographs of people in public places, including public streets, see *Campbell v MGN Ltd.* [2004] UKHL 22 in which Hope L (at para. 122) stated that where people appear incidentally in a photographed street scene, generally they cannot object to its publication. However, if the street scene is used purely as a background for a photograph of a specific person, then the publication of such a photograph without the authorisation of that person is a different matter and the question to be addressed is whether there is public interest in having the contents of such a photograph published. It would appear, that Hope L, by so stating, was heading towards granting recognition to an image right, when no such right exists under United Kingdom law.

Furthermore, on the issue of the legal right to take photographs of people in public places and to publish them as elements of news stories, Kearns P also stated:

> A finding in favour of the plaintiffs would also give rise to a situation where a newspaper might feel itself inhibited from publishing a photograph of any public person attending, for example a funeral, or leaving or entering a court building or polling station. In any of these situations it is not difficult to imagine circumstances where a claimant could invoke some consideration of privacy.[80]

The issue of the granting of a prior restraint of publication of a news story and thus the restricting of the right of freedom of expression at an interlocutory stage was central to the 2010 Irish High Court case of *Murray v Newsgroup Newspapers*.[81] In *Murray*, a case concerning the publication of images of a convicted sex offender, Irvine J held that for a restraint of the right of freedom of expression to be granted at the interlocutory stage, the applicant must present the court with a 'convincing case' that the prohibition sought is 'likely' to be granted by a trial court.[82] In order to do so, Irvine J held that:

> the applicant must show that the interference with freedom of expression sought is justified by one of the recognised exceptions[83] to that right and that the proposed restriction will be proportionate to the aim to be achieved.[84]

Irvine J went on to state 'the court must scrutinise an application for an injunction seeking a prior restraint of a publication with "particular care"'.[85] He also held that such an applicant has an onus to convince the court that the balance of convenience lies in his favour.[86] Irvine J concluded that the applicant had 'failed to demonstrate sufficient significant inconvenience such as would justify a curtailment on the freedom of expression of the defendant newspapers'.[87]

80 ibid
81 *Murray v Newsgroup Newspapers Limited* [2010] IEHC 248
82 ibid para 68
83 Note: The "recognised exceptions" to the right of freedom of expression as referred to by Irvine J in *Murray* are those as specified by Article 10(2) of the Council of *Europe Convention for the Protection of Human Rights and Fundamental Freedoms*, as incorporated into the European Convention on Human Rights Act 2003.
84 *Murray v Newsgroup Newspapers Limited* [2010] IEHC 248, para 68
85 ibid para 68
86 ibid para 85
87 ibid

2.4.5.4) *Personal rights*

On Personal Rights, Art. 40.3.1° of the Constitution states: 'The State guarantees in its laws to respect, and, as far as practicable, by its laws to defend and vindicate the personal rights of the citizen.'[88] In addition, Art. 40.3.2° provides:

> The State shall, in particular, by its laws protect as best it may from unjust attack and, in the case of injustice done, vindicate the life, person, good name, and property rights of every citizen.[89]

The use of the words "in particular" in Art. 40.3.2° signals that other, unspecified rights are also contemplated. While the right of freedom of expression is not an absolute right and it is subject to restriction as provided for under the previously mentioned Art. 40.6.1(i) of the Constitution, Hamilton CJ held in the Irish Supreme Court case of *Proinsias De Rossa v Independent Newspapers Plc.*[90] that that right must also be balanced with the personal rights guaranteed by Article 40.3.1°.[91] The implication of *De Rossa* for photograph publishers is that they must be mindful of the constitutionally guaranteed personal rights of others, when they are deciding whether or not to publish a particular photograph. Many unenumerated, fundamental rights – those personal rights which are not specifically mentioned in the Constitution – have been identified and confirmed to exist by the courts, by reference to the use of the words "in particular" in setting out specific personal rights in Art. 40.3.2°. For example, a right to marital privacy was established by the Irish Supreme Court in the 1973 case of *McGee v Attorney General.*[92] In the 1987 case of *Kennedy and Arnold v Ireland,*[93] which involved the tapping by the government of two journalists' private telephones, the Irish High Court recognised the right to personal privacy in one's telephone conversations as being another unenumerated personal right.

2.4.5.5) *Private property rights*

The right to the private ownership of personal property is guaranteed by Art. 43.1 of the Constitution:

88 Constitution of Ireland *(Art. 40.3.1)* (on Personal Rights)
89 ibid *Art. 40.3.2°*
90 *Proinsias de Rossa v Independent Newspapers Plc* [1999] 4 IR 432
91 ibid 456
92 *McGee v Attorney General and Anor* [1973] IESC 2
93 *Kennedy and Arnold v Ireland* [1987] 1 IR 587 (HC), 593

> The State acknowledges that man, in virtue of his rational being, has the natural right, antecedent to positive law, to the private ownership of personal goods.[94]

Under Art. 43.1.2°: 'The State accordingly guarantees to pass no law attempting to abolish the right of private ownership or the general right to transfer, bequeath, and inherit property.'[95] However, Art. 43 recognises that the exercise of the rights guaranteed by it 'ought, in civil society, to be regulated by the principles of social justice'.[96] Consequently, Art. 43 makes provision for the State to place limitations on the exercise of the private property rights guaranteed by it for the purpose of 'reconciling their exercise with the exigencies of the common good'.[97] Of central importance to the creators of photographs is the recognition by the Irish High Court in the 1994 case of *Phonographic Performance (Ireland) Limited v William Austin Cody and Princes Investments Limited*,[98] that the creators of literary, dramatic, musical and artistic works have, as a right of private property under Art. 40.3.2° and Art.43.1, the right not to have their created works stolen or plagiarised.[99] As shall be discussed in Chapter 3, the Copyright and Related Rights Act 2000, as amended, (hereinafter "CRRA") includes a "photograph" within its definition of an "artistic work".

2.4.6) Photographers' and photograph publishers' statutory rights

Since the Irish state gained its independence from the United Kingdom in 1922, the Oireachtas has passed a wide range of statutes designed to create and/or protect both legal and statutory personal rights. Recent examples of such are the CRRA, as amended; the Defamation Act 2009, as amended; the Non-Fatal Offences Against the Person Act 1997, as amended, (Section 10 of which deals with "harassment and the interference with one's personal privacy"); and the Data Protection Acts 1998–2018.[100] No statute of the Oireachtas grants one either a specific or a general legal right to create a photograph. However, the right of freedom of expression is recognised in Irish statute law via the European Convention on Human Rights Act 2003, as amended, which incorporated the ECHR into Irish statute law. If individuals have, since 2003, a statutory right of freedom of expression and the right to exercise that right through the publication

94 Constitution of Ireland *(Art. 43.1.1°)* (on Private Property)
95 ibid *Art. 43.1.2°*
96 ibid *Art. 43.2.1°*
97 ibid *Art. 43.2.2°*
98 *Phonographic Performance (Ireland) Limited v William Austin Cody and Princes Investments Limited* [1998] 4 IR 504
99 ibid 511
100 Note: In Ireland, there is no statute which explicitly grants a general right to personal privacy. One could take the view, that the Data Protection Acts 1988–2018 have become surrogate general privacy acts.

of photographs, then, by definition, they must also have an implied statutory right to create photographs for such publications. Freedom of expression is also recognised indirectly through the Defamation Act 2009, as amended. Section 44 of the Act made provision for the legal recognition of the Press Council of Ireland as the Press Council in Ireland[101] and Schedule 2 of the Act specified the minimum requirements for such a body.[102] Under Schedule 2, the first expressed principal object of the Press Council is for it 'to ensure the protection of the freedom of expression of the press'.[103] The CRRA, as amended, confers a wide range of legal rights on both the authors of photographs and photograph publishers. Consequently, Chapter 3 examines copyright law in detail.

2.4.7) Common law right to take photographs

The taking and publication of photographs are, both in practical terms and from a legal perspective, two separate activities. Since the public became fascinated with photography in the latter part of the 19th century, it had been generally understood, that there was a common law right to take a photograph in a public place or a privately owned place to which the public is admitted without any photography restrictions being imposed as a condition of admittance.[104] The common law right to take a photograph of another person was recognised in 1916 in the English High Court case of *Sports and General Press Agency Limited v "Our Dogs" Publishing Company Limited*.[105] In *Sports and General*, which concerned the taking of photographs at a dog show, Horridge J held that nobody had a legal right to prevent another person from taking a photograph of them, just as a person could not legally prevent another from giving either a non-libellous or non-wrongful description of him.[106] Horridge J also stated that the dog show organisers could not legally prevent a person conveniently positioned outside the show and with a view of the show from taking pictures of it.[107] On appeal to the Court of Appeal, Swinfen Eady LJ, while confirming the previously mentioned decision of Horridge J, held that the right to take photographs on a piece of property was not part of the property rights attached to that property. However, he held that the right to take photographs on a piece of private property could be made subject to a contract

101 Defamation Act 2009, s 44
102 ibid sch 2
103 ibid sch 2, s 2
104 Note: Chapter 4 discusses a range of legal mechanisms, rights and interests that may be implemented to either restrict or prohibit the taking of photographs on publicly owned and privately owned places to which members of the public are permitted access.
105 *Sports and General Press Agency Limited v "Our Dogs" Publishing Company Limited* [1916] 2 K.B. 880
106 ibid 884
107 ibid

of admission to that property.[108] As a consequence of this judgement, it has become common practice for the promoters of events taking place on privately owned properties, that are open to the public through the purchase of an admission ticket, to include a term in their contract of admission contained on the admission tickets, which prohibits admitted people from taking photographs within the event's venue without prior approval of the event organisers. Also, when event organisers are granting sole photography rights to photographers, it is common practice to do so via a written contract.

In the English High Court case of *Bernstein of Leigh (Baron) v Skyviews and General Ltd.*,[109] (a trespass and invasion of privacy case involving aerial photography), Griffiths J rejected the view that a landowner owned the airspace over his lands up to the sky and he went on to held that there is no law which, in general, prevents the taking of a photograph. Having held that the defendant's aircraft did not infringe the plaintiff's rights in his airspace, he determined that the act of taking an aerial photograph was not a trespass into the plaintiff's airspace and could not be turned into one.[110] In general, the over-flight of an aircraft for the purpose of taking a once-off aerial photograph, as opposed to undertaking continuous aerial photography, would not amount to harassment and an actionable nuisance. However, one should not take as a given, that the judgement in *Bernstein* would prevent an aggrieved person, in every circumstance, from the taking an action against an aerial photographer. Aerial photography has traditionally been undertaken from either helicopters or small planes. Due to their increased availability and lower costs compared to aircraft hire, the use of drones for aerial photography is growing in popularity. Chapter 5 discusses the legal restrictions on the use of drones.

The question of the legal right to take a photograph in a public place has not featured in cases at the Irish Superior Courts. In a few instances, such a right has been raised among other legal issues during cases in the lower Irish courts. For example, two public order cases determined at District Court level dealt with, among other more central issues, the right to take photographs in public places and particularly of members of An Garda Síochána (the Irish police) performing their duties in public places. In one case, two members of An Garda Síochána were convicted for assaulting a member of the public who had used a mobile phone camera to photograph gardaí (members of An Garda Síochána), who were in attendance at a disturbance on a street. One of the arresting gardaí had seized the arrested individual's mobile phone and deleted the images recorded on it. Both gardaí were fined for assault and ordered to pay compensation to the individual, while one of them was also convicted and fined for criminal damage as a result of his illegal seizure of the mobile phone

108 *Sports and General Press Agency, Limited v "Our Dogs" Publishing Company Limited* [1917] 2 KB 125, 127–128

109 *Bernstein of Leigh (Baron) v Skyviews and General Ltd.* [1978] QB 479

110 ibid 487–488

and the deletion of the images.[111] A person's lack of an appreciation that their wrongful and direct interference with the goods of another without lawful authority was an offence will not absolve their liability. Not all interferences with the goods of another may be tortious, as the interferer may have lawful authority to do so.[112] In the more recent case, in 2012, four individuals had been attempting to gain entry to a pub. The gardaí were called and they ordered the four to "move on". Two complied and two failed to do so. While one of the latter two was being arrested, the other had photographed the gardaí making the arrest. He was arrested and charged with having committed an alleged public order offence. In that case, the District Court judge stated that it is not an offence to take a photograph of another person being arrested.[113] One should note that a personal dislike by a member of An Garda Síochána to being photographed while performing his/her legal duties in a public place does not make the taking of such photographs an illegal act. An individual does not have a legal right to compel a photographer to delete a photograph taken of them. This issue was central to a 2018 Dublin Civil Circuit Court case in which the Court awarded damages against Irish Rail to a claimant, who was held to have been falsely imprisoned following her refusal to delete photographs that she had taken of an Irish Rail worker during a disturbance at a railway station.[114]

While one has a common law right to take a photograph in a privately owned place to which one is freely admitted without any photography restrictions being imposed as a condition of entry, that in itself does not create either an absolute or an exclusive right to take photographs on that privately owned property without the permission of the property owner. The owner of a private property to which a person has been freely admitted without any restriction on photography has the right to request that person to desist from taking either any further photographs or photographs of particular items or places while on the property. Also, the publication of images created while on privately owned property, whether admitted with or without a restriction on taking photographs, is a separate legal issue to the actual taking of the photographs. Such a publication could be subject to any prior restrictions agreed as part of the grant of permission by the property owner to take the photograph while on the property. It could also breach the private property owner's property rights. The right to

111 ——'Gardaí Fined for Assaulting Man Who Was Filming Row' *Irish Examiner* (Cork, 05 December 2009) <www.irishexaminer.com/ireland/gardai-fined-for-assaulting-man-who-was-filming-row-107224.html> accessed 01 April 2018

112 Note: See Chapter 5 on the legal powers of seizure by members of An Garda Síochána and the United Kingdom's Police.

113 Bernie English, 'Judge Appalled By Arrest Scenes' *Limerick Post* (Limerick, 16 July 2012) <www.limerickpost.ie/2012/07/16/judge-appalled-by-arrest-scenes/> accessed 01 April 2018

114 Ray Managh, 'Marketing Executive Awarded €16K After Trinity Ball Revellers Step into Middle of DART Ticket Row' *Irish Independent* (Dublin, 01 February 2018) <www.independent.ie/irish-news/courts/marketing-executive-awarded-16k-after-trinity-ball-revellers-step-into-middle-of-dart-ticket-row-36554981.html> accessed 01 April 2018

take photographs on private property was a central issue in the 2017 Irish High Court case of *Matute v Medtronic Ireland Ltd. and Others.*[115] It should be noted, that *Matute* concerned a specific set of circumstances and it does not give rise to a general legal right to take photographs while on privately owned property upon which the property owner has photography restrictions or prohibitions in place. In *Matute*, the plaintiff's engineer had been refused permission by the defendant to take photographs within the latter's factory during a joint engineering inspection relating to a damages claim by the plaintiff against his employer (the defendant). Photographs supplied by the defendant to the plaintiff's engineer were deemed by the latter as unacceptable for use in his preparation of an engineer's report for the plaintiff.[116] Barr J stated that in civil litigation a claimant has 'a right to be allowed to put his case together in as full a manner as is possible, so that he can present his case fully at the trial of his action'.[117] Barr J ordered that the plaintiff's engineer was to be permitted to take whatever photographs of the plaintiff's work station that he deemed were necessary for his civil claim.[118]

2.5) Brief conclusions

Although they are related, the creation and publication of photographs are two distinct activities both in practical terms and also from a rights perspective. Photographers and photograph publishers enjoy a range of legal rights which are derived both directly and indirectly from a number of sources at the global, European, European Union and national levels, namely international treaties and conventions, the Constitution of Ireland, statutory legislation and the common law. The creation of a photograph is one of the methods and stages involved in the process through which a person may express and communicate his/her ideas, beliefs or other information with others. The right to take a photograph in a public place or in a place to which members of the public are admitted without any restrictions on the taking of photographs is founded in the common law. It is also founded in the legal right of freedom of expression and in particular its sub-set – the right of artistic expression. The right to publish a created photograph is founded upon the rights of freedom of expression, including its sub-sets of artistic and commercial expression, and freedom of communication. These rights are not absolute rights. The right to take and/or publish a photograph may be restricted by either legislative provisions, the rights of others or the courts when they are protesting and/or enforcing any competing rights.

115 *Matute v Medtronic Ireland Ltd. and Others* [2017] IEHC 431
116 ibid paras 2–4 and paras 6–19
117 ibid para 22
118 ibid para 28

References

Books

Alston P and Goodman R, *International Human Rights* (Oxford University Press 2013)

Barendt E, *Freedom of Speech* (2nd edn, Oxford University Press 2005)

Boyle K and Shah S, 'Thought, Expression, Association and Assembly' in Daniel Moeckli, Sangeeta Shah and Sandesh Sivakumaran (eds), *International Human Rights Law* (2nd edn, Oxford University Press, 2014)

Campbell T, *Rights: A Critical Introduction* (Routledge 2006)

Coleman J, *Rights and Their Foundations* (Garland 1994)

Donnelly J, *Universal Human Rights in Theory and Practice* (Cornell University Press 2012)

Doyle O and Carolan E, *The Irish Constitution: Governance and Values* (Thomson Round Hall 2008)

Hogan G and Whyte G, *J.M. Kelly: The Irish Constitution* (4th edn, Lexis Nexis 2003)

Holderness M, Poppelmann B and Klehm M, *The Right Thing: An Author's Rights Handbook for Journalists* (International Federation of Journalists 2011)

Jones H and Benson C, *Publishing Law* (4th edn, Routledge 2011)

Jones P, *Rights* (The Macmillan Press Ltd. 1994)

Kearns P, *Freedom of Artistic Expression: Essays on Culture and Legal Censure* (Hart Publishing 2013)

McGonagle M, *Media Law* (2nd edn, Thompson Round Hall 2003)

McMahon B and Binchy W, *Law of Torts* (4th edn, Bloomsbury Professional 2013)

Stone R, *Textbook on Civil Liberties and Human Rights* (Oxford University Press 2004)

Wacks R, *Understanding Jurisprudence: An Introduction to Legal Theory* (3rd edn, Oxford University Press 2012)

Journal articles

Daly T, 'Strengthening Irish Democracy: A Proposal to Restore Free Speech to Article 40.6.1(i) of the Constitution' (2009) 31 *Dublin University Law Journal* 228

Diggelmann O and Cleis M, 'How the Right to Privacy Became a Human Right' (2014) 14(3) *Human Rights Law Review* 441

Kennedy R, 'Was It Author's Rights All the Time? Copyright as a Constitutional Right in Ireland' (2011) 33 *Dublin University Law Journal* 253

O'Flaherty M, 'Freedom of Expression: Article 19 of the International Covenant on Civil and Political Rights and the Human Rights Committee's General Comment No. 34' (2012) 12(4) *Human Rights Law Review* 627

—— 'Limitations on Freedom of Opinion and Expression: Growing Consensus or Hidden Fault Lines?' (2012) 106 *American Society of International Law* 347

Newspaper articles

English B, 'Judge Appalled By Arrest Scenes' *Limerick Post* (Limerick, 16 July 2012) <www.limerickpost.ie/2012/07/16/judge-appalled-by-arrest-scenes/> accessed 01 April 2018

Managh R, 'Marketing Executive Awarded €16K After Trinity Ball Revellers Step Into Middle of DART Ticket Row' *Irish Independent* (Dublin, 01 February 2018) <www.independent.ie/irish-news/courts/marketing-executive-awarded-16k-after-trinity-ball-revellers-step-into-middle-of-dart-ticket-row-36554981.html> accessed 01 April 2018

O'Keeffe C, 'Gardaí Fined for Assaulting Man Who Was Filming Row' *Irish Examiner* (Cork, 05 December 2009) <www.irishexaminer.com/ireland/gardai-fined-for-assaulting-man-who-was-filming-row-107224.html> accessed 01 April 2018

Official Reports and Publications

Council of the European Union, *EU Human Rights Guidelines on Freedom of Expression Online and Offline* (Brussels, 12 May 2014) <www.consilium.europa.eu/uedocs/cms_data/docs/pressdata/EN/foraff/142549.pdf> accessed 31 March 2018

Dáil Éireann Debate 10 November 2011, vol 746, col 318 Human Rights Issues <http://oireachtasdebates.oireachtas.ie/debates%20authoring/DebatesWebPack.nsf/takes/dail2011111000046?opendocument> accessed 28 March 2018

United Nations, General Assembly, Resolutions Adopted By the General Assembly During Its First Session, *Calling of an International Conference on Freedom of Information* Res 59(1) <www.un.org/documents/ga/res/1/ares1.htm> accessed 28 March 2018

—— Office of the High Commissioner for Human Rights, *Human Rights Committee* <www.ohchr.org/EN/HRBodies/CCPR/Pages/CCPRIntro.aspx> accessed 28 March 2018

—— Office of the High Commissioner for Human Rights, Committee on Economic, Social and Cultural Rights, *General Comment No. 17: Article 15(1)(c) – Right of Everyone to Benefit From the Protection of the Moral and Material Interests Resulting From Any Scientific, Literary or Artistic Production of Which He or She Is the Author* (E/C.12/GC/17) (Geneva, 12 January 2006) <http://tbinternet.ohchr.org/_layouts/treatybodyexternal/TBSearch.aspx?Lang=en&TreatyID=9&DocTypeID=11> accessed 28 March 2018

—— Office of the High Commissioner for Human Rights, Human Rights Committee, *General Comment No. 34 on Article 19 of the International Covenant on Civil and Political Rights* (on Freedom of Expression) CCPR/C/GC/34 (Geneva, 12 September 2011) <www2.ohchr.org/english/bodies/hrc/docs/gc34.pdf> accessed 28 March 2018

—— Office of the High Commissioner for Human Rights, Human Rights Council Resolutions, *Resolution 20/8: The Promotion, Protection and Enjoyment of Human Rights on the Internet* (A/HRC/RES/20/8) (Geneva, 16 July 2012) <http://ap.ohchr.org/documents/dpage_e.aspx?si=A/HRC/RES/20/8> accessed 28 March 2018

—— *The Universal Declaration of Human Rights* <www.un.org/en/universal-declaration-human-rights/index.html> accessed 28 March 2018

3 Photographers' and photograph publishers' rights under copyright law

3.1) Introduction

While one has a general common law right to take photographs, the legal right relating to any created photograph is another matter. The primary source of photographers' legal rights over their created works is copyright law. Chapter 3 examines the legal rights of photographers and photograph publishers as provided through copyright law. It discusses the nature, scope and practical application of the now statutory rights collectively known as copyright and moral rights. It also discusses how photographers' and photograph publishers' rights under copyright law are currently restricted through legislative provisions pertaining to copyright and a number of proposed legislative reforms, which may further restrict those rights.

3.2) Development of photographers' and photograph publishers' rights under copyright law

The right to copyright in a work has existed in Ireland since the early medieval days of the Brehon Law.[1] Over time, this right was developed and refined both by the common law and through the enactment of statutes and statutory instruments by the Parliament of the United Kingdom and since 1922 by the Oireachtas. Irish copyright law has been further developed and harmonised through Ireland's membership of the EU, its ratification of international conventions and treaties dealing with intellectual property and as a consequence of court judgements. The right to possess a copyright in a photograph has been granted legal standing in relatively recent times. This legal right is however subject to limitations, restrictions and exemptions. The Constitution of Ireland does not make mention of a right to copyright. However, Article 40.3.2° of the Constitution, on personal rights, guarantees that the State will protect,

1 Note: For a discussion on Brehon Law, see Fergus Kelly, *A Guide to Early Irish Law* (Dublin Institute for Advanced Studies 1998).

among other things, the property rights of every citizen from unjust attack.[2] Also, in relation to private property, Article 43.1.1° of the Constitution recognises one's right to private ownership of property.[3] Keane J recognised the right to copyright as a property right under these two Articles in the 1994 Irish High Court case of *Phonographic Performance (Ireland) Limited v William Austin Cody and Princes Investments Limited*.[4] Such recognition by Keane J was applied by Charleton J in the 2010 Irish High Court cases of *EMI Records (Ireland) Ltd. and Others v UPC Communications Ireland Ltd.*[5] and *EMI Records (Ireland) and Others v Eircom Ltd.*[6] The view that a legal right to copyright has existed in Ireland since the time of the Brehon Law is recognised by the Irish courts of today.[7]

While a right to intellectual property has a particular significance and a strong constitutional status in Irish law, a common law right to copyright in books and musical and dramatic works was recognised in the 1758 English High Court case of *Duke of Queensbury v Shebbeare*.[8] While *Queensbury* concerned copyright in an unpublished work, the 1769 English High Court case of *Millar v Taylor*[9] recognised a right to copyright in a published work. In *Millar*, the Court held that such a right had not been abolished by the Copyright Act 1709 (Statute of Anne).[10] However, the House of Lords subsequently held in *Donaldson v Beckett*[11] that the common law right to a perpetual copyright had been removed by the 1709 Act.[12]

The passing of a number of statutes has resulted in photographers being conferred with a statutory right to own the copyright to any photographs created by them. The Copyright Act 1709[13] was the first copyright statute enacted in the United Kingdom. That statute did not make provision for a copyright in a photograph. Through the inclusion of photographs as fine art within the terms of the Fine Arts Copyright Act 1862,[14] photographs were given a statutory copyright protection. The common law right to copyright

2 Constitution of Ireland, *Art. 40.3.2°* (on Personal Rights)
3 ibid *Art. 43.1.1°* (on Private Property Rights)
4 *Phonographic Performance (Ireland) Limited v William Austin Cody and Princes Investments Limited* [1998] 4 IR 504, 511
5 *EMI Records (Ireland) Ltd. and Others v UPC Communications Ireland Ltd.* [2010] IEHC 377, para 85
6 *EMI Records (Ireland) Ltd. and Others v Eircom Ltd.* [2010] IEHC 108, paras 28–29
7 For example, see *EMI Records and Others v Eircom Ltd.* [2010] IEHC 108
8 *Duke of Queensbury v Shebbeare* (1758) 2 Eden 329, 330
9 *Millar v Taylor* (1769) 4 Burr 2303
10 ibid 2417
11 *Donaldson v Beckett* (1774) 1 ER 837
12 ibid 847
13 Copyright Act 1709
14 Fine Arts Copyright Act 1862, s 1
Note: Fine art photographs are those which are produced for their aesthetic value. While photography is recognised as a branch of fine art, many photographers, and not just artists who use paint brushes, will argue about whether or not photographs in general

was abolished by the Copyright Act 1911.[15] Following the foundation of Saorstát Éireann (the Irish Free State) in 1922, the Industrial and Commercial Property (Protection) Act 1927[16] was enacted and it included provisions relating to the copyright in photographs. Section 154(1) of the Act granted a right to copyright in, among other types of works, an artistic work[17] and S.158(2) of the Act detailed the rights of a copyright owner.[18] Remedies for infringement of copyright were provided for under S.159 and S.160 of the Act.[19] An artistic work was defined by S.177(1) as including "photographs"[20] and S.171 defined the duration of the term of copyright in a photograph as being 'fifty years from the making of the original negative from which the photograph was directly or indirectly derived'.[21] The Act abrogated the common law right to copyright[22] and S.4 of the Act repealed the whole of the Copyright Act 1911.[23] As a consequence of the Irish Supreme Court's decision in *Performing Rights Society v Urban District Council of Bray*,[24] the Copyright (Preservation) Act 1929 was enacted to ensure the continuation of any copyright, which had previously existed in accordance with the terms of the Copyright Act 1911 and prior to the signing of the Treaty between Ireland and Great Britain on 6 December 1921.[25]

The Copyright Act 1963, as amended,[26] was the first stand-alone statute dealing with copyright enacted by the state. It was designed to consolidate statutes dealing with copyright and to take account of the development in communications technologies, such as the broadcasting of television programmes; the expansion and diversification of the recording industry and of Ireland's obligations under international agreements dealing with copyright.[27] Save for Section 59,[28] the entire 1963 Act, the entire Copyright (Amendment) Act 1987,

---

or a particular photograph is a work of fine art. To a great extent, the argument is a subjective matter.

15 Copyright Act 1911, s 31
16 Industrial and Commercial Property (Protection) Act 1927
17 ibid s 154(1)
18 ibid s 158(2)
19 ibid s 159–160
20 ibid s 177(1)
21 ibid s 171
22 ibid s 176
23 ibid s 4 and first schedule
24 *Performing Rights Society v Urban District Council of Bray* [1930] AC 377, 379–380
25 Copyright (Preservation) Act 1929, ss 1–3
26 Note: The Copyright Act 1963 was amended by the Copyright (Amendment) Act 1987 and the Intellectual Property (Miscellaneous Provisions) Act 1988.
27 Dáil Deb 28 November 1962, vol 198, col 240 <http://oireachtasdebates.oireachtas.ie/Debates%20Authoring/DebatesWebPack.nsf/takes/dail1962112800045?opendocument> accessed 09 April 2018
28 Note: Section 59 of the Copyright Act 1963 amended Section 70 of the Industrial and Commercial Property (Protection) Act 1927, which dealt with copyright in registered designs.

and Sections 2 and 3 of the Intellectual Property (Miscellaneous Provisions) Act 1988 were repealed by the Copyright and Related Rights Act 2000 (hereinafter "CRRA").[29] The CRRA, as amended, is the current legislation governing copyright in Ireland. A major piece of legislation, the CRRA has been amended by the Copyright and Related Rights (Amendment) Acts of 2004[30] and 2007[31] and also by a number of statutory instruments, principally the European Communities (Copyright and Related Rights) Regulations 2004[32] and the European Union (Copyright and Related Rights) Regulations 2012.[33] These two statutory instruments gave further effect to specific aspects of the EC Copyright Directive – Directive 2001/29/EC.[34] Article 2 of the Directive relates to the exclusive reproduction rights[35] of authors. Article 3 concerns the exclusive rights of authors to communicate and make available[36] their works to the public, while Article 4 deals with authors' exclusive right to distribute[37] their works to the public by sale or otherwise.

29 Copyright and Related Rights Act 2000, second schedule, part 1
Note: In many respects the actual wording of the Copyright and Related Rights Act 2000 is very close to that of the United Kingdom's Copyright, Designs and Patents Act 1988.

30 Copyright and Related Rights (Amendment) Act 2004

31 Copyright and Related Rights (Amendment) Act 2007

32 European Communities (Copyright and Related Rights) Regulations 2004, SI 2004/16

33 European Union (Copyright and Related Rights) Regulations 2012, SI 2012/59
Note also: The European Communities (Enforcement of Intellectual Property Rights) Regulations 2006, SI 2006/360 gave legal effect to certain aspects of Directive 2004/48/EC of the European Parliament and of the Council on 29 April 2004 on the enforcement of intellectual property rights.

34 Directive 2001/29/EC of the European Parliament and of the Council of 22 May 2001 on the harmonisation of certain aspects of copyright and related rights in the information society [2001] OJ L167/10 <http://eur-lex.europa.eu/LexUriServ/LexUriServ.do?uri=OJ:L:2001:167:0010:0019:EN:PDF> accessed 09 April 2018

35 ibid art 2

36 ibid art 3
Note: A website hyperlink to a protected work published on the Internet without the consent of the work's copyright owner could, in specific circumstances, amount to an infringement of the Article 3 right to communicate. In the CJEU case of *Case C160/15 GS Media BV v Sanoma Media Netherlands BV* (8 September 2016), the Court, at para 55, held: 'in order to establish whether the fact of posting, on a website, hyperlinks to protected works, which are freely available on another website without the consent of the copyright holder, constitutes a "communication to the public" within the meaning of that provision, it is to be determined whether those links are provided without the pursuit of financial gain by a person who did not know or could not reasonably have known the illegal nature of the publication of those works on that other website or whether, on the contrary, those links are provided for such a purpose, a situation in which that knowledge must be presumed.'

37 ibid art 4

3.3) Copyright and Related Rights Act 2000

3.3.1) Statutory recognition of copyright as a property right

Like the 1963 Act,[38] the CCRA, as amended, formally recognises copyright as a property right, which from an economic point of view makes it an important right and asset for a photographer to possess. Section 17(1) of the Act states:

> Copyright is a property right whereby, subject to this Act, the owner of the copyright in any work may undertake or authorise other persons in relation to that work to undertake certain acts in the State, being acts which are designated by this Act as acts restricted by copyright in a work of that description.[39]

3.3.2) Statutory definitions relevant to copyright in photographs

Section 2(1) of the Act includes a number of inter-related definitions of relevance to copyright in photographs and they are drawn-together through S.17 of the Act. Such definitions include:

> "Photograph" means a recording of light, or any other radiation on any medium on which an image is produced, or from which an image may by any means be produced and which is not part of a film.[40]

This broad definition of a "photograph" would include both traditional still film photography and other modern methods of photographic image capture, such as digital camera sensors, thermal imaging, magnetic resonance imaging, ultra sound and x-rays, on which still photographic images may be recorded. "Film" is defined as 'a fixation on any medium from which a moving image may, by any means, be produced, perceived or communicated through a device'.[41] The word "film" as defined by S.2(1) of the Act refers to what one could also call a movie and not to a piece of still photographic film. While noting that many Sections within the Act treat films separately from photographs, this book deals purely with still photographs. Photographs are specified within the Act's definition of an "artistic work" and, interestingly, a photograph is the only type of artistic work that is defined by the Act. The artistic quality of a photograph

38 Copyright Act 1963, s 47
39 Copyright and Related Rights Act 2000, s 17(1)
40 ibid s 2(1)
41 ibid
Note: Section 2(1) of the CRRA defines a "fixation" as: 'the embodiment of sounds or images or any combination of sounds or images, or the representation thereof, from which they can be perceived, reproduced or communicated through a device'.

has no bearing on whether a photograph qualifies as an artistic work.[42] The CRRA states that a "copyright work" is a work in which a copyright subsists and that a "work" includes an "artistic work".[43]

3.3.3) *Originality in an artistic work and the subsistence of copyright*

Section 17(2)(a) of the Act states that 'Copyright subsists, in accordance with this Act, in (a) original literary, dramatic, musical or artistic works, (b) sound recordings, films, broadcasts or cable programmes, (c) the typographical arrangement of published editions, and (d) original databases.'[44] Notably, the term "original" is only used in respect of sub-sections (a) and (d). As photographs, as previously defined, are classed as "artistic works", copyright may subsist in them. The CRRA is silent on what specifically constitutes an "original" artistic work. It is rather unfortunate that the drafters of the Act, who would or ought to have been aware of the past legal problems caused by the inclusion of the non-defined term "original" as also contained in previous Copyright Acts and in the United Kingdom's Copyright, Designs and Patents Act 1988,[45] did not include such a definition or alternatively had not refrained from including the word "original" in the CRRA. Consequently, it was left to the courts to determine what constituted an "*original*" artistic work. Instead of taking the commonly accepted meaning of the word "original" (*first, initial, something from which a copy is made*), the courts in justification for the decisions in their judgements created their own interpretations of the meaning of the word, when used in relation to copyright. In the past, the courts mandated that certain prerequisites must be demonstrated to exist in a work before it will be classified as being "original", including that it must be an expression of the author's thoughts and that its author must expend a degree of knowledge, labour, judgement and skill in producing the work.[46] Determining the degree or extent of work, labour and skill necessary to be present in a work for it to be classed as an original work and thus qualify for copyright protection is to a great extent a subjective judgement.

The definition of "artistic work" in S.2(1) of the CRRA includes "prints".[47] The Act does not specify what constitutes a print. A photographic print made from an original photographic image contained on either a frame of negative

42 ibid
43 ibid
44 ibid s 17(2)(a)
45 Copyright Act 1911, s 1(1); Copyright Act 1963, s 8(1) and Copyright, Designs and Patents Act 1988, s 1(1)
46 See: *University of London Press v University Tutorial Press* [1916] 2 Ch 601, 608–609; *G.A. Cramp and Sons Ltd. v Frank Smythson Ltd.* [1944] AC 329, 340 and *Antiques-portfolio.com Plc v Rodney Fitch and Co. Ltd.* [2001] FSR 23, para 30
47 Copyright and Related Rights Act 2000, s 2(1)

or positive film or on a digital camera's sensor would be a copy of such an image. The author of the original image would be its first copyright owner and therefore permitted to make a copy of that image. Photographic prints created from frames of still film using film enlargers, photocopiers, dye-sublimation, digital inkjet or any other type of electronic photograph printer would all have to meet the originality requirement of an artistic work for them to be eligible to benefit from copyright protection. Leggatt LJ held in the English High Court case of *The Reject Shop Plc v Robert Manners*[48] that using a photocopier to create enlarged, printed copies of drawings did not create a copyright in the enlarged drawings, as he viewed the process of enlargement as being mechanical rather than one that required an input of artistic skill and labour. The question of originality in a photograph has been considered by the Court of Justice of the European Union (hereinafter "CJEU"). In the 2012 case of *Painer v Standard Verlags GmbH*,[49] the Court referred to Directive 93/98/EEC,[50] which defined the level of originality required for a photograph to qualify for copyright protection. Directive 2006/116/EC repealed Directive 93/98/EC and it contains a similarly worded definition, namely:

> A photographic work within the meaning of the Berne Convention is to be considered original if it is the author's own intellectual creation reflecting his personality, no other criteria such as merit or purpose being taken into account.[51]

3.3.4) *Copyright does not subsist in ideas, infringing works or copies of made-available works*

Ideas may not be copyrighted. Section 17(3) of the CRRA states: 'Copyright protection shall not extend to the ideas and principles which underlie any element of a work'.[52] Also, copyright does not subsist in a work which infringes the copyright in another work[53] or in a copy taken from a work which has been previously made available to the public.[54]

48 *The Reject Shop Plc v Robert Manners* [1995] FSR 870, 876
49 Case 145/10 *Painer v Standard Verlags GmbH* [2012] ECDR 6, paras 15–17
50 Council Directive 93/98/EEC of 29 October 1993 harmonizing the term of protection of copyright and certain related rights [1993] OJ L290/9, recital 17 <http://eur-lex.europa.eu/LexUriServ/LexUriServ.do?uri=CELEX:31993L0098:en:NOT> accessed 11 April 2018
51 Directive 2006/116/EC of the European Parliament and of the Council of 12 December 2006 on the term of protection of copyright and certain related rights [2006] OJ L372/12, recital 16 <http://eur-lex.europa.eu/LexUriServ/LexUriServ.do?uri=CELEX:32006L0116:EN:NOT> accessed 11 April 2018
52 Copyright and Related Rights Act 2000, s 17(3)
53 ibid s 17(5)
54 ibid s 17(6)

3.3.5) Author of a photograph and first owner of copyright in a photograph

Under S.21 of the CRRA, the "author" of a work is the person who creates the work and in the case of a "photograph" that is the "photographer".[55] The Act also provides for the joint authorship of works.[56] The first owner of the copyright in a photograph is the author of the work unless:

(a) the work is made by an employee in the course of employment, in which case the employer is the first owner of any copyright in the work, subject to any agreement to the contrary,
(b) the work is the subject of Government or Oireachtas copyright,
(c) the work is the subject of the copyright of a prescribed international organisation, or
(d) the copyright in the work is conferred on some other person by an enactment.[57]

Also, S.23(2) of the CRRA states:

> Where a work, other than a computer program, is made by an author in the course of employment by the proprietor of a newspaper or periodical, the author may use the work for any purpose, other than for the purposes of making available that work to newspapers or periodicals, without infringing the copyright in the work.[58]

The question of whether a joint ownership of the first copyright in a photograph exists could potentially arise in a number of situations, for example where a photo stylist or an assistant photographer is involved in a photo shoot.[59] Ideally, the issue of copyright ownership in created photographs should be explicitly stated in any photographer's contract *for* services. Joint copyright ownership is also of relevance to press photographers, who are employed by newspapers or periodicals and who may wish to use their created photographs for other purposes like including them in exhibitions; personal, printed promotional materials or selling prints of them to third parties. Many press photographers work through photo agencies on a freelance or on a contractual basis. In some instances, images photographed by a number of photographers at an event may be pooled and later selected from by the photo agency for publication. Depending upon the terms of the contract between the photographer and the photo agency, the

55 ibid s 21(h)
56 ibid s 22(1)
57 ibid s 23(1)
58 ibid s 23(2)
59 For example see: *Celebrity Pictures Ltd. and Tyson Sadlo v B. Hannah Ltd.* [2012] EWPCC 32

owner of the copyright in such photographs may be either an individual photographer or a joint ownership between either an individual photographer or a pool of photographers and the photo agency.[60]

3.3.6) *Presumption of knowing a work's author and first copyright owner*

The CRRA grants a presumption in respect of knowledge of the author of a work and, by definition, the first copyright owner to a work, S.2(7) of the Act states: 'The author of a work shall be deemed to be known where it is possible for a person, without previous knowledge of the facts, to ascertain the identity of the author of the work by reasonable enquiry.'[61] This presumption is relevant to claims of copyright infringement and to the topic of orphan works, which will be discussed further.

3.3.7) *Duration of copyright in a photograph*

Under S.24(1) of the CRRA, the duration of the copyright in a photograph expires '70 years after the date of the death of its author, irrespective of the date on which it has been first lawfully made available to the public'.[62] In accordance with S.35 of the Act, the term of copyright in respect of a photograph commences on 'the first day of January in the year following the event that gives rise to that term'.[63] A similar term of copyright exists in respects of an anonymous or pseudonymous artistic work lawfully made available to the public provided there is no doubt concerning the author's identity, the author has disclosed his/her identity or where his/her identity becomes known within 70 years from the date on which the work was first lawfully made available.[64] It could be a difficult task for anybody other than a photographer himself to accurately state whether or not particular images contained within his/her lifetime's collection of work were or were not ever made available to the public by him either under his/her own name or anonymously or pseudonymously and if they were the individual dates on which each such image was first made available. Consequently, if photographers wish to have a clearer and longer copyright duration to subsist in their works, it would be better for them to

60 See: Mathilde de Rocquigny, 'France: Ownership of Rights Concerning Agency Photographs' *European Audiovisual Observatory IRIS Merlin*, IRIS 2001–2:14/32 (Regional Court in Nanterre, 1 Chamber A, 13 December 2000 – case of *Francis Apesteguy et autres v Société Gamma Presse Image*) <http://merlin.obs.coe.int/iris/2001/2/article32.en.html> accessed 14 April 2018

61 Copyright and Related Rights Act 2000, s 2(7)

62 ibid s 24(1)

63 ibid s 35

64 ibid s 24(2), s 24(3)

only make their works available during their lifetime under their own names and not anonymously or pseudonymously.

Once an author's term of copyright in an unpublished photograph has expired, it may be possible for a third party to obtain a copyright in it by making it available to the public. Section 34 of the Act states:

> Following the expiration of the copyright in a work, any person who lawfully makes available to the public for the first time a work which was not previously so made available, shall benefit from rights equivalent to the rights of an author, other than the moral rights, for 25 years from the date on which the work is first lawfully made available to the public.[65]

In addition to making provision for a court to grant orders for the disclosure of information concerning the origin and distribution of infringing works and for the recall, removal or destruction of copyright infringing works, the European Communities (Enforcement of Intellectual Property Rights) Regulations 2006 amended the CRRA and inserted a new S.34A, which contains a presumption as to the ownership of the copyright in a work made available to the public in accordance with S.34:

> In civil proceedings for infringement of a right conferred in respect of a work made available to the public under section 34, where copies of the work bear or incorporate a statement, label or other mark that a named person is the owner of rights in the work under that section, the statement, label or mark shall be admissible as evidence of the fact stated or indicated and shall be presumed to be correct, unless the contrary is proved.[66]

3.3.8) Qualification for copyright protection

In general, copyright shall not subsist in a work unless the qualification requirements, as specified in the CRRA, in respect of the work's author and the country, territory, state or area in which the work is first lawfully made available to the public are satisfied.[67] A work will qualify for copyright protection if 'its author was at the material time a qualifying person'.[68] Qualifying persons are defined by the Act as including, among others, an Irish citizen and 'a citizen or subject of, or an individual domiciled or ordinarily resident in the State, or in any country, territory, state or area to which the relevant provisions of this Part extend'.[69]

65 ibid s 34
66 European Communities (Enforcement of Intellectual Property Rights) Regulations 2006 SI 2006/360, reg 6
67 Copyright and Related Rights Act 2000, s 182
68 ibid s 183(1)
69 ibid s 183(2)

Being an artistic work, a photograph qualifies for copyright protection 'where it is first lawfully made available to the public (a) in the State; or (b) in any country, territory, state or area to which the relevant provision of this Part extends'.[70] On making available to the public, S.184 states:

> lawfully making available to the public a work in one country, territory, state or area shall be deemed to be the first lawful making available to the public of the work even where the work is simultaneously lawfully made available to the public elsewhere; and for this purpose, lawfully making available to the public of a work elsewhere within the previous 30 days shall be deemed to be simultaneous.[71]

3.3.9) Registration of copyright is not a legal requirement for copyright to subsist

There is no state copyright registration system in Ireland. For a copyright to subsist in a photograph, it is not a legal requirement under the CRRA that the copyright must be registered. Under S.175 of the Act, the Controller of Patents, Designs and Trade Marks licenses and maintains a register of copyright licensing bodies[72] and for copyright licensing purposes, a copyright owner may register a copyright in a photograph with one of the registered copyright licensing bodies. Normally, licensed copyright licensing bodies deduct a commission on any copyright royalties collected on behalf of their members.

3.3.10) Copyright owner's rights

Under S.37(1) of the CRRA, and subject to the exemptions contained within Chapter 6 of the Act (as discussed further), the owner of the copyright to a work (a photograph) has an exclusive right to undertake or to authorise others to undertake acts, which the CRRA terms "*acts restricted by copyright*". A copyright owner has an exclusive right:

(a) to copy the work;
(b) to make available to the public the work;

70 ibid s 184(1)
71 ibid s 184(2)
Note: Section 188(1) of the CRRA, as amended, provides for the extension of the provisions for the qualification of works for copyright protection, as specified in Sections 183 and 184, to any convention country, state or area. Under the Third Schedule to the Act, the list of agreements, treaties and conventions which shall be reckonable for the purpose of the extension of the qualification of copyright protection to works under Section 188 of the Act includes, among others, the Berne Convention and the WIPO Agreement.
72 Irish Patents Office, *Register of Copyright Licensing Bodies* <www.patentsoffice.ie/en/Copyright/Regulation-of-Copyright-Licensing-Bodies/> accessed 12 April 2018

(c) to make an adaptation of the work or to undertake either of the acts referred to in paragraph (a) or (b) in relation to an adaptation.[73]

Section 39(2) of the CRRA gives the owner of the copyright in a work "reproduction rights" – that is the right to make copies of that work or to authorise other people to do so.[74] Copying includes the storage of the copyrighted work in any medium and in relation to an artistic work the making of three-dimensional copies of a two dimensional work and the making of two dimensional copies of a three-dimensional work.[75] The owner of a copyright has a "making available right". That is the right to make either the original work or copies of the work available to the public or to authorise others to do so.[76] A copyright owner also has distribution,[77] rental and lending rights.[78] The owner of the copyright to a photograph would be eligible to benefit from these rights. Section 42(2)(a) of the CRRA states that "rental" 'means making a copy of a work available for use, on terms that it is to be or may be returned after a limited period of time, for direct or indirect economic or commercial advantage', while S.42(2)(b) states that "lending" 'means making a copy of a work available for use, on terms that it is to be or may be returned after a limited period of time, otherwise than for direct or indirect economic or commercial advantage, through an establishment to which members of the public have access'.[79]

A number of exclusions to the previously mentioned renting and lending rights are specified under S.42(3) of the Act, which states:

> References in this Part to "rental" or "lending" shall not include the making available of copies of a work for the purposes of:
>
> (a) performing, playing or showing in public, broadcasting or inclusion in a cable programme service,
> (b) exhibition in public, or
> (c) on the spot reference use.[80]

73 Copyright and Related Rights Act 2000, s 37(1)
74 Copyright and Related Rights Act 2000, s 39(2)
75 ibid s 39(1)
76 ibid s 40(8)
Note: Under Section 40(4) of the CRRA, where a person who provides facilities for the making available of a copy of a work has been advised by the owner of the copyright in that work that those facilities are being used to infringe that copyright and he/she fails to remove the infringing material, that person shall be liable for the infringement of the copyright in the work.
77 ibid s 41(1)
78 ibid s 42(6)
79 ibid s 42(2)
80 ibid s 42(3)

The making available and lending rights of a copyright holder were amended by the Copyright and Related Rights (Amendment) Act 2007 Act.[81] In relation to the making available rights, S.5 of the 2007 Act amended S.40(1)(g) of the CRRA by deleting the words "without payment of remuneration to the owner of the copyright in the work"[82] and S.9 of the 2007 Act repealed S.69 of the CRRA.[83] Section 6 of the 2007 Act inserted a new S.42(7) in the CRRA to create a new exemption for public libraries to a copyright holder's lending rights. It states:

> The lending right in relation to a work does not apply at any time in a period during which a scheme for the remuneration of authors is in effect, pursuant to Section 42A, in relation to works of a class in which that work is included, whether the author, or (in the case of a work of joint authorship) any of the authors, is a participant in that scheme or not.[84]

Section 7 of the 2007 Act[85] inserted a new S.42(A) in the CRRA to authorise the Minister to establish a Public Lending Remuneration Scheme under which the authors of qualifying works would receive remuneration for the lending of their works by public libraries.[86] The Copyright and Related Rights (Public Lending Remuneration Scheme) Regulations 2008,[87] as amended by the 2013 Regulations,[88] established this Scheme.[89] The authors of qualifying works may register their works with the Registrar of the Public Lending Rights Remuneration Scheme in order to receive a remuneration for the lending of their works by public libraries. This Scheme applies to books and not to stand-alone photographs. As a consequence of the creation of the previously mentioned lending right exemption under S.42(7) of the Act and as membership of the Scheme by authors of books is voluntary, it would be prudent for any photographer, who has published a photography book, to register as a member of the Scheme,

81 Copyright and Related Rights (Amendment) Act 2007, s 6(b)
82 ibid s 5
83 ibid s 9
84 Copyright and Related Rights Act 2000, s 42(7)
85 Copyright and Related Rights (Amendment) Act 2007, s 7
86 Copyright and Related Rights Act 2000, s 42(A)
87 Copyright and Related Rights (Public Lending Remuneration Scheme) Regulations 2008 SI 2008/597
88 Copyright and Related Rights (Public Lending Remuneration Scheme) (Amendment) Regulations 2013 SI 2013/221
89 Public Lending Remuneration Office, *About the PLR Scheme* <www.plr.ie/about-plr/> accessed 12 April 2018
Note: In June 2013, the Chief Executive Officer of the Local Government Management Agency was designated as the Registrar of the Scheme by the Minister for the Environment, Community and Local Government through the Copyright and Related Rights (Public Lending Remuneration Scheme) (Amendment) Regulations 2013 SI 2013/221, reg 4.

which is administered by the Public Lending Remuneration Office. By doing so, they would have a possibility of receiving some level of remuneration for the lending-out of copies of their works by public libraries.

Making an adaptation of a work is an act restricted to the owner of the copyright in that work and S.43(1)(a) of the CRRA states that for the purposes of S.37 of the Act, 'an adaptation is made when it is recorded in writing or otherwise'.[90] In addition, S.43(2)(c) states that 'an adaptation of an artistic work includes a collage of the work with other works, an arrangement or other alteration of the work'.[91]

The rights granted through S.37(1) of the CRRA to the owners of the copyright in photographs are very important to them from an economic[92] perspective. However, in many instances the enforcement of these rights is extremely problematic due to the theft of photographers' images and their subsequent unauthorised usage by third parties on Internet websites, social media sites and in printed materials and photographers' inability to obtain payment for such unauthorised usage from the owners and/or client users of such sites.

3.3.11) Infringement of copyright

The purpose of the infringement provisions of the CRRA is to protect the rights of copyright holders in qualifying works. Section 37(2) of the CRRA states that 'the copyright in a work is infringed by a person who without the licence of the copyright owner undertakes, or authorises another to undertake, any of the acts restricted by copyright'.[93] Furthermore, S.37(3) states that 'references to the undertaking of an act restricted by the copyright in a work shall relate to the work as a whole or to any substantial part of the work and to whether the act is undertaken directly or indirectly'.[94] One may infringe the copyright in a work by either copying the work in its entirety or a substantial part of it. In the case of photographs, the issue of a "substantial part" of the work is problematic, as the Act does not define what constitutes a "substantial part" of a photograph. On a normal reading, one would view a copy image of a copyrighted photograph as being a substantial part of the copyrighted photograph, if it contains a straight crop and copy of the majority percentage of the copyrighted

90 Copyright and Related Rights Act 2000, s 43(1)(a)
Note: For an example of an adaptation of a photograph see: Noel Barker, 'New Tubridy Sketch After Objection By Photographer' *Irish Examiner* (Cork, 28 February 2014) <www.irishexaminer.com/ireland/new-tubridy-sketch-after-objection-by-photographer-260369.html> accessed 12 April 2018

91 ibid s 43(2)(c)

92 Note: See: The British Photographic Council, *British Photographic Council Industry Survey Shows True Value of Photographers' Copyright* (July 2010) <www.british-photographic-council.org/survey/2010> accessed 12 April 2018

93 Copyright and Related Rights Act 2000, s 37(2)

94 ibid s 37(3)

photograph. It has been for the courts to determine what constitutes a "substantial part" of a photograph and judges views have differed. They have looked at the actual subject matter content captured in a photograph while determining whether a photograph is a copy of another. *Creation Records Ltd. v News Group Newspapers*[95] and *Temple Island Collections Limited v New English Teas Limited*[96] are two example cases. In the English High Court case of *Creation Records*, Lloyd J stated that a basis proposition of copyright law is that where two works are created using the same source that does not result in one work being a copy of the other.[97] The English Patents County Court case of *Temple Island Collections* concerned not the originality of two in-camera created photographs, but rather the originality of two greyscale[98] photographic prints. Both prints featured a number of similar constituent elements, namely a south-bound, spot-coloured[99] red London Routemaster bus on Westminster Bridge with Big Ben and the House of Parliament in the background under a white sky. They were shot from different angles – one was from road level, while the other was from below road level and also showed the River Thames. The defendant admitted having prior sight of the claimant's photograph. Birss J determined that the claimant's work had been substantially copied and that there had been a copyright infringement. Although an idea cannot be copyrighted, it would appear that the Court's decision was based more on the constituent elements of the idea as expressed in the two photographs rather than the actual expression of such elements through the photographs.

In addition to the previously mentioned provisions relating to copyright infringement under S.37(2) of the CRRA in Ireland, under S.44(2) a copy of a copyrighted work

> shall be an infringing copy (a) where the making of it constitutes an infringement of the copyright in the work concerned or (b) where it has been or is to be imported into the State, and its making in the State would have constituted an infringement of the copyright in the work concerned, or a breach of an exclusive licence agreement relating to that work.[100]

While one may infringe the copyright in a copyrighted photograph by creating an unauthorised adaptation of it,[101] one may also commit a secondary

95 *Creation Records Ltd. v News Group Newspapers* [1997] EWHC Ch 370
96 *Temple Island Collections Limited v New English Teas Limited* [2012] EWPCC 1
97 *Creation Records Ltd. v News Group Newspapers* [1997] EWHC Ch 370, para 15
98 Note: A greyscale photograph is one in which all colour is reduced to a range of grey shades.
99 Note: Spot-colouring is a printing process through which a colour is added to a specific section of a greyscale image.
100 Copyright and Related Rights Act 2000, s 44(2)
101 ibid s 43

infringement of a copyrighted work by dealing with an infringing copy of the work[102] or by providing another party with the means for making infringing copies of the work.[103] In addition, if one transmits a copy of a copyrighted work without the permission of the copyright owner via a telecommunications system (which would include by telephone, fax, email or through the Internet), such a transmission and subsequent reception of the copy of the copyrighted work would amount to an infringement of the copyright.[104]

3.3.12) Exempted acts permitted in respect of copyrighted works

The CRRA provides a number of exemptions to the rights available under copyright, whereby certain activities undertaken by third parties will not constitute an infringement to the copyright in an artistic work. Such exempted acts, which do have limitations, relate to fair dealing for research or private study;[105] for criticism or review purposes or for reporting of current events;[106] incidental inclusion of a copyrighted material;[107] educational,[108] library and archive activities;[109] and public administration.[110] The CRRA defines "Fair dealing" with an artistic work for research or private study purposes as:

> the making use of a literary, dramatic, musical or artistic work, . . . for a purpose and to an extent which will not unreasonably prejudice the interests of the owner of the copyright.[111]

The test, therefore, is one of reasonableness. The Act further states that fair dealing with a work for the purposes of criticism or review of either that work or another work 'shall not infringe any copyright in the work where the criticism or review is accompanied by a sufficient acknowledgement'.[112] However, in relation to the reporting of current events there is a specified exclusion in respect of use of photographs under S.51(2), which states:

> fair dealing with a work (other than a photograph) for the purpose of reporting current events shall not infringe copyright in that work, where the report is accompanied by a sufficient acknowledgement.[113]

102 ibid s 45
103 ibid s 46(1)
104 ibid s 46(2)
105 ibid s 50(1)
106 ibid s 51(2)
107 ibid s 52(1)
108 ibid ss 53–58
109 ibid ss 58–70
110 ibid ss 71–77
111 ibid s 50(4)
112 ibid s 51(1)
113 ibid s 52(2)

One may ask why are photographs granted an exemption to fair dealing for the purposes of reporting current events under S.51(2) of the Act? The Copyright Act 1963 did not contain such an exemption for photographs and during the Dáil Éireann[114] and Seanad Éireann[115] debates on the Copyright and Related Rights Bill 1999, discussion relating to S.51 did not make any mention as to why a photograph should or should not be granted this exemption. However, it is noted that the wording of S.51(2) of the Act is virtually identical to that of S.30(2) of the United Kingdom's Copyright, Designs and Patents Act 1988, which relates to "fair dealing for the purposes of reporting current events". Without such an exemption, the income which photographers (particularly freelance photographers) may derive from the publication and re-publication of their photographs would be in serious jeopardy and would impact on their livelihoods. The copyright in a copyrighted work, including photographs, is not infringed if it is included in another work in an incidental manner.[116] The CRRA does not define what constitutes an "incidental" inclusion. This exception may possibly apply if a copyrighted photograph is included in another photograph, but in the background and not forming the majority of the contents of the latter photograph. However, if such an inclusion is undertaken in a manner which unreasonably prejudices the interests of the owner of the copyright to that work, then it would not come within this exemption.[117]

Sections 53–58 of the CRRA provide for a broad range of exemptions, subject to limitations, in respect of education, libraries and archives.[118] Under S.53(1) of the Act, a copyrighted, published artistic work may be copied without infringing its copyright if it is 'copied in the course of instruction or of preparation for instruction'.[119] This exemption does not apply to unpublished artistic works. Also, the exemption does not apply unless:

(a) the copying is done by or on behalf of a person giving or receiving instruction,
(b) the copying is not by means of a reprographic process, and
(c) the copy is accompanied by a sufficient acknowledgement.[120]

114 Dáil Deb 11 November 1999, vol 510, col 1091 <http://oireachtasdebates.oireachtas.ie/debates%20authoring/debateswebpack.nsf/takes/dail1999111100006?opendocument> accessed 16 April 2018

115 Seanad Deb 30 June 1999, vol 160, col 66 <http://oireachtasdebates.oireachtas.ie/debates%20authoring/debateswebpack.nsf/takes/seanad1999063000008?opendocumen t> accessed 16 April 2018

116 Copyright and Related Rights Act 2000, s 52(1)

117 ibid s 52(3)

118 ibid ss 53–58

119 ibid s 53(1)

120 ibid s 53(2)

Due to the CRRA's definition of a "reprographic process",[121] this S.53(1) exemption may not be availed of to copy photographs published either in books or in an electronic format or to copy published, stand-alone photographs. Section 58 of the CRRA, as amended by S.8 of the Copyright and Related Rights (Amendment) Act 2007, also grants an exemption to educational establishments in respect of the lending by them of copyrighted works.[122] Sections 59–70 of the CRRA, as amended, provide exemptions, subject to limitations, in respect of the copying of copyrighted works by prescribed libraries and archives.[123]

For the purposes of public administration, the CRRA also provides for exemptions to the rights of copyright owners. Under S.71(1) of the Act, 'The copyright in a work is not infringed by anything done for the purposes of parliamentary or judicial proceedings or for the purpose of reporting those proceedings.'[124] Thus, the copyright in photographs prepared for a client as part of his/her evidence in a court case would not be infringed by the making of copies of them for or by his/her opponent in the case. A similar exemption exists in respect of statutory inquiries.[125] Under S.73 of the Act, 'Any material which is comprised in records which are open to public inspection may be copied, and a copy may be supplied to any person, without infringement of copyright.'[126] There is a limitation to this exemption in that no use other than for public record inspection purposes may be made of a copy of a public record containing copyrighted material without the copyright owner's permission.[127] This limitation must be clearly marked on any copy of a public record made available to the public.[128] From a photographer's perspective, unless such a mark is clearly displayed on the facing side of any hardcopy photographs made

121 Note: Section 2(1) of the CRRA defines "reprographic process" as: 'a process for (a) making facsimile copies, or (b) involving the use of an appliance for making multiple copies, and includes, in relation to a work held in electronic form, any copying by electronic means, but does not include the making of a film or sound recording'.

122 ibid s 58

123 ibid ss 59–70

Note (1): Section 2(3) of the CRRA states that references in the Act to "prescribed archives" apply equally to "prescribed museums".

Note (2): See: Copyright and Related Rights (Educational Establishments and Establishments to which Members of the Public have Access) Order 2000, SI 2000/409 and Copyright and Related Rights (Librarians and Archivists) (Copying of Protected Material) Regulations 2000, SI 2000/427.

Note (3): Sections 61, 62, 64, 65, 67 and 68 of the CRRA were amended by the European Union (Certain Permitted Uses of Orphan Works) Regulations 2014 SI 2014/490 to give effect to Directive 2012/28/EU of the European Parliament and of the Council of 25 October 2012 on certain permitted uses of orphan works. The topic of orphan works will be discussed further below.

124 ibid s 71(1)

125 ibid s 71(2)

126 ibid s 73

127 ibid s 74(2)

128 ibid s 74(3)

available the practical benefit of this limitation and marking requirement would be of little use.

The European Communities (Copyright and Related Rights) Regulations 2004[129] were introduced to give further effect to Directive 2001/29/EC[130] and they inserted a new S.87 in the CRRA. Under the new S.87(1), temporary acts of reproduction do not infringe the copyright in a work where such acts are:

> transient or incidental and which are an integral and essential part of a technological process and whose sole purpose is to enable (a) a transmission in a network between third parties by an intermediary, or (b) a lawful use, of a work or other subject-matter to be made, and which acts have no independent economic significance.[131]

The CRRA grants a copyright infringement exemption to cover the reproduction of copyrighted works by Internet intermediaries, which is a necessity in the course of their provision of transmission services to and between their clients. A 2011 decision by the German Federal Supreme Court (Bundesgerichtshof) (hereinafter "BGH") may act as words of caution for photographers regarding the possibility or not of an infringement by intermediaries, and in particular by search engines, of their copyright in photographs which they have published on the Internet. The BGH determined that the search engine Google had not infringed the copyright in photographs by displaying thumbnail copies of them in the results generated following a search for an image topic using Google's image search facility. The Court referred to its decision in a similar case in 2010 in which it held that because the plaintiff had not taken any technically possible measures to prevent search engines accessing copies of her images, that she had not objected to her images being displayed as thumbnails by the search engine.[132]

129 European Communities (Copyright and Related Rights) Regulations 2004 SI 2004/16

130 Directive 2001/29/EC of the European Parliament and of the Council of 22 May 2001 on the harmonisation of certain aspects of copyright and related rights in the information society [2001] OJ L167/10 <http://eur-lex.europa.eu/LexUriServ/LexUriServ.do?uri=OJ:L:2001:167:0010:0019:EN:PDF> accessed 16 April 2018

131 Copyright and Related Rights Act 2000, s 87(1)
Note: In Case C-360/13 *Public Relations Consultants Association Ltd. v The Newspaper Licensing Agency Ltd. and Others* (5 June 2014), the CJEU, at para 63, held that 'Article 5 of Directive 2001/29 must be interpreted as meaning that the on-screen copies and the cached copies made by an end-user in the course of viewing a website satisfy the conditions that those copies must be temporary, that they must be transient or incidental in nature and that they must constitute an integral and essential part of a technological process, as well as the conditions laid down in Article 5(5) of that directive, and that they may therefore be made without the authorisation of the copyright holders.'

132 Note (1): See: Anne Yliniva-Hoffmann, 'Germany: BGH Rules Again on Thumbnail Admissibility' *European Audiovisual Observatory IRIS Merlin*, IRIS 2012-1:1/17 <http://merlin.obs.coe.int/iris/2012/1/article17.en.html> accessed 16 April 2018
Note (2): See: Anne Yliniva-Hoffmann, 'Germany: BGH Rules that Google Image Search Engine Does Not Breach Copyright' *European Audiovisual Observatory IRIS Merlin*,

This BGH decision shifts the onus onto the copyright owner to prevent images being located on the Internet and copied by search engines. It is similar to saying that because a person's house does not have a burglar alarm installed, a burglar is legally entitled to conclude that its owner would not object if he broke into it. While one may prevent a search engine's crawler from finding photographs on a website through, for example, the inclusion of a "robots.txt" file in a website's software code, in reality doing so would defeat a commercial photographer's ability to sell copies of images displayed on his/her website, as only individuals who would know the exact URLs for the website's image galleries would be able to find them. Also, even though they are not always successful, the use of search engine image finders, like Google's "Image Search", are handy tools for photographers to use in tracking down the unauthorised use of their copyrighted images by other websites. Some social media websites do take notice of the rights of image copyright holders. For example, one may insert a Pinterest "pinterest nopin"[133] meta tag on one's website. Upon seeing this meta tag, Pinterest's web crawler will prevent copyright protected images being pinned from such websites to Pinterest by its account holders.[134]

Frequently referred to as "freedom of panorama", one may photograph buildings, sculptures, models of buildings and works of artistic craftsmanship that are permanently on public display and situated either in a public place or in a premises that is open to the public without infringing any copyright in such works.[135] Also, one may subsequently make created photographic copies of such artistic works available to the public without infringing the copyright in the original artistic works.[136]

It is not an infringement of the copyright in an artistic work if a copy of it is made for the purpose of including such a copy in an advertisement to sell that work.[137] If that copy of the original work is later 'sold, rented or lent, or offered or exposed for sale, rental, loan, or otherwise made available to the public', then it would be an infringement of the copyright in the original work.[138]

Where one is the author of, but not the copyright owner to, an artistic work, one may make another subsequent copy of that work without infringing the copyright in that work 'provided the author does not repeat or imitate the main design of the earlier work'.[139] In essence, for a photographer to benefit from

IRIS 2010–6:1/18 <http://merlin.obs.coe.int/iris/2010/6/article18.en.html> accessed 16 April 2018

133 Pinterest, *Prevent Saves to Pinterest From Your Website* <https://help.pinterest.com/en/articles/prevent-people-saving-things-pinterest-your-site> accessed 16 April 2018

134 Matt McGee, 'Flickr Uses "Nopin" Meta Tag to Keep Some Images Off Pinterest' *Marketing Land* (25 February 2012) <http://marketingland.com/flickr-uses-nopin-meta-tag-to-keep-some-images-off-pinterest-6811> accessed 16 April 2018

135 Copyright and Related Rights Act 2000, s 93(2)(c)

136 ibid s 93(3)

137 ibid s 94(1)

138 ibid s 94(2)

139 ibid s 95

this exemption, his/her copy image would have to look substantially different to his/her previously created image. When selling photographs, photographers should carefully evaluate the effect of selling their copyright in their images along with the images on their legal ability to subsequently create very similar images.

3.3.13) Dealings with rights in copyrighted works

The copyright in an artistic work is a property right independent of any property rights attached to that physical work. In accordance with S.120(1) of the CRRA, 'the Copyright in a work is transmissible by assignment, by testamentary disposition or by operation of the law, as personal or moveable property'.[140] Also, under S.120(2)

> a transmission of the copyright in a work by assignment, by testamentary disposition or by operation of law may be partial, so as to apply (a) to one or more but not all of the acts the copyright owner has the right to undertake or authorise, and (b) to part but not the whole of the period for which the copyright in the work is to subsist.[141]

Thus, the owner of the copyright in a work could decide, for example, to assign, license or transmit by testament the right to make the work available to the public without a right to make an adaptation of the work. For an assignment in whole or in part of a copyright in a work to have legal effect, it must be in writing and signed by the assignor or on his/her behalf.[142] A copyright licence granted by a copyright owner to a third party is:

> binding on every successor in title to his or her interest in the copyright, except a purchaser in good faith for valuable consideration and without notice (actual or constructive) of the licence or a person deriving title from such a purchaser.[143]

A copyright licence may be granted on either a non-exclusive or an exclusive basis.[144] An "exclusive licence" is defined by the CRRA as:

> a licence in writing which is signed by or on behalf of an owner or prospective owner of the copyright which authorises the licensee, to the exclusion of all other persons, including the person granting the licence, to exercise a

140 ibid s 120(1)
141 ibid s 120(2)
142 ibid s 120(3)
143 ibid s 120(4)
144 ibid s 122(1)

right which would otherwise be exercisable exclusively by the copyright owner and references to an exclusive licensee shall be construed accordingly.[145]

In the course of business, photographers frequently grant copyright licences to third parties for either a specific or an indefinite duration on a non-exclusive basis. If a photographer were to grant an exclusive licence to a third party, they would be excluding themself (and possibly to their own financial detriment) from undertaking for the duration of the licence any of the acts restricted by the copyright in a work.[146]

3.3.14) Moral rights

In addition to the previously discussed, range of economic rights granted to the owner of the copyright in artistic works, the CRRA, as amended, also grants a number of moral rights, namely a *Paternity Right*, an *Integrity Right* and a *Right Against False Attribution to a Work.* Furthermore, the CRRA grants a *Privacy Right* to people who commission the creation of photographs for private or domestic purposes. Under S.107 of the Act, the author of a work has the right to 'be identified as the author and that right shall also apply in relation to an adaptation of the work'.[147] An author who uses a pseudonym, initials or other form of identification has the right to use such a form to identify his/ her work.[148] The right to be identified as the author is known as the *paternity right.* However, under S.108 there are a number of exemptions to this right and any acts done under Sections 52, 53(5), 71, 72 or 88 of the CRRA, which relate respectively to the incidental inclusion of copyright material; anything done for the purposes of examinations; parliamentary and judicial proceedings; statutory inquiries; and anonymous or pseudonymous works do not infringe the paternity right.[149] The paternity right does not apply to 'anything done by or with the authority of the copyright owner where the copyright in the work originally vested in an employer under Section 23'.[150] It also does not apply to a work created for the purpose of reporting current events[151] or a newspaper,

145 ibid s 122(1)

146 Note: When photographers are granting third parties permission to use their images, if they do so through a licence agreement, they would generally use their own licence agreements. In recent years, some photographers have been using "*Copyleft*" and "*Creative Commons*" licensing systems, rather than drafting and using their own licences. As these licensing systems operate within copyright law, they will not be discussed in this book.
Copyleft, *What Is Copyleft?* <https://copyleft.org/> accessed 16 April 2018
Creative Commons, *What We Do: What Is Creative Commons?* <https://creativecommons.org/about/> accessed 18 April 2018

147 Copyright and Related Rights Act 2000, s 107(1)

148 ibid s 107(2)

149 ibid s 108(1)

150 ibid s 108(2)

151 ibid s 108(3)

periodical and other specified types of publications.[152] Furthermore, it does not apply to works in which either a Government or Oireachtas copyright subsists, or to works in which the copyright originally vested in a prescribed international organisation unless the work's author had previously been identified as its author in copies of the work that had been made available to the public.[153] The paternity right does not apply in respect of an artistic work whose author died before the commencement of Part II (on Copyright) of the Act.[154] In addition, a paternity right in respect of an artistic work shall not apply:

(a) where copyright first vested in the author, to anything which by virtue of an assignment of copyright made or licence granted before the commencement of Part II of this Act may be done without infringing copyright,
(b) where copyright first vested in a person other than the author, to anything done by or with the licence of the copyright owner.[155]

Section 109 of the CRRA concerns the "*Integrity Right*" and states:

> the author of a work shall have the right to object to any distortion, mutilation or other modification of, or other derogatory action in relation to, the work which would prejudice his or her reputation and that right shall also apply in relation to an adaptation of the work.[156]

Like the previously mentioned paternity right, the integrity right is similarly restricted by the terms of S.12(1) and S.12(2) of Part I of the First Schedule to the Act.[157] Also, S.110 and S.111 of the Act contain a wide range of exemptions and qualifications to this integrity right. One infringes an integrity right by possessing, dealing in or making available

> a work or a copy of a work or an adaptation thereof which has, and which he or she knows or has reason to believe has, been subjected to any distortion, mutilation or other modification or other derogatory action within the meaning of Section 109.[158]

152 ibid s 108(4)
153 ibid s 108(5)
154 ibid first sch, part I, s 12(1)
Note: Commencement date: 12 December, 2000. Copyright and Related Rights Act (Commencement) Order 2000, SI 2000/404.
155 ibid first sch, part I, s 12(2)
156 ibid s 109(1)
157 ibid first sch, part I, ss 12(1)–12(2)
158 ibid s 112

Authors have a right not to have works falsely attributed to them.[159] The "*Right against False Attribution to a Work*" also applies to adaptations of works.[160] An "attribution" is defined by S.113(5) of the Act as being 'a statement, express or implied, as to who is the author of the work'.[161] This right is infringed if one undertakes any one of a number of specified actions, such as the sale of a work or a copy of a work with a false attribution while 'knowing or having reason to believe that the attribution is false'.[162] Court cases concerning the false attribution of artistic works are a rarity and particularly so in relation to photographs.[163] In addition to the previously mentioned integrity rights granted to the owners of the copyright in photographs, S.114(1) of the CRRA grants, subject to a few specified exceptions, a privacy right to people, who commission photographers to create photographs for private or domestic purposes.[164] The making available of a work or copies of a work subject to S.114 without the authority of the work's commissioner is an infringement of this right to privacy. Although this right may be waived in writing[165] in favour of a commissioned photographer, it is a right against rather than a right to a photographer. Consequently, this right to privacy will be discussed in Chapter 4. The S.107 paternity right, the S.109 integrity right and the S.114 right to privacy in a photograph subsist for the same duration[166] as that of the copyright (as specified by S.24) in the photograph. But, the S.113 right against the false attribution of a work subsists for 20 years after the death of the person on whom that right is conferred.[167] A right against false attribution of authorship existed under the Copyright Act 1963 and it had a similar duration limitation.[168] Although this moral right was discussed during the Oireachtas Select Committee on Enterprise and Small Business Debate on the Copyright and Related Rights Bill 1999, there was no specific discussion relating to the duration period of the right.[169] It would appear that the 20-year duration limitation was simply carried over to the CRRA resulting in this moral right having a shorter duration period than

159 ibid s 113(1)
160 ibid s 113(4)
161 ibid s 113(5)
162 ibid s 113(2)
163 For example see: *Clark v Associated Newspapers Ltd.* [1998] EWHC Patents 345
164 Copyright and Related Rights Act 2000, s 114(1)
Note: This S.114 right to privacy does not apply to photographs taken before the commencement date of Part 2 of the Act (12 December, 2000).
Copyright and Related Rights Act 2000, first sch, para 13.
Copyright and Related Rights Act (Commencement) Order 2000, SI 2000/404.
165 ibid s 116
166 ibid s 115(1)
167 ibid s 115(2)
168 Copyright Act 1963, s 54(5)
169 Oireachtas Select Committee on Enterprise and Small Business Deb 17 Feb 2000 <http://oireachtasdebates.oireachtas.ie/Debates%20Authoring/DebatesWebPack.nsf/committeetakes/BUS2000021700003> accessed 16 April 2018

that of the other previously mentioned moral rights. It is also noted, that it is of a similar duration to that provided for under the United Kingdom's Copyright, Designs and Patents Act 1988[170] and its preceding Act, the Copyright Act 1956.[171] The statutory right against false attribution of authorship has its origin in the Fine Arts Copyright Act 1862, which also specified a 20-year limitation period following an author's death.[172] It would be appropriate for the legislature to amend the duration of this moral right to that of the other moral rights.

In contrast to copyright, any moral rights attached to a work are not assignable or alienable.[173] Under S.107 and S.109 of the CRRA, only the author of a work may be granted respectively a paternity or an integrity right.[174] The right against false attribution of authorship of a work may apply to anybody,[175] while the right to privacy in a work commissioned for private and domestic purposes only applies to the commissioner of such a work.[176] Section 119 of the CRRA concerns the transmission of moral rights upon death and it states that upon the death of any person entitled to a paternity right, an integrity right or a privacy right in a photograph:

> (a) the right passes by testamentary disposition to such person as the person entitled to the right may direct,
> (b) where there is no direction as to whom the right passes but the copyright in the work concerned forms part of an estate, the right passes to the person to whom the copyright passes, and
> (c) where the right does not pass under paragraph (a) or (b), it is exercisable by the personal representatives of the person entitled to the right.[177]

In relation to the right against false attribution, S.119(5) of the Act provides that:

> Any infringement of the right conferred by Section 113 in relation to a false attribution of a work after the death of a person is actionable by the personal representatives of that person.[178]

170 Copyright, Designs and Patents Act 1988, s 86(2)
171 Copyright Act 1956, s 43(5)
172 Fine Arts Copyright Act 1862, s 7
173 Copyright and Related Rights Act 2000, s 118
174 ibid ss 107 and 109
175 ibid s 113(1)
176 ibid s 114(1)
177 ibid s 119(1)
178 ibid s 119(5)

3.3.15) Remedies available for infringement of copyright and moral rights

The CRRA grants copyright owners a range of remedies for the infringement of their copyright. It also grants to exclusive licensees of the copyright to a work 'except as against the copyright owner, the same rights and remedies in respect of matters occurring after the grant of the licence as if the licence had been an assignment'.[179] Under S.135(2) of the Act, such rights and remedies 'are concurrent with those of the copyright owner'.[180] An infringement of copyright is actionable by a copyright owner[181] and in such an action 'all relief by way of damages, injunction, account of profits or otherwise is available to the plaintiff as it is available in respect of the infringement of any other property right'.[182] A court may award damages for an infringement of copyright.[183] In addition to granting compensation for any financial loss suffered by a plaintiff from an infringement of his/her copyright, a court may award either aggravated or exemplary damages or both.[184] However, under S.128(2) of the Act, and without prejudice to any other remedy available to a court, if it is shown in such an action that at the time of the infringement that the defendant 'did not know and had no reason to believe that copyright subsisted in the work to which the action relates, the plaintiff is not entitled to damages against the defendant'.[185] In order for a defendant to benefit from this prohibition on the award of damages against them for a proven infringement of copyright, he or

179 ibid s 135(1)
180 ibid s 135(2)
181 ibid s 127(1)
182 ibid s 127(2)
Note: Case C-441/13 *Pez Hejduk v EnergieAgentur.NRW GmbH* (22 January 2015) at the CJEU concerned the infringement of an Austrian photographer's copyright in her photographs through the uploading of them by a third party on a Germany-based website. In *Pez Hejduk*, the CJEU, at para 38, held that 'in the event of an allegation of infringement of copyright and rights related to copyright guaranteed by the Member State of the court seised, that court has jurisdiction, on the basis of the place where the damage occurred, to hear an action for damages in respect of an infringement of those rights resulting from the placing of protected photographs online on a website accessible in its territorial jurisdiction. That court has jurisdiction only to rule on the damage caused in the Member State within which the court is situated.' *Pez Hejduk* concerned a preliminary ruling on the interpretation of Article 5(3) of Council Regulation (EC) No 44/2001 of 22 December 2000 on jurisdiction and the recognition and enforcement of judgements in civil and commercial matters, which relates to "Special Jurisdiction" (Brussels Regulation). Council Regulation (EC) No 44/2001 of 22 December 2000 on jurisdiction and the recognition and enforcement of judgements in civil and commercial matters [2001] OJ L12/1
<http://eur-lex.europa.eu/LexUriServ/LexUriServ.do?uri=OJ:L:2001:012:0001:0023:en:PDF> accessed 18 April 2018
183 ibid s 128(1)
184 ibid s 128(3)
185 ibid s 128(2)

she would have to rebut an application of any of the presumptions which exist under S.139 of the Act.[186] Of primary relevance here is the presumption that copyright subsists in a work until the contrary is proved.[187] Also, under S.139(3) 'where the subsistence of copyright in a work is proved or admitted, or is presumed under sub-Section (2), the plaintiff shall be presumed to be the owner or, as the case may be, the exclusive licensee of the copyright, until the contrary is proved'.[188] While the owners of the copyright in photographs have a legal right to initiate civil actions for an infringement of their copyright, the associated legal costs could make doing so prohibitive. Such cases are very infrequent in Ireland.[189]

Section 97(1) of the United Kingdom's Copyright, Designs and Patents Act 1988, as amended, contains a provision that is closely worded to that of the previously mentioned S.128(2) of the CRRA.[190] Central to the defence's case in the Patents County Court case of *Hoffman v Drug Abuse Resistance Education (UK) Ltd.*[191] was this S.97(1) defence. In *Hoffman*, the defendant had commissioned a third-party website design firm to design two websites for it. In doing so, the design firm copied 19 of the claimant's images from a government sponsored (Department of Health) website entitled "*Talk to Frank*". The defendant advanced a S.97 defence that its website designer had believed that the website from which the images had been copied ("*Talk to Frank*") was covered by Crown copyright and thus it was not illegal for it to copy and use the images in question without infringing the claimant's copyright. However, Birss J held that a belief in the existence of a reproduction permission under Crown copyright did not mean that a copyright did not subsist in a work.[192] The claimant had previously rejected a Department of Health offer of £50,000 to settle the claim.[193] The claimant had sought compensation from the court

186 ibid s 139(2)
187 ibid
188 ibid s 139(3)
189 Note (1): For an example of a recently concluded civil case concerning infringement of copyright in photographs, see: Jane Last, 'Owner of Theliberal.ie Website Apologises, Agrees to Pay Damages for Copyright Breaches' *Irish Independent* (Dublin, 11 July 20017) <www.independent.ie/irishnews/courts/owner-of-theliberalie-website-apologises-agrees-to-pay-damages-for-copyright-breaches-35914639.html>
Note (2): See also: —— 'Private Alexandra College in Court After Transition Year Students Start T-Shirt Business' *Irish Independent* (Dublin, 2 February 2013) <www.independent.ie/national-news/courts/private-alexandra-college-in-court-after-transition-year-students-start-tshirt-business-3368858.html> accessed 24 April 2018
190 Copyright, Designs and Patents Act 1988, s 97(1)
Note: Section 97(1) states: 'Where in an action for infringement of copyright it is shown that at the time of the infringement the defendant did not know, and had no reason to believe, that copyright subsisted in the work to which the action relates, the plaintiff is not entitled to damages against him, but without prejudice to any other remedy.'
191 *Hoffman v Drug Abuse Resistance Education (UK) Ltd.* [2012] EWPCC 2
192 ibid para 31
193 ibid paras 33–47

based on the National Union of Journalists (NUJ) *Rate for the Job*[194] without advancing any detailed supporting evidence on same. Birss J discounted the multi-annual use fees sought and awarded £10,000 in damages plus interest to the claimant. *Hoffman* illustrates how a judge may decide the quantum of damages to be awarded in the absence of a detailed and supportable damages claim being advanced by a claimant.[195] Ideally, the NUJ *Rate for the Job* should be the standard rates to be used by a court when it is determining the quantum of damages to be awarded to a claimant and without the claimant having to prove an actual specific figure for his/her financial loss as a result of a copyright infringement.

Among the other remedies available to a copyright owner for an infringement of his/her copyright under the Irish Act is the right to seek a court order for the delivery-up of infringing copies of the work from any person, who in the course of business, is in possession of infringing copies of the copyrighted work and any article used to make infringing copies.[196] An application to the court for such an order must be made within 6 years from the date on which the infringing copy of the work was made.[197] Also, under S.144(3) of the Act an order for delivery-up in criminal proceedings taken under S.142 may not be made 'after the expiration of 6 years from the date on which the proceedings under that Section were initiated'.[198] A copyright owner may also apply to a District Court for a seizure order[199] and a District Court, on being satisfied that any seized copy is an infringing copy, may order that the copy be either destroyed or delivered-up to the owner of the copyright or otherwise dealt with

194 National Union of Journalists, London Freelance, *Rate for the Job* <www.londonfreelance.org/rates/newrates.html#Photography> accessed 16 April 2018
Note: The *Rate for the Job* is the scale of fees obtained by NUJ members, including freelance photographer members, for various types of work done and is updated regularly.

195 Note (1): See also: *Sheldon v Daybrook House Promotions Ltd.* [2013] EWPCC 26
Note (2): For examples of how the courts have used the "User Principle" (the royalties that would have been paid by a willing licensee to a willing licensor) when determining the quantum of damages to be awarded in copyright infringement cases, see: *Absolute Lofts South West London Ltd. v Artisan Home Improvements Ltd. & Anor* [2015] EWHC 2608 (IPEC) and *Jodie Aysha Henderson v All Around the World Recordings Ltd.* [2014] EWHC 3087 (IPEC).
Note (3): Under Section 128(3) of the CRRA, a court may award aggravated or exemplary damages or both in a copyright infringement case. Under Section 97(2) of the United Kingdom's Copyright, Designs and Patents Act 1988, a court may award additional damages for a "flagrant" infringement of copyright. For a UK example, see report of the 2015 Intellectual Property Enterprise Court case of *Jonathan Clive Wendal Webb v VA Events and Others* (5 March 2015) (Claim No. IP14S01982) (IPEC) available at <www.webbaviation.co.uk/IP14S01982_Approved_Judgment.pdf> accessed 24 April 2018

196 Copyright and Related Rights Act 2000, s 131

197 ibid s 144(1)

198 ibid s 144(3)

199 ibid s 132(1)

as the Court may determine.[200] One should exercise caution prior to seeking a District Court seizure order, as under S.132(5):

> After the implementation of an order under this Section, the court may, on the application of a person aggrieved by it, award damages against the applicant for the court order as it considers just, on being satisfied that:
>
> (a) no infringement of copyright has been established and
> (b) the information on which the copyright owner applied for the order was given maliciously.[201]

In instances where it is impracticable for a copyright owner to apply to the District Court for a seizure order under S.132, he or she may himself seize an infringing copy of a copyrighted work if 'it is found being hawked, carried about or marketed'.[202] The CRRA places a number of specific restrictions and requirements on a copyright owner in exercising this right, including a requirement to inform a member of An Garda Síochána in the District Court area in which the seizure is to be made of the location and time of the seizure in advance of making such a seizure.[203] While S.133(5) of the Act states: 'A person exercising the right to seize and detain conferred by subsection (1) may enter premises to which members of the public have access',[204] this right under S.133(1) is effectively of little benefit to a copyright owner, as S.133(6) states:

> A person exercising the right to seize and detain conferred by subsection (1) may not seize anything in the possession, custody or control of a person at his or her permanent or regular place of business, trade or profession, and may not use any force.[205]

With reference to the conversion or detention by any person of infringing copies of a copyrighted work, articles used to create infringing copies or copyright protection-defeating devices, a copyright owner is entitled under S.134 to all rights and remedies as he/she would be entitled to if he/she were the owner of the infringing copies, articles or devices since they were made.[206] However, under S.134(2) of the CRRA and in accordance with S.12(2) of the Statute of Limitations 1957, as amended,[207] a six-year limitation is placed on the bringing

200 ibid s 132(2)
201 ibid s 132(5)
202 ibid s 133(1)
203 ibid s 133
204 ibid s 133(5)
205 ibid s 133(6)
206 ibid s 134(1)
207 Note: The Statute of Limitations 1957 was amended by the Statute of Limitations (Amendment) Act 1991 and the Statute of Limitations (Amendment) Act 2000

of an action to enforce the rights granted under S.134(1).[208] This six-year limitation period may be postponed in the case of a fraud or a mistake and it shall not begin to run until the plaintiff has discovered the fraud or mistake or could have discovered it through reasonable diligence.[209]

The European Union (Copyright and Related Rights) Regulations 2012[210] inserted a new S.40(5)(a) in the CRRA to give legal effect to Article 8 of EC Directive 2001/29/EC.[211] Section 40(5)(a) of the Act states:

> The owner of the copyright in a work may, in respect of that work, apply to the High Court for an injunction against an intermediary to whom paragraph 3[212] of Article 8 of Directive 2011/29/EC of the European Parliament and of the Council of 22 May 2001 on the harmonisation of certain aspects of copyright and related rights in the information society applies.[213]

While such a remedy would be available to a photographer whose photographs are being illegally displayed in breach of copyright on a third party's website, the legal costs associated with an injunction application to the High Court to order a website's Internet service provider (website host), to prevent the continuation of the infringement of such copyright would be prohibitive.

In addition to the previously mentioned remedies granted by the CRRA in respect of the infringement of the copyright in a work, the Act also grants remedies to the owner of a moral right attached to a work and granted by the Act for the infringement of that moral right. A moral right owner may apply to the appropriate court for damages or other relief, where there is claimed to be an infringement of such a right.[214]

208 Copyright and Related Rights Act 2000, s 134(2)
209 Statute of Limitations 1957, s 71(1) and s 72(2)
210 European Union (Copyright and Related Rights) Regulations 2012, SI 2012/59
211 ibid reg 2
212 Directive 2001/29/EC of the European Parliament and of the Council of 22 May 2001 on the harmonisation of certain aspects of copyright and related rights in the information society [2001] OJ L167/10, art 8 <http://eur-lex.europa.eu/LexUriServ/LexUriServ.do?uri=OJ:L:2001:167:0010:0019:EN:PDF> accessed 16 April 2018
Note: Paragraph 3 of Art. 8 of this Directive states: 'Member States shall ensure that rightholders are in a position to apply for an injunction against intermediaries whose services are used by a third party to infringe a copyright or related right.'
213 Copyright and Related Rights Act 2000, s 40(5)(a)
Note: For an example of such an injunction application see: *EMI Records (Ireland) Ltd. and Others v UPC Communications Ireland Ltd. and Others* [2013] IEHC 274.
214 Copyright and Related Rights Act 2000, s 137
Note: Section 2 of the CRRA defines "appropriate court" as being either the District Court, Circuit Court or the High Court depending upon the value of the damages sought by a claimant.

3.3.16) Criminal offences relating to copyright

Infringement of copyright is a criminal offence. Many individuals are either unaware of or do not recognise this fact. This is possibly because while copyright is legally classified by the CRRA as being a property right, it is not tangible like a piece of real property. Also, it is possible that many people do not view the copyright in a work as being a property and do not see anything wrong with copyright infringement. Sections 140 and 141 detail a number of offences in relation to copyright infringement. Section 140(1) of the Act states:

> A person who, without the consent of the copyright owner:
>
> (a) makes for sale, rental or loan,
> (b) sells, rents or lends, or offers or exposes for sale, rental or loan,
> (c) imports into the State, otherwise than for his or her private and domestic use,
> (d) in the course of a business, trade or profession, has in his or her possession, custody or control, or makes available to the public, or
> (e) otherwise than in the course of a business, trade or profession, makes available to the public to such an extent as to prejudice the interests of the owner of the copyright,
>
> a copy of a work which is, and which he or she knows or has reason to believe is, an infringing copy of the work, shall be guilty of an offence.[215]

Other offences relating to articles that have been specifically designed or adapted for the making of copies of a work and to copyright protection–defeating devices are also specified by the Act.[216] Also, the showing of a copyrighted artistic work in public without the authorisation of the copyright owner is a criminal offence and the person who caused it to be shown is guilty of an offence, if he/she was aware or had reason to believe that the doing so would infringe the copyright in the work.[217] A person found guilty of a S.140(1), S.140(3) or a S.140(4) offence is liable on summary conviction to a fine not exceeding £1,500 [€1,904][218] in respect of each infringing copy or to a term of imprisonment not exceeding 12 months or both.[219] If convicted on indictment, one is liable for a fine not exceeding £100,000 [€126,974] or to a term of imprisonment not

215 ibid s 140(1)
Note: For the purposes of Section 140, S.140(2) defines a "loan" as: 'a loan for reward and in particular does not include a loan to a family member or friend for private and domestic use, and "lends" shall be construed accordingly'.
216 ibid s 140(3) and s 140(4)
217 ibid s 140(5)(c)
218 Note: Under S.6(3) of the Fines Act 2010, this maximum fine upon summary conviction would now be a Class "C" fine of €1,000–€2,500.
219 Copyright and Related Rights Act 2000, s 140(7)(a)

exceeding five years or both.[220] Similar penalties apply in respect of the offence of infringing the copyright in an artistic work by showing it in public.[221] Section 141 makes it an offence to make a false claim to copyright for financial gain. A person found guilty of this offence 'shall be liable on conviction on indictment to a fine not exceeding £100,000 [€126,974] or to imprisonment for a term not exceeding 5 years, or both'.[222]

It is common practice for professional photographers to implement any of a number of copyright protection measures[223] in order to protect their copyright. Such measures include the overprinting of a copyright watermark on any photographs published by them on their own websites; the inclusion of a copyright notice within the metadata file[224] of any photographs, which they either publish on their own websites or provide to their clients in a digital format; the inclusion of anti-copying or reproduction measures on disks of images supplied to their clients for image viewing and/or selection purposes; and the printing of a copyright notice on either the facing or rear side of any hardcopy photographic prints supplied to clients. The removal and/or alteration of rights management information metadata files contained within copyrighted photographs published on the Internet is a massive problem for photographers. The CRRA does offer some remedies to rights owners in respect of such infringements through its criminalisation of the act of unlawful interference with rights management information. Under S.375(1), where a copyright holder provides rights management information in respect of a copyrighted work, he/she has the same rights and remedies, as he/she has against a copyright infringer, against anyone who, among other specified actions, removes or alters the rights management information from a copyrighted work or who makes available, sells, rents or lends a copy of that copyrighted work with the rights management information removed or altered.[225] A person who undertakes any of the actions specified in S.375(1) shall be guilty of an offence.[226] It is the norm for photographers to insert rights management information (metadata files) into their digital images' files. However, the Act does not make any mention of this type of data file or the illegality of the unauthorised removal of information from a photograph's metadata file. The prosecution of offences under either S.140 or S.376 of the Act is extremely

220 ibid s 140(7)(b)
221 ibid s 140(8)
222 ibid s 141
223 Note: Section 2(1) of the CRRA defines a "rights protection measure" as: 'any process, treatment, mechanism or system which is designed to prevent or inhibit the unauthorised exercise of any of the rights conferred by this Act'.
224 Note: A metadata file is a digital data file that contains descriptive data relating to other data. A digital photograph's data file may include a metadata file, which details the rights management information and other particulars relating to the photograph.
225 ibid s 375(1)
226 Copyright and Related Rights Act 2000, s 376(2)

rare in Ireland.[227] On the prosecution of S.376 offences, the Irish Professional Photographers' and Videographers' Association (IPPVA) has stated, that its members have no knowledge of any prosecutions having been taken in respect of an illegal removal of rights management information from a photograph.[228] The initiation of either a S.140 or a S.376 prosecution is made difficult by the necessity to identify the actual individual who either infringed the copyright in a photograph or removed the rights management information from a photograph's metadata file. Then, it would be necessary to prove that that individual did so knowing that doing so constituted an offence under the Act. In addition to the previously mentioned offences specified under the CRRA, a person who uses a computer to infringe the copyright in a photograph could, in certain circumstances, be prosecuted under the Criminal Justice (Theft and Fraud Offences) Act 2001, as amended. Section 9(1) of the Act makes it an offence for a person to dishonestly operate or to cause another to operate a computer with the intention of either making a gain for himself or another person or causing a loss to another.[229] For the successful conviction of an individual charged with a S.9(1) offence, it would be necessary for the prosecution to prove both that the individual had acted dishonestly and that he/she intended to either make a gain for himself or to cause a loss to another person.

3.4) Copyright protection under international conventions and treaties

Ireland is a party to a number of international copyright conventions and treaties, namely the Berne Convention for the Protection of Literary and Artistic Works, the Agreement on Trade-related Aspects of Intellectual Property Rights

227 Note (1): For an example of such a case see: *Director of Public Prosecutions v McGoldrick* [2005] IE CCA 84. *McGoldrick* concerned the possession for trade of copyright infringing videocassette recordings of movies and not the infringement of the copyright in a still photograph.
Note (2): One may initiate a private prosecution for copyright infringement. In the Irish High Court case of *Kelly and Anor v District Court Judge Ryan* [2013] IEHC 321, Hogan J, at paras 14–22, stated that the right to initiate a private prosecution in respect of an offence still existed under Irish law and was not abolished by the Criminal Procedure Act 1967, as amended by the Criminal Justice Act 1999, except where barred from doing so by a number of statutes. While one has the legal right to initiate a private prosecution for a Section 140 or Section 376 offence, Hogan J stated, at para 42D, that its continuation would be dependent upon the express consent of the Director of Public Prosecutions.

228 Department of Business, Enterprise and Innovation, Copyright Review Committee, *The Irish Professional Photographers' Association Submission to the Committee for the Review of Irish Copyright Law* (July 2011) 4 <https://dbei.gov.ie/en/Consultations/Consultations-files/Irish-Professional-Photographers-Association.pdf> accessed 18 April 2018

229 Criminal Justice (Theft and Fraud Offence) Act 2001, s 9(1)
Note: Upon conviction on indictment of such an offence, under Section 9(2) of the CRRA a person is liable to a fine or imprisonment for a term of up to 10 years or both.

(TRIPS) and the World Intellectual Property Organisation (WIPO) Copyright Treaty. The CRRA, as amended, and a number of statutory instruments have updated Irish legislation to incorporate the provisions of these conventions and treaties.[230]

Ireland became a party to the 1886 Berne Convention for the Protection of Literary and Artistic Works in 1927.[231] Essentially, Berne lays down a set of basic minimum rights of protection for authors of various types of qualifying literary and artistic works. It also provides for exceptions and limitations to such rights. The countries that are parties to Berne may individually determine the specific terms of protection and any limitations on such protection, which they will apply to qualifying works. A number of the provisions of Berne are of direct relevance to photographers. Photographs are included as literary and artistic works for protection purposes under Art. 2(1) of the Convention.[232] For a work to benefit from copyright protection under Berne, it is irrelevant whether a qualifying work has been published or not[233] and no formalities, such as the registration of a copyright in a work, are required of an author for him to enjoy and exercise the rights protected under Berne.[234] While Berne states that it is a matter for the legislature of each of the State Parties to Berne to determine the duration of the term of the protection offered within their individual jurisdictions in respect of a photograph, it also states that such protection shall run for a minimum of 25 years from when a photograph was created.[235]

In respect of EU Member States, Art.1 of Council Directive 93/98/EEC states that the term of protection in artistic works within the meaning of Berne (photographs) runs for 'the life of the author and for 70 years after his death, irrespective of the date when the work is lawfully made available to the public'.[236] Berne reserves to authors the exclusive right to authorise the reproduction of their works.[237] However, under what has become known as the "Berne Three Step Test", signatory countries to Berne may permit exceptions to this exclusive reproduction right in special cases provided such reproductions are not incompatible

230 Copyright and Related Rights Act 2000, third schedule
231 World Intellectual Property Organisation, *Treaties and Contracting Parties: Berne Convention, Ireland* <www.wipo.int/treaties/en/remarks.jsp?cnty_id=971C> accessed 17 April 2018
232 Berne Convention for the Protection of Literary and Artistic Works, art 2(1) <www.wipo.int/treaties/en/ip/berne/trtdocs_wo001.html> accessed 17 April 2018
233 ibid art 3(1)(a)
234 ibid art 5(2)
235 ibid art 7(4)
236 Council Directive 93/98/EEC of 29 October 1993 harmonizing the term of protection of copyright and certain related rights [1993] OJ L290/9, art 1(1) <http://eur-lex.europa.eu/LexUriServ/LexUriServ.do?uri=CELEX:31993L0098:en:NOT> accessed 17 April 2018
237 Berne Convention for the Protection of Literary and Artistic Works, art 9(1) <www.wipo.int/treaties/en/ip/berne/trtdocs_wo001.html> accessed 17 April 2018

with the normal exploitation of an author's work and do not prejudice an author's legitimate interests in an unreasonable manner.[238] Berne also grants artistic works' authors an exclusive right in relation to adaptations and alterations to their works.[239] Independent of an author's economic rights, Art. 6*bis*(1) of Berne grants the author of a work the right to claim to be its author and the right to object to any distortion or modification of that work, which would adversely affect his/her reputation.[240] The term of duration of these moral rights is provided for under Art. 6(2).[241] Berne includes provisions for the free use of works covered by it, such as for the making of quotations and for teaching purposes.[242] Berne says that the Signatory States may decide the conditions under which photographs may be reproduced and made available to the public for the purpose of reporting on current events. to Signatory States.[243]

For an author of a work protected under Berne to be regarded as its author and thus entitled to institute infringement proceedings to protect his/her rights, the appearance of his/her name or his/her pseudonym on that work will be sufficient proof of him/her being its author unless the contrary is proven.[244] The Berne Convention makes provision for the seizure of infringing copies of protected works.[245] It also recognises the artists' resale right, also known as "droit de suite" (the right to follow), which permits authors of works of art to receive a commission on the resale of their works.[246] Under Berne, this right may only be claimed by an author if the country to which he/she belongs has introduced legislation permitting this right and to the extent permitted.[247] The artists' resale right 'forms an integral part of copyright and is an essential prerogative for authors' according to Directive 2001/84/EC.[248] Through the European Communities (Artist's Resale Right) Regulations 2006,[249] which transposed Directive 2001/84/EC into Irish law, and as amended,[250] artists in Ireland have obtained, subject to specific provisions, a right to receive a royalty on the resale value of any original works of art, which they sell. Photographs

238 ibid art 9(2)
239 ibid art 12
240 ibid art 6*bis*(1)
241 ibid art 6(2)
242 ibid art 10
243 ibid art 10*bis*(2)
244 ibid art 15(1)
245 ibid art 16(1)
246 ibid art 14*ter*(1)
247 ibid art 14*ter*(2)
248 Directive 2001/84/EC of the European Parliament and of the Council of 27 September 2001 on the resale right for the benefit of the author of an original work of art [2001] OJ L272, para 4 <http://eur-lex.europa.eu/LexUriServ/LexUriServ.do?uri=CELEX:32001L0084:EN:NOT> accessed 17 April 2018
249 European Communities (Artist's Resale Right) Regulations 2006, SI 2006/312
250 The 2006 Regulations were amended by the European Communities (Artist's Resale Right) (Amendment) Regulations 2011, SI 2011/709

are included within the definition of "an original work of art" contained in Directive 2001/84/EC.[251] Copies of works of art that are covered by the Directive and which are made in limited numbers by an artist or under his/her authority are also considered as being original works of art under the Directive.[252] Regulation 3(1) of the 2006 Regulations recognises the artists' resale right[253] and the sale of an original work of art is considered as a resale under Reg. 5(2), if the following conditions are met:

(a) the buyer, the seller or, if the sale takes place through an agent, the agent of the buyer or the seller, is acting in the course of a business of dealing in works of art and
(b) the sale price is not less than €3,000.[254]

Regulation 9(1) details the scale of royalty percentages payable upon a resale of an original work of art up to a maximum royalty amount of €12,500.[255] The duration of an artist's resale right in an artistic work is the same as that of the copyright in such a work.[256] The 2006 Regulations had stipulated that this right extinguished upon the author's death.[257] But, the 2011 Amendment Regulations extended the duration of a resale right by re-defining it as being 'the lifetime of the author and for 70 years after his or her death'.[258] In addition, the 2011 Amendment Regulations introduced the right to transmit a resale right 'by testamentary disposition or in accordance with the rules of intestate succession as personal or moveable property'.[259] Thus, the heirs of

251 Directive 2001/84/EC of the European Parliament and of the Council of 27 September 2001 on the resale right for the benefit of the author of an original work of art, art 2(1) <http://eur-lex.europa.eu/LexUriServ/LexUriServ.do?uri=CELEX:32001L0084:EN:NOT> accessed 17 April 2018

252 ibid art 2(2)

253 European Communities (Artist's Resale Right) Regulations 2006, SI 2006/312, reg 3(1)

254 ibid reg 5(2)

255 ibid reg 9(1)

256 Directive 2001/84/EC of the European Parliament and of the Council of 27 September 2001 on the resale right for the benefit of the author of an original work of art, art 8(1) <http://eur-lex.europa.eu/LexUriServ/LexUriServ.do?uri=CELEX:32001L0084:EN:NOT> accessed 17 April 2018
Note (1): Art. 8(1) of Directive 2001/84/EC states that the term of protection of the resale right shall correspond to that specified in Art. (1) of Council Directive 93/98/EEC. <http://eur-lex.europa.eu/LexUriServ/LexUriServ.do?uri=CELEX:32001L0084:EN:NOT> accessed 17 April 2018
Note (2): Art. (1) of Council Directive 93/98/EEC of 29 October 1993 harmonising the term of protection of copyright and certain related rights [1993] OJ L290/9 specifies the duration of authors' right in artistic works. <http://eur-lex.europa.eu/LexUriServ/LexUriServ.do?uri=CELEX:31993L0098:en:NOT> accessed 17 April 2018

257 European Communities (Artist's Resale Right) Regulations 2006, SI 2006/312, reg 10

258 European Communities (Artist's Resale Right) (Amendment) Regulations 2011, SI 2011/709, reg 10(1)

259 ibid reg 4A

artists may benefit from the resale right. Although the previously mentioned provisions in the Berne Convention have been incorporated into Irish law through the CRRA, as amended, and Ireland's implementation of EU Copyright Directives, other countries outside of the EU may rely directly on Berne. Consequently, Berne is of relevance to Irish photographers doing business in any non-EU countries.

Ireland is a member of the World Trade Organisation and a signatory to its Agreement on Trade-related Aspects of Intellectual Property Rights (TRIPS).[260] With some exceptions, TRIPS embraces the provisions of the Berne Convention. Articles 9–14 of TRIPS deal with the area of copyright and related rights. Under Art. 9(1), compliance with Arts. 1–21 of the Berne Convention is a requirement. However, member countries do not have rights or obligations under TRIPS in respect of the moral rights granted under Art. 6*bis* of Berne.[261] The scope of copyright protection under TRIPS extends to the expression of ideas, but not to the ideas themselves.[262] Although adherence to the Berne "Three Step Test" relating to limitations and exceptions is covered under the compliance requirement of Article 9 as previously mentioned, TRIPS reiterates the requirement to adhere to this test in Article 13.[263]

Ireland is also a member of the World Intellectual Property Organisation (WIPO) and it ratified the 1996 WIPO Copyright Treaty in 2009.[264] Essentially, the WIPO Copyright Treaty updates Berne by taking into account recent technological developments. On the duration of the protection of photographic works, Art.9 of WIPO states that the provisions of Art.7(4) of Berne is not to be applied by States Parties.[265] As previously mentioned, under Art.7(4) of Berne, photographs were granted copyright protection for the life of the author and 25 years after his/her death in contrast to the general term of protection for artistic works of 50 years after an author's death. The effect of Art. 9 of WIPO was to remove this distinction in Berne and to increase the term of protection for photographs to 50 years after the author's death. Article 11 stipulates the obligations on parties contracting to the Treaty to provide legal protection and remedies against the circumvention of technological measures used by authors to prevent unauthorised acts in respect of their works.[266] Article 12 contains similar stipulations in relation to the circumvention of any rights management information (digital rights management information)

260 World Trade Organisation, *TRIPS Agreement (as Amended on 23 January 2017)* <www.wto.org/english/docs_e/legal_e/31bis_trips_01_e.htm> accessed 17 April 2018
261 ibid art 9(1)
262 ibid art 9(2)
263 ibid art 13
264 World Intellectual Property Organisation, *Administered Treaties: Contracting Parties* <www.wipo.int/treaties/en/ShowResults.jsp?treaty_id=16> accessed 17 April 2018
265 WIPO Copyright Treaty, Art 9 <www.wipo.int/treaties/en/ip/wct/trtdocs_wo033.html> accessed 17 April 2018
266 ibid art 11

employed by an author in his/her work or the unauthorised removal or alteration of same by third parties in order to infringe an author's rights.[267] Articles 6 and 7 of Directive 2001/29/EC[268] deal specifically with the obligations contained in Art. 11 and Art. 12 of WIPO and the transposition of the provisions of this Directive was completed with the commencement of the European Communities (Copyright and Related Rights) Regulations 2004.[269]

3.5) Erosion of photographers' rights under copyright law

The enactment of copyright law reform measures instigated at EU and national levels allied with proposals for further copyright reform and marketplace activities are either eroding or may have the potential to further erode some of the existing rights available to photographers through their ownership of the copyright in their works.

3.5.1) Copyright reforms resulting from EU law

At an EU level, a number of additional exemptions to existing copyright holders' rights either have been or are due to be implemented. Directive 2012/28/EU of the European Parliament and of the Council on certain permitted uses of orphan works[270] was transposed into Irish law through the European Union (Certain Permitted Uses of Orphan Works) Regulations 2014.[271] These Regulations also amended the CRRA. An orphan work is a copyrighted work whose copyright holder, following a diligent search, is either unidentifiable or untraceable.[272] The CRRA, as amended, had not previously made any mention of such works. This Directive permits specified uses of particular types of both published and unpublished works held by EU Member States' publicly accessible libraries, educational establishments and museums; archives; film or audio heritage institutions

267 ibid art 12

268 Directive 2001/29/EC of the European Parliament and of the Council of 22 May 2001 on the harmonisation of certain aspects of copyright and related rights in the information society [2001] OJ L167/10, arts 6–7 <http://eur-lex.europa.eu/LexUriServ/LexUriServ.do?uri=OJ:L:2001:167:0010:0019:EN:PDF> accessed 17 April 2018

269 European Communities (Copyright and Related Rights) Regulations 2004, SI 2004/16

270 Directive 2012/28/EU of the European Parliament and of the Council of 25 October 2012 on certain permitted uses of orphan works OJ L299/5 <http://eur-lex.europa.eu/LexUriServ/LexUriServ.do?uri=OJ:L:2012:299:0005:0012:EN:PDF> accessed 19 April 2018

271 European Union (Certain Permitted Uses of Orphan Works) Regulations 2014 SI 2014/490

272 Directive 2012/28/EU of the European Parliament and of the Council of 25 October 2012 on certain permitted uses of orphan works OJ L299/5, art 2(1) <http://eur-lex.europa.eu/LexUriServ/LexUriServ.do?uri=OJ:L:2012:299:0005:0012:EN:PDF> accessed 19 April 2018

and public-service broadcasting organisations while they undertake activities relating to their public-interest roles.[273] Both published and unpublished works are covered by the Directive including, among others, books, newspapers, magazines and journals.[274] At present, the Directive does not cover stand-alone photographs. However, Art. 10 of the Directive provides for the on-going review of the operation of the Directive and the possible inclusion of, in particular, stand-alone photographs within the scope of the Directive.[275] The institutions covered by the Directive possess vast quantities of orphan, stand-alone photographs within their collections.[276] The cost of obtaining rights clearance for their usage would be significantly higher than the cost of copying them. It is cheaper to copy a stand-alone photograph than to copy a book. Having a legal right to use stand-alone photographs would offer these institutions great potential to derive a financial return from them.[277] It would provide a major saving for these institutions and also their funders, which are mainly the State. An institution wishing to make use of a suspected orphan work contained within its collection must undertake a diligent search for the work's copyright owner and the research sources searched must, at a minimum, include those specified in the Directive's Annex.[278] The Directive does not specify what actually constitutes a "diligent" search. Where a work is granted orphan work status, that status applies throughout the EU.[279] Under Art. 6(1), permitted uses of orphan works include making them available to the public and reproducing them for digitisation, indexation, cataloguing, preservation and restoration purposes.[280] The manner through which orphan works may be made available to the public is not specified by the Directive. The prescribed types of institutions may generate income from their use of their orphan works, but only for the exclusive purpose of covering the cost of digitising and making the works available to the public.[281] While the Directive does not currently permit the overt commercialisation of orphan works, such a restriction could be removed at a future

273 ibid art 1(1)
274 ibid art 1(2) and art 1(3)
275 ibid art 10
276 Note: See: Vuopala A, *Assessment of the Orphan Works Issue and Costs for Rights Clearance* (European Commission, May 2010) <www.ec.europa.eu/information_society/activities/digital_libraries/doc/reports_orphan/anna_report.pdf> accessed 15 December 2013 <www.ace-film.eu/wp-content/uploads/2010/09/Copyright_anna_report-1.pdf> accessed 14 April 2018
277 Note: See: Intellectual Property Office, *Impact Assessment BIS1063: Orphan Works* (15 June 2012) <http://webarchive.nationalarchives.gov.uk/20140603102744/www.ipo.gov.uk/consult-ia-bis1063-20120702.pdf> accessed 18 April 2018
278 Directive 2012/28/EU of the European Parliament and of the Council of 25 October 2012 on certain permitted uses of orphan works OJ L299/5, art 3 <http://eur-lex.europa.eu/LexUriServ/LexUriServ.do?uri=OJ:L:2012:299:0005:0012:EN:PDF> accessed 18 April 2018
279 ibid art 4
280 ibid art 6(1)
281 ibid art 6(2)

date. Identified authors and rights holders of what were suspected orphan works must be named in any use of such works by an institution of the type specified by the Directive.[282] This stipulation may be of benefit to rights holders who wish to determine if their works are being used under the Orphan Works Directive. Under Art. 5 of the Directive, a rights holder has the possibility of putting an end to one of his/her works being classified as an orphan works'.[283] Where a copyright holder of a suspected orphan work is identified and located following a diligent search by an institution or the copyright holder himself finds out that his/her work is being used as an orphan work, the copyright holder may either prohibit or put an end to the use of his/her work as an orphan work. In effect, this is an after-the-event opt-out rather than an opt-in to the orphan works scheme. Institutions covered by the Directive must maintain and furnish specified records of their diligent searches of orphan works to a national authority[284] and the latter must furnish same to the Office for Harmonization in the Internal Market – now known as the European Union Intellectual Property Office (EUIPO).[285] The EUIPO manages a searchable database of works granted orphan works status. Before rights holders may take benefit of the Art. 5 opt-out, they must know of its existence and how it operates. One suspects that the general public is not aware of the orphan works scheme. Should stand-alone photographs come within the terms of the Directive, it will be necessary that the EUIPO's online database would be searchable by image. For such to work would require the EUIPO to set up a massive online photo archive and to undertake a major publicity campaign across the EU to advise EU citizens of its existence.

An onus is placed on the Member States to make provision for the payment of a fair compensation to rights holders making use of the Art. 5 opt-out in respect of pre-opt-out usage of their works as orphan works.[286] The Directive does not specify what constitutes a "fair compensation", but Recital 18 of the Directive gives a degree of clarity and states:

> For the purposes of determining the possible level of fair compensation, due account should be taken, inter alia, of Member States' cultural promotion objectives, of the non-commercial nature of the use made by the organisations in question in order to achieve aims related to their public-interest missions, such as promoting learning and disseminating culture, and of the possible harm to right holders.[287]

282 ibid art 6(3)
283 ibid art 5
284 ibid art 3(5)
285 ibid art 3(6)
Note: See: European Union Intellectual Property Office, About Us <https://euipo.europa.eu/ohimportal/en/the-office> accessed 19 August 2018
286 ibid art 6(5)
287 ibid recital 18

Thus, it would appear that rights holders may not receive their commercial rates of remuneration. In addition to transposing this Directive into Irish law, the European Union (Certain Permitted Uses of Orphan Works) Regulations 2014[288] also inserted two new sections (S.70A and S.236A) into the CRRA which deal with specified acts of reproduction and the making available of orphan works by specified relevant bodies.[289] Under the Regulations, an orphan work may be used for the 'sole purpose of covering the costs incurred by it in digitising the orphan work concerned and making it available to the public'.[290] The Regulations allocated a number of functions concerning orphan works to the Controller of the Irish Patents Office including the receipt and transmission of records on orphan works' diligent searches to the EUIPO [291] and the responsibility to determine the fair compensation, if any, due to a rights holder, who has put an end to the use of his/her work as an orphan work and who not reached a compensation agreement with a relevant body that had used his/her work as an orphan work.[292] While the Regulations do provide that a rights holder who is dissatisfied with the level of compensation being awarded by the Controller may petition the High Court, the costs associated with doing so would, in the main, make it prohibitive.[293]

Under the Directive, the management of rights and particularly extended collective licences relating to use of orphan works is a matter for Member States.[294] Aside from Directive 2012/28/EU on orphan works, Directive 2014/26/EU of the European Parliament and of the Council[295] is relevant to photographers. When licensing others to use their copyrighted works, photographers generally negotiate the fees payable to them directly with prospective licensees. In some instances, photographers grant a licensing and collection agency the right to both licence their works and to collect the relevant licensing fees from licensees on their behalf. Directive 2014/16 deals with the collective management of copyright and related rights and it places a duty on Member States to regulate the management of copyright and related rights by collective management organisations.[296] The European Union (Collective Rights Management) (Directive 2014/26/EU) Regulations 2016 transposed Directive

288 European Union (Certain Permitted Uses of Orphan Works) Regulations 2014 SI 2014/490
289 ibid reg 12
290 ibid reg 8(4)
291 ibid reg 5(4)
292 ibid reg 11
293 ibid reg 15
294 ibid recital 24
295 Directive 2014/26/EU of the European Parliament and of the Council of 26 February 2014 on collective management of copyright and related rights and multi-territorial licensing of rights in musical works for online use in the internal market [2014] OJ L84/72 <http://eur-lex.europa.eu/LexUriServ/LexUriServ.do?uri=OJ:L:2014:084:0072:0098:EN:PDF> accessed 20 April 2018
296 ibid art 1

2014/26/EU into Irish law.[297] The Regulations cover the activities, duties and responsibilities of both collective management organisations (CMOs) and Independent Management Entities (IMEs), as defined by the Regulations.[298] The monitoring of the compliance by CMOs and IMEs with their duties and responsibilities under the Regulations is undertaken by the Controller of Patents, Designs and Trade Marks.[299]

In addition to the previously mentioned EU Directives, Directive (EU) 2017/1564[300] implements the Marrakesh Treaty.[301] This Directive permits exceptions to copyright holders' existing reproduction and making available rights to provide for the reproduction and making available of works in formats accessible by people, who are blind, visually impaired or otherwise print disabled. In practical terms, it is unlikely that this Directive will have any impact on photographers' rights in respect of their copyrighted stand-alone photographs.

With a stated aim of further harmonising EU law on copyright and related rights, the European Union is currently debating a proposed new directive on Copyright in the Digital Single Market.[302] There are two direct references to images and photographs within the proposed directive, namely in Recital 8 (on data mining) and Recital 25 (on cultural heritage collections and licensing mechanisms). The articles of the proposed directive cover a range of matters including, briefly: Art. 3 (text and data mining); Art. 4 (use of works in cross-border teaching); Art. 5 (cultural heritage collections); Art. 7 (collective management organisations (CMOs) and use of out-of-commerce works by cultural heritage institutions with an opt-out for rights holders of the class of works covered by a CMO licence agreement); Art. 8 (cross-border uses of Art. 7 works); Art. 11, Art. 18 and Art. 21 (reproduction, communication and making available neighbouring rights for press publishers in relation to their digital (online) press publications; those rights to expire 20 years after publication of a press publication and will also apply to publications published before the date

297 European Union (Collective Rights Management) (Directive 2014/26/EU) Regulations 2016, SI 2016/156

298 ibid reg 2

299 ibid reg 33

300 Directive (EU) 2017/1564 of the European Parliament and of the Council of 13 September 2017 on certain permitted uses of certain works and other subject matter protected by copyright and related rights for the benefit of persons who are blind, visually impaired or otherwise print-disabled and amending Directive 2001/29/EC on the harmonisation of certain aspects of copyright and related rights in the information society [2017] OJ L242/6 <https://eur-lex.europa.eu/legal-content/EN/TXT/HTML/?uri=CELEX:32017L1564&from=EN> accessed 20 April 2018

301 Marrakesh Treaty to facilitate access to published works for persons who are blind, visually impaired or otherwise print disabled <www.wipo.int/treaties/en/ip/marrakesh/> accessed 20 April 2018

302 Proposal for a Directive of the European Parliament and of the Council on Copyright in the Digital Single Market <https://eur-lex.europa.eu/legal-content/EN/TXT/HTML/?uri=CELEX:52016PC0593&from=EN> accessed 27 April 2018

on which Member States must transpose the Directive into national law); Art. 12 (in respect of works transferred or licensed to publishers, the latter to have a right to a share of any fair compensation for uses of works made under exceptions or limitations to a transfer or licence agreement), Art. 13 (the use of effective content recognition technologies by information society service providers that store and grant public access to large amounts of user uploaded works to prevent the availability of works identified by their rights owners through their services) and Arts. 14–16 (fair remuneration for authors of licensed or transferred works). The operation of the proposed Art. 13 will require reproduction and making available licence agreements between copyright owners of works and service providers and a monitoring by service providers of works uploaded to their platforms to prevent copyright infringements by users of such platforms. A general monitoring of the uploading of works by service providers could have the effect of preventing copyright owners from uploading their works or in having such works removed by service providers.

3.5.2) *Copyright law review and reform in the United Kingdom*

In contrast to the previously mentioned copyright reform measures relating to orphan works as implemented in Ireland, in the United Kingdom a somewhat different approach was adopted. As the United Kingdom undertook a review of its copyright law prior to a similar review being undertaken in Ireland, it will be discussed firstly. The 2011 report on the review of the UK's intellectual property framework by an independent review committee chaired by Prof. Hargreaves made recommendations relating to specific aspects of copyright, namely: copyright licensing, orphan works and limits to copyright.[303] Following the publication of the Hargreaves Report, the Copyright, Designs and Patents Act 1988 (hereinafter "CDPA") was amended by the Enterprise and Regulatory Reform Act 2013. The 2013 Act inserted new sections in the CDPA relating to the licensing of orphan works;[304] extended collective licensing;[305] the authorisation and regulation of licensing bodies;[306] and the Copyright Tribunal.[307] Regulations covering the Use of Orphan Works,[308] the Licensing of Orphan

303 Intellectual Property Office, *Digital Opportunity: A Review of Intellectual Property and Growth, An Independent Report by Professor Ian Hargreaves* (May 2011), 8 <www.ipo.gov.uk/ipreview-finalreport.pdf> accessed 20 April 2018
304 Copyright, Designs and Patents Act 1988, s 116A
305 ibid s 116B
306 ibid s 116C
307 ibid s 116D
308 The Copyright and Rights in Performances (Certain Permitted Uses of Orphan Works) Regulations 2014, SI 2014/2861

Works,[309] Extended Collective Licensing[310] and the Regulation of Relevant Licensing Bodies[311] were also implemented. The Comptroller-General of Patents, Designs and Trade Marks was designated as the authorising body in respect of these schemes.[312]

While stand-alone photographs are not specifically mentioned in the Copyright and Rights in Performances (Certain Permitted Uses of Orphan Works) Regulations 2014, the Regulations do include photography (i.e. embedded photographs) as a category of works coming within the Regulations.[313] Under Reg. 6 of the Regulations, a relevant body covered by the Regulations may use an orphan work to create revenue 'otherwise than for the exclusive purpose of covering the costs of the relevant body in digitising orphan works and making them available to the public' or 'in order to achieve aims which are not related to its public interest mission'.[314] Consequently, relevant bodies may make full commercial use of orphan works within their collections. Regulation 2 specifies the types of bodies, which are permitted under the Regulations to make use of orphan works.[315] In accordance with the Copyright and Rights in Performances (Licensing of Orphan Works) Regulations 2014, the Comptroller-General (the authorising body) may grant a licence to a relevant body to use an orphan work once he/she has been provided with the prescribed information by that body.[316] While an orphan work may be licensed by the Comptroller-General for use in the United Kingdom on a non-exclusive basis, it may not be sub-licensed.[317] Licences for the use of orphan works may not exceed a seven-year term,[318] but the Comptroller-General may renew a licence for a further seven-year term.[319] The Licensing of Orphan Works Regulations 2014 prescribe how a copyright holder to a work may object to his/her work being licensed as an orphan work and how the copyright holder may, if authorised by the Comptroller-General, receive a payment in respect of the use of that work as an orphan work.[320]

309 The Copyright and Rights in Performances (Licensing of Orphan Works) Regulations 2014, SI 2014/2863
310 The Copyright and Rights in Performances (Extended Collective Licensing) Regulations 2014, SI 2014/2588
311 The Copyright (Regulation of Relevant Licensing Bodies) Regulations 2014, SI 2014/898
312 The Copyright and Rights in Performances (Licensing of Orphan Works) Regulations 2014, SI 2014/2863, reg 2
313 The Copyright and Rights in Performances (Certain Permitted Uses of Orphan Works) Regulations 2014, SI 2014/2861, sch, part 2, para 3
314 ibid sch, part 1, reg 6
315 ibid reg 2(1)
316 The Copyright and Rights in Performances (Licensing of Orphan Works) Regulations 2014, SI 2014/2863, reg 6(1)
317 ibid reg 6(2)
318 ibid reg 6(2)(b)
319 ibid reg 8(1)
320 ibid reg 12 and reg 13

The Copyright and Rights in Performances (Extended Collective Licensing) Regulations 2014 set out the regulation of the extended collective licensing of works protected by copyright,[321] while the Copyright (Regulation of Relevant Licensing Bodies) Regulations 2014, among other matters, prescribe the criteria, which authorised licensing bodies must adopt as a code of practice and adhere to.[322] In the United Kingdom, extended collective licensing is an "opt-out"[323] rather than an "opt-in" scheme.

In relation to a limiting of copyright, the Hargreaves Report proposed the creation of a payment-free, limited private copying exception.[324] Consequently, a new S.28B was inserted in the CDPA by the Copyright and Rights in Performances (Personal Copies for Private Use) Regulations 2014[325] to permit the payment-free, private copying for personal use of a copyrighted work, which was owned by the person making the private copy.[326] Also, in instances where a copyright owner of a work has included copying prevention measures in his/her work, under S.28B the Secretary of State could, on receipt of a complaint, order the copyright owner to provide the complainant with the means to defeat such copying prevention measures.[327] In the High Court judicial review case of *The Queen (on the application of British Academy of Songwriters, Composers and Authors and Others v Secretary of State and Others*,[328] Green J held that Directive 2001/29/EC[329] requires Member States that permit the introduction of an exception to the reproduction right under Art. 2 of the Directive for an Art. 5(2)(b) (private copying) purpose to implement a mechanism to compensate the copyright holder for his/her reproduction rights irrespective of whether such a compensation mechanism may or may not actually result in the copyright owner being paid compensation.[330] Having referred to the "fair compensation" requirement of Art. 6(5) of the Directive, Green J determined

321 The Copyright and Rights in Performances (Extended Collective Licensing) Regulations 2014, SI 2014/2588

322 The Copyright (Regulation of Relevant Licensing Bodies) Regulations 2014, SI 2014/898

323 The Copyright and Rights in Performances (Extended Collective Licensing) Regulations 2014, SI 2014/2588, reg 16

324 Intellectual Property Office, *Digital Opportunity: A Review of Intellectual Property and Growth, An Independent Report by Professor Ian Hargreaves* (May 2011), 49 <www.ipo.gov.uk/ipreview-finalreport.pdf> accessed 20 April 2018

325 Copyright and Rights in Performances (Personal Copies for Private Use) Regulations 2014, SI 2014/2361, reg 2

326 Copyright, Designs and Patents Act 1988, s 28B

327 ibid s 296ZEA

328 *The Queen (on the application of British Academy of Songwriters, Composers and Authors and Others v Secretary of State and Others* [2015] EWHC 1723 (Admin)

329 Directive 2001/29/EC of the European Parliament and of the Council of 22 May 2001 on the harmonisation of certain aspects of copyright and related rights in the information society [2001] OJ L167/10, art 5(2)(b) <http://eur-lex.europa.eu/LexUriServ/LexUriServ.do?uri=OJ:L:2001:167:0010:0019:EN:PDF> accessed 20 April 2018

330 *The Queen (on the application of British Academy of Songwriters, Composers and Authors and Others v Secretary of State and Others* [2015] EWHC 1723 (Admin), para 181

that it was unlawful to implement S.28B without any compensation mechanism being put in place.[331]

The Copyright and Rights in Performances (Quotation and Parody) Regulations 2014 introduced a new exemption in copyright law in respect of quotations and parody.[332] As it is not possible to quote from a photograph, one cannot envisage how an exemption for quotation purposes would impinge on photographers' rights in their works. The Regulations provide a fair dealing exemption in respect of parody in a work, which would include photographs.[333]

3.5.3) Copyright law review and reform in Ireland

The Irish government established the Copyright Review Committee (hereinafter "CRC") in 2011.[334] The CRC was tasked with identifying and suggesting solutions to barriers existing under current copyright legislation to innovation; examining the appropriateness of having a US-style "fair use" doctrine in Ireland and recommending changes to EU law, which would enable changes to be made to existing Irish copyright law.[335] Its 2013 Report recommended a range of changes to the CRRA. There are many similarities between the CRC's recommendations and those contained in the previously mentioned, previously produced Hargreaves Report.[336] To a great extent, the CRC's Report is a comparative assessment of the CRRA's existing copyright exceptions and limitations with those permitted under the EU Copyright Directive 2001/29/EC. While making some recommendations, which would assist in protecting and enforcing photographers' and photograph publishers' existing rights, many of the CRC's recommendations could, if implemented, have the effect of further reducing their existing rights.[337]

331 ibid para 273
Note (1): See also the CJEU case of Case C-572/13 *Hewlett-Packard Belgium SPRL v Reprobel SCRL* (12 November 2015) on the issue of fair compensation.
Note (2): See: 'Academic Behind Copyright Law Changes Warns that Rights Holders Could Lose Even More Control of Content by Taking Test Cases to Court' *Out-Law.com* (07 March 2014) <www.out-law.com/en/articles/2014/october/academic-behind-copyright-law-changes-warns-that-rights-holders-could-lose-even-more-control-of-content-by-taking-test-cases-to-court/> accessed 21 May 2018

332 The Copyright and Rights in Performances (Quotation and Parody) Regulations 2014, SI 2014/2356

333 ibid reg 5

334 Department of Business, Enterprise and Innovation, *Modernising Copyright: The Report of the Copyright Review Committee* (Dublin 2013) <www.djei.ie/en/Publications/Publication-files/CRC-Report.pdf> accessed 21 April 2018

335 ibid 8

336 Intellectual Property Office, *Digital Opportunity: A Review of Intellectual Property and Growth, An Independent Report by Professor Ian Hargreaves* (May 2011) <www.ipo.gov.uk/ipreview-finalreport.pdf> accessed 20 April 2018

337 Note: For a discussion of the CRC Report and the potential impact of some of its recommendations on photographers' and photograph publishers' current legal rights under

Following the publication of the CRC Report, the Copyright and Other Intellectual Property Law Provisions Bill 2018[338] was introduced in the Oireachtas. The Bill proposes a number of amendments to the CRRA which are of relevance to photographers and photograph publishers. Offering little by way of an increase in the protection or greater enforcement of photographers' existing rights under the CRRA, the Bill primarily proposes a further erosion of their rights through an expansion of the exemptions to copyright. Chiefly among the Bill's proposed amendments to the CRRA are matters relating to the CRRA's S.16 on jurisdiction of the courts (District and Circuit Courts to have jurisdiction to hear intellectual property claims):[339] S.24 on the duration of copyright (proposed new, clearer S.24(1): irrespective of whether or not an artistic work has ever been lawfully made available to the public, its copyright term will expire 70 years after death of its author);[340] S.34 on rights relating to the making available of previously unpublished works;[341] S.37 on rights of a copyright owner (proposed incorporation of "rights management information" within the definition of a "work");[342] S.51 on fair dealing for criticism of review;[343] S.57 on educational establishments' exemptions;[344] S.66 (copying by librarians and archivists);[345] a new S.68A (exemption for format shifting by librarians and archivists);[346] a new S.69A (exemption for fair dealing by libraries and archivists);[347] S.52 on fair dealing (proposed creation of an exemption for caricature, parody and pastiche);[348] S.94 on advertising of sale of artistic works;[349] S.198 on delivery of certain published materials to prescribed libraries (a new sub-section (4A) to cover the deposit of digital publications, which would bring

Irish copyright law, see: Michael O'Flanagan, 'Copyright Reform: A Modernisation or the Start of the Death of Copyright for Photographers? – Part 1' (2014) 19(4) *Communications Law – The Journal of Computer, Media and Telecommunications Law* 114

338 Copyright and Other Intellectual Property Law Provisions Bill 2018 <www.oireachtas.ie/viewdoc.asp?DocID=37989&&CatID=59> accessed 21 April 2018

339 ibid s 5
Note: At present, under Section 127 of the CRRA, an infringement of a copyright is actionable by its copyright owner. Thus, the proposed new Section 16A neither adds anything to that existing right nor does it make it any easier or less expensive for a copyright owner to take an action against a copyright infringer.

340 ibid s 7

341 ibid s 9

342 ibid s 10

343 ibid s 11

344 ibid s 14

345 ibid s 16

346 ibid s 17

347 ibid s 18

348 ibid s 12

349 ibid s 22

the contents of published websites within the scope of its terms);[350] S.375–376 (on rights management information) and a proposed new S.377 (making, among other matters, the removal or alteration of rights management information from a copyrighted work and the making available of a copyrighted work with its rights management information removed a copyright infringement).[351] The Bill also proposes to amend the fines applicable to offences under the CRRA[352] and to rename the Controller of the Irish Patents Office as the Controller of Intellectual Property and the Irish Patents Office as the Intellectual Property Office of Ireland.[353]

It is unfortunate that the Bill does not propose to implement the CRC recommended expansion of the Small Claims Court's remit to permit its hearing of intellectual property claims (either with a jurisdiction level of the District Court as recommended by the CRC or without same) and the creation of a specialist intellectual property court within the Circuit Court.[354] In its Regulatory Impact Analysis on the 2018 Bill, (a cost/benefit analysis), the Department of Business, Enterprise and Innovation stated, among other reasons, that an expansion of the remit of the Small Claims Court would necessitate the training of Small Claims Registrars in IP law.[355] It also suggested that there is not enough of a demand for the types of court access recommended by the CRC, because few intellectual property infringement claims are currently taken to court.[356] That does not mean that such court access would not be availed of by copyright owners if it were available as a cost-effective route for taking copyright infringement actions. A primary reason for the current low number of civil court cases

350 ibid s 27
Note: Under Section 27 of the 2018 Bill a "digital publication" is 'any publication published online or offline which is made available to the public in a medium other than in print (including any publication in any digital or electronic or other technological form, but does not include any sound recording or film or any combination thereof)'. This proposal would permit the prescribed bodies to collect, copy and make available copies of published websites. Photographers publishing stand-alone photographic images on their own and other websites should consider embedding a clearly visible, over-printed copyright watermark on their images before they upload them to the Internet. Doing so would also assist in minimising the possibility of such published stand-alone images being categorised as orphan works at any future date.

351 ibid ss 34–36

352 ibid s 44

353 ibid s 4 and s 40

354 Department of Business, Enterprise and Innovation, *Modernising Copyright: The Report of the Copyright Review Committee* (Dublin 2013), 10 <www.djei.ie/en/Publications/Publication-files/CRC-Report.pdf> accessed 23 April 2018

355 Department of Business, Enterprise and Innovation, Intellectual Property Unit, *Regulatory Impact Analysis: Copyright and Other Intellectual Property Law Provisions Bill 2018* (Dublin 2018) <https://dbei.gov.ie/en/Legislation/Legislation-Files/Regulatory-Impact-Analysis-Copyright-Other-IP-Law-Provisions-Bill-2018.pdf> accessed 23 April 2018

356 ibid

concerning copyright infringement is the significant legal and other costs associated with taking such actions in either the District or Circuit Court relative to the value of the loss incurred by a copyright owner through a copyright infringement. On reading the previously mentioned Regulatory Impact Analysis, one is left with the view that this is obvious to the Department.[357]

3.5.4) Forsaking rights under copyright for publicity

All photographers need to publicise their businesses as part of their marketing strategy to both hold on to their existing clients and more importantly to obtain new business. They will use many avenues to generate publicity, including social media and photo sharing websites and by entering photographic competitions. By doing so, they may be voluntarily permitting their rights under copyright to be eroded. Social media websites such as Facebook, Twitter, Instagram, YouTube, Pinterest, Flickr, Tumblr and Reddit permit the uploading of photographs to them. The terms of service of such websites frequently include terms under which a user (a photographer) of the website grants royalty-free reproduction and making available rights to both the websites and other users of those websites. Such granted rights may be in the form of a royalty-free, unrestricted, indefinite, irrevocable, worldwide licence to the website. In some instances, the rights granted may provide for the commercial exploitation of uploaded material. These websites' terms of service may also include a requirement that their users (including photographers) grant the websites an indemnity against any claims from third parties resulting from the uploading of material (photographs) to them. Numerous photographers, both professional and amateur, submit entries to photographic competitions that are organised at international and national levels by magazines, newspapers, photographic societies and websites. At a national level, some local authorities and commercial firms, including sections of the print media, organise photographic competitions for the sole purpose of acquiring a body of photographic images without having to pay commercial photography rates, which they may subsequently use in the production of both their own printed promotional materials and online presence. In submitting entries to photographic competitions, entrants would most likely have to grant reproduction and making available rights to the competitions' organisers on terms similar to the previously mentioned and an indemnity.

While some people might say that any publicity is good publicity, for a full-time professional photographer, publicity on its own does not pay the bills. Photographers should carefully balance the possible gains to be made from using such websites for publicity purposes with the legal rights, which they would be giving away (principally their reproduction and making available rights) and also with any potential losses that could occur as a result of a consequential legal action. Many photographers insert rights management information (copyright

357 ibid

notice) metadata files (known as EXIF data) into the digital files of images that they intend will be uploaded to the Internet either by themselves or their clients. Photographers should note that some social media[358] websites and other website operators strip out this metadata file while photographs are being uploaded to their websites. In addition to the possibility of giving an "in the public domain" appearance to stripped images that have been uploaded to the Internet, this practice of metadata stripping makes the tracing by copyright owners of the unauthorised reproduction of their copyrighted photographs on the Internet a more difficult task.

3.5.5) Clients grabbing photographers' copyright and moral rights

When issuing commercial photography contracts to photographers, there is a current practice among many corporate and state clients to require contracted photographers to transfer to them their rights under copyright and also to waive their moral rights[359] in respect of any images, which they create for such clients. In practical terms, it is a case of photographers either accepting the offered contract or walking away. As many photographers are in need of work and income, they are effectively forced to agree to a copyright assignment and a moral rights waiver without being paid an additional fee by those clients for their acquisition of those rights.[360] Copyright is a property right under the CRRA and while the state has a duty under Art. 40.3.2° of the Constitution to protect the property rights of copyright holders, such a duty would appear to receive little attention or respect from organs of the state[361] that engage in rights grabbing when issuing commissions to photographers. As Irish government departments and other organs of the state frequently engage in copyright and moral rights grabbing through their tender contracts, it is unlikely that the state will voluntarily take the initiative to curb this activity. However, commercial photographers do

358 'Many social media sites still remove image rights from photos' *International Press Telecommunications Council* (19 January 2016) <https://iptc.org/news/many-social-media-sites-still-remove-image-rights-information-from-photos/> accessed 22 April 2018 See also: 'German Photographer Sued Facebook for Removing EXIF Data, and He Won' *Petapixel.com* (22 November 2016) <https://petapixel.com/2016/11/22/german-photographer-sued-facebook-removing-exif-data-won/> accessed 24 April 2018

359 Note: The waiver of moral rights is legally permitted by S.116 of the CRRA. However, S.118 of the Act prohibits the assignment or alienation of moral rights.

360 Note: See also: Copyright Review Committee, *The Irish Professional Photographers' Association Submission to the Committee for the Review of Irish Copyright* Law (July 2011), 2–3 <www.djei.ie/en/Consultations/Consultations-files/Irish-Professional-Photographers-Association.pdf> accessed 20 April 2018

361 Note: For an example of rights grabbing through the terms of a tender contract as practised by an Irish government department, see: Office of Government Procurement, *Request for Tenders Dated 2nd May 2017 to Establish a Multi Supplier Framework Agreement for the provision of Professional Photography and Videography Services*, appendix 7, sch A, para 6. Tender Reference No.: EMS022F. <https://irl.eu-supply.com/ctm/Supplier/PublicTenders> accessed 24 April 2018

have the option of either not accepting rights grabbing terms in tender contracts for photography services, when they submit tenders, or refusing to submit tenders for contracts containing such clauses. In addition, professional photographers' representative organisations, like the IPPVA and the NUJ, could take an active lead on behalf of their members to stop rights grabbing through tender contracts by publicly naming and shaming tender requesters engaging in such practice.

3.6) Brief conclusions

In Ireland, photographers' rights under copyright law are broad in scope and, in general terms, the protections offered to photographers through copyright law are good. However, the exercise of such rights and the attainment of the protection afforded to them are under attack by copyright infringers and vested interest groups. Existing rights of copyright holders need to be actively enforced by the State and new legislation is required to permit an effective protection and financially affordable enforcement of copyright owners' rights in their photographs. The unauthorised use of photographers' copyrighted works by third parties, particularly online, is perhaps one of the biggest problems facing professional photographers on a daily basis. In addition, the current exemptions to the rights of copyright holders, as permitted under the CRRA, are also detrimental to the rights of copyright holders – particularly their reproduction and economic rights and also to their moral rights. The CRRA should be amended by converting the existing permitted exempted acts into acts permitted under licence from copyright owners.

References

Books

Clark R, *Irish Copyright and Design Law* (Butterworths 2001)
Clark R, Smyth S and Hall N, *Intellectual Property Law in Ireland* (3rd edn, Bloomsbury Professional 2010)
Derclaye E, *Copyright and Cultural Heritage: Preservation and Access to Works in a Digital World* (Edward Elgar 2010)
Kelly C and Murphy A, *Copyright and Related Rights Act 2000* (Roundhall, Sweet & Maxwell 2002)
Kelly F, *A Guide to Early Irish Law* (Dublin Institute for Advanced Studies 1998)
Michalos C, *The Law of Photography and Digital Images* (Sweet and Maxwell 2004)
Nagle E, *Intellectual Property Law* (Thomas Reuters 2012)
Stokes S, *Art and Copyright* (2nd edn, Hart Publishing 2012)

Journal articles

Hughes J, 'The Photographer's Copyright: Photograph as Art, Photograph as Database' (2012) 25(2) *Harvard Journal of Law and Technology* 328
O'Flanagan M, 'Copyright Reform: A Modernisation or the Start of the Death of Copyright for Photographers? – Part 1' (2014) 19(4) *Communications Law – The Journal of Computer, Media and Telecommunications Law* 114

—— 'Copyright Reform: A Modernisation or the Start of the Death of Copyright for Photographers? – Part 2' (2015) 20(1) *Communications Law – The Journal of Computer, Media and Telecommunications Law*

Ong B, 'Why Moral Rights Matter: Recognizing the Intrinsic Value of Integrity Rights' (2003, Summer) *Columbia Journal of Law and the Arts* 297

O'Sullivan M, 'The Pluralistic, Evolutionary, Quasi-legal Role of the GNU General Public Licence in Free/libre/open Source Software (FLOSS)' (2004) 26(8) *European Intellectual Property Review* 340

—— 'Creative Commons and Contemporary Copyright: A Fitting Shoe or "A Load of Old Cobblers"?' (2008, January) 13(1–7) *First Monday*

—— 'Irish Artistic Copyright Law: A Menagerie of Holy Cows and the Turtle Doves?' (2015) 1 *Intellectual Property Quarterly* 31

Petri G, 'The Public Domain vs. the Museum: The Limits of Copyright and Reproduction of Two-Dimensional Works of Art' (2014) 12(1):8 *Journal of Conservation and Museum Studies* 1

Sheehan R, 'Colmcille and the Irish Copyright Tradition' (2009) 14(1) *The Bar Review* 19

Newspaper articles and other online articles and press releases

—— 'Academic Behind Copyright Law Changes Warns that Rights Holders Could Lose Even More Control of Content By Taking Test Cases to Court' *Out-Law.com* (07 March 2014) <www.out-law.com/en/articles/2014/october/academic-behind-copyright-law-changes-warns-that-rights-holders-could-lose-even-more-control-of-content-by-taking-test-cases-to-court/> accessed 21 May 2018

—— 'Aerial Photographer's Damages Claim Achieves Record Height' *Editorial Photographers United Kingdom and Ireland* (10 March 2015) <www.epuk.org/news/aerial-photographer-s-damages-claim-achieves-record-height> accessed 20 May 2018

—— 'Ballagh Gets €5,000 for Royalties Loss After Resale Law Failure' *The Irish Times* (Dublin, 1 July 2006) <www.irishtimes.com/news/ballagh-gets-5-000-for-royalties-loss-after-resale-law-failure-1.1024606> accessed 22 May 2018

—— 'British Photographic Council Industry Survey Shows True Value of Photographers' Copyright' *The British Photographic Council* (July 2010) <www.british-photographic-council.org/survey/2010> accessed 12 April 2018

—— 'Court Report – The Case of the Missing 33 © Scripts' *Webb Aviation*, <www.webbaviation.co.uk/court-report.html> accessed 20 May 2018

—— 'German Photographer Sued Facebook for Removing EXIF Data, and He Won' *Petapixel.com* (22 November 2016) <https://petapixel.com/2016/11/22/german-photographer-sued-facebook-removing-exif-data-won/> accessed 24 April 2018

—— 'Many Social Media Sites Still Remove Image Rights From Photos' *International Press Telecommunications Council* (19 January 2016) <https://iptc.org/news/many-social-media-sites-still-remove-image-rights-information-from-photos/> accessed 22 April 2018

—— 'Prevent Saves to Pinterest From Your Website' *Pinterest* <https://help.pinterest.com/en/articles/prevent-people-saving-things-pinterest-your-site> accessed 16 April 2018

—— 'Private Alexandra College in Court After Transition Year Students Start T-shirt Business' *Irish Independent* (Dublin, 02 February 2013) <www.independent.ie/national-news/courts/private-alexandra-college-in-court-after-transition-year-students-start-tshirt-business-3368858.html> accessed 24 April 2018

Barker N, 'New Tubridy Sketch After Objection By Photographer' *Irish Examiner* (Cork, 28 February 2014) <www.irishexaminer.com/ireland/new-tubridy-sketch-after-objection-by-photographer-260369.html> accessed 12 April 2018

Blazquez F, Cappello M, Fontaine G and Valais S, 'Exceptions and Limitations to Copyright' *European Audiovisual Observatory IRIS Plus* (IRIS 2017–1) <https://rm.coe.int/iris-plus-2017-1-exceptions-and-limitations-to-copyright/168078348b> accessed 13 April 2018

Bron C, 'Germany: Liability of Website Operators for Users' Infringements' *European Audiovisual Observatory IRIS Merlin* (IRIS 2010–1:1/13) <http://merlin.obs.coe.int/iris/2010/1/article13.en.html> accessed 13 April 2018

De Rocquigny M, 'France: Ownership of Rights Concerning Agency Photographs' *European Audiovisual Observatory IRIS Merlin* (IRIS 2001–2:14/32) <http://merlin.obs.coe.int/iris/2001/2/article32.en.html> accessed 14 April 2018

Last J, 'Owner of Theliberal.ie Website Apologises, Agrees to Pay Damages for Copyright Breaches' *Irish Independent* (Dublin, 11 July 20017) <www.independent.ie/irish-news/courts/owner-of-theliberalie-website-apologises-agrees-to-pay-damages-for-copyright-breaches-35914639.html> accessed 20 April 2018

Lucey A, 'Second Judge Excuses Himself From Copyright Breach Case Involving MEP' *Irish Examiner* (Cork, 22 March 2014) <www.irishexaminer.com/ireland/second-judge-excuses-himself-from-copyright-breach-case-involving-mep-262860.html> accessed 18 April 2018

McGee M, 'Flickr Uses "Nopin" Meta Tag to Keep Some Images Off Pinterest' *Marketing Land* (25 February 2012) <http://marketingland.com/flickr-uses-nopin-meta-tag-to-keep-some-images-off-pinterest-6811> accessed 16 April 2018

O'Sullivan M, 'Former GAA President Sued Over Copyright of Photos Used in His Book' *Irish Independent* (Dublin, 22 March 2014) <www.independent.ie/irish-news/courts/former-gaa-president-sued-over-copyright-of-photos-used-in-his-book-30115201.html> accessed 22 April 2018

Yliniva-Hoffmann A, 'Germany: BGH Rules that Google Image Search Engine Does Not Breach Copyright' *European Audiovisual Observatory IRIS Merlin* (IRIS 2010–6:1/18) <http://merlin.obs.coe.int/iris/2010/6/article18.en.html> accessed 16 April 2018

—— 'Germany: BGH Rules Again on Thumbnail Admissibility' *European Audiovisual Observatory IRIS Merlin* (IRIS 2012–1:1/17) <http://merlin.obs.coe.int/iris/2012/1/article17.en.html> accessed 16 April 2018

Official reports and publications

Dáil Éireann Debate 28 November 1962, vol 198, col 240 Copyright Bill 1962 <http://oireachtasdebates.oireachtas.ie/Debates%20Authoring/DebatesWebPack.nsf/takes/dail1962112800045?opendocument> accessed 09 April 2018

Dáil Éireann Debate 11 November 1999, vol 510, col 1091 Copyright and Related Rights Bill 1999 <http://oireachtasdebates.oireachtas.ie/debates%20authoring/

debateswebpack.nsf/takes/dail1999111100006?opendocument> accessed 16 April 2018

Department of Business, Copyright Review Committee, *The Irish Professional Photographers' Association Submission to the Committee for the Review of Irish Copyright Law* (July 2011) <https://dbei.gov.ie/en/Consultations/Consultations-files/Irish-Professional-Photographers-Association.pdf> accessed 18 April 2018

—— Enterprise and Innovation, *Consultation on Transposition of the Orphan Works Directive and the Use of Orphan Works* (Dublin, 20 March 2014) <https://dbei.gov.ie/en/Consultations/Consultations-files/Orphan-Works-Directive-2012_28_EU-Consultation-on-Transposition-and-Functioning-under-Irish-Law.pdf> accessed 18 April 2018

—— Intellectual Property Unit, *Regulatory Impact Analysis: Copyright and Other Intellectual Property Law Provisions Bill 2018* (Dublin 2018) <https://dbei.gov.ie/en/Legislation/Legislation-Files/Regulatory-Impact-Analysis-Copyright-Other-IP-Law-Provisions-Bill-2018.pdf> accessed 23 April 2018

—— *Modernising Copyright: The Report of the Copyright Review Committee* (Dublin 2013) <www.djei.ie/en/Publications/Publication-files/CRC-Report.pdf> accessed 21 April 2018

European Commission, *Proposal for a Directive of the European Parliament and of the Council on Copyright in the Digital Single Market* <https://eur-lex.europa.eu/legal-content/EN/TXT/HTML/?uri=CELEX:52016PC0593&from=EN> accessed 27 April 2018

House of Commons Debate 28 April 1988, vol 132, cols 565–566 Copyright, Designs and Patents Bill <http://hansard.millbanksystems.com/commons/1988/apr/28/copyright-designs-and-patents-bill-lords#column_565> accessed 14 April 2018

House of Lords Debate 08 December 1987, vol 491, cols 111–115 Copyright, Designs and Patents Bill <http://hansard.millbanksystems.com/lords/1987/dec/08/copyright-designs-and-patents-bill-hl-1#column_111> accessed 14 April 2018Intellectual Property Office, *Digital Opportunity: A Review of Intellectual Property and Growth, An Independent Report by Professor Ian Hargreaves* (May 2011) <www.ipo.gov.uk/ipreview-finalreport.pdf> accessed 20 April 2018

—— *Factsheet – Orphan Works Licensing Scheme and Extended Collective Licensing* <http://webarchive.nationalarchives.gov.uk/20140603094109/www.ipo.gov.uk/orphanworks-licensing.pdf> accessed 20 April 2018

—— *Impact Assessment BIS1063: Orphan Works* (15 June 2012) <http://webarchive.nationalarchives.gov.uk/20140603102744/www.ipo.gov.uk/consult-ia-bis1063-20120702.pdf> accessed 18 April 2018

Irish Patents Office, *Register of Copyright Licensing Bodies* <www.patentsoffice.ie/en/Copyright/Regulation-of-Copyright-Licensing-Bodies/> accessed 12 April 2018

Office of Government Procurement, *Request for Tenders Dated 2nd May 2017 to Establish a Multi Supplier Framework Agreement for the Provision of Professional Photography and Videography Services.* Tender Reference No.: EMS022F. <https://irl.eu-supply.com/ctm/Supplier/PublicTenders> accessed 24 April 2018

Oireachtas Select Committee on Enterprise and Small Business Debate 17 February 2000, Copyright and Related Rights Bill 1999 <http://oireachtasdebates.oireachtas.ie/Debates%20Authoring/DebatesWebPack.nsf/committeetakes/BUS2000021700003> accessed 16 April 2018

Public Lending Remuneration Office, *About the PLR Scheme* <www.plr.ie/about-plr/> accessed 17 April 2018

Seanad Éireann Debate 30 June 1999, vol 160, col 66 Copyright and Related Rights Bill 1999 <http://oireachtasdebates.oireachtas.ie/debates%20authoring/debates-webpack.nsf/takes/seanad1999063000008?opendocument> accessed 16 April 2018

Vuopala A, *Assessment of the Orphan Works Issue and Costs for Rights Clearance* (European Commission, May 2010) <www.ec.europa.eu/information_society/activities/digital_libraries/doc/reports_orphan/anna_report.pdf> accessed 15 December 2013 <www.ace-film.eu/wp-content/uploads/2010/09/Copyright_anna_report-1.pdf> accessed 14 April 2018

World Intellectual Property Organisation, *Administered Treaties: Contracting Parties* <www.wipo.int/treaties/en/ShowResults.jsp?treaty_id=16> accessed 17 April 2018

—— *Treaties and Contracting Parties: Berne Convention, Ireland* <www.wipo.int/treaties/en/remarks.jsp?cnty_id=971C> accessed 17 April 2018

Websites of interest

Copyleft, *What Is Copyleft?* <https://copyleft.org/>

Creative Commons, *What We Do: What Is Creative Commons?* <https://creativecommons.org/about/> accessed 16 April 2018

European Union Intellectual Property Office, *About Us* <https://euipo.europa.eu/ohimportal/en/the-office> accessed 19 August 2018

Irish Professional Photographers' and Videographers' Association <www.irishphotographers.com> accessed 16 April 2018

National Union of Journalists, London Freelance, *Rate for the Job* <www.londonfreelance.org/rates/newrates.html#Photography> accessed 16 April 2018

4 Legal restrictions imposed on photographers and photograph publishers to protect and enforce the personal rights of others

4.1) Introduction

Chapter 2 discussed the legal rights to create and/or publish photographs; the legal basis of these rights; the extent to which and how they are or may be protected and enforced by both the state and rights owners; the balancing of these rights by the courts with the rights of others; how photographers' and publishers' rights are or may be eroded; and what is or should be done by the state to reduce such an erosion of rights. Chapter 3 then examined the nature, scope and practical application of one discrete set of rights of particular importance to the day-to-day business of photographers, namely rights under copyright law. None of the rights pertaining to the taking or publishing of photographs are absolute rights. They may be restricted in support of other interests. While photographers and publishers of photographs are free to enjoy their freedom of expression rights, including both artistic and commercial expression, they have both a legal and moral duty to respect and not infringe the legal and moral rights of others. The protection and enforcement of the guaranteed legal private rights of others, irrespective of whether those rights are founded on provisions of the Constitution of Ireland or are given recognition through statutes, EU law, international treaties and conventions or the common law, may result in the restriction of photographers' and publishers' rights. In determining whether or not to enforce the protection of photographers' and publishers' freedom of expression rights, the courts must balance those rights with any competing rights. As highlighted by Sajó J and Tsotsoria J in their joint dissenting opinion in the 2015 ECtHR case of *Delfi AS v Estonia*,[1] the protection of the right of freedom of expression may not be used as a means to impose duties on the holders of that right.[2] While guaranteeing freedom of the press, Art. 40.6.1°.i of the Constitution goes on to state separately:

> the State shall endeavour to ensure that organs of public opinion . . . shall not be used to undermine public order or morality or the authority of the state.[3]

1 *Delfi AS v Estonia* App No 64569/09 (ECHR, 16 June 2015)
2 ibid para 38
3 Constitution of Ireland (*Art. 40.6.1°.i*) (on Personal Rights)

As a consequence of Art. 40.6.1°.i, the state has the legal power to introduce legislative measures, which could result in restricting photographers' and photograph publishers' right of freedom of expression. The ECtHR held in the case of *Müller et al. v Switzerland*[4] that the right of freedom of expression guaranteed under Art. 10(1) of the Convention[5] includes freedom of artistic expression.[6] This Art. 10 right may be restricted in accordance with Art. 10(2) of the Convention, which states:

> The exercise of these freedoms, since it carries with it duties and responsibilities, may be subject to such formalities, conditions, restrictions or penalties as are prescribed by law and are necessary in a democratic society, in the interests of national security, territorial integrity or public safety, for the prevention of disorder or crime, for the protection of health or morals, for the protection of the reputation or rights of others, for preventing the disclosure of information received in confidence, or for maintaining the authority and impartiality of the judiciary.[7]

Central to Art. 10(2) is the requirement that any restrictions imposed by a State Party on the right of freedom of expression must be prescribed for in law and they must be necessary for the attainment of the objectives specified in Art. 10(2). It is these limitations and restrictions that will be examined in this and the following chapter. Chapter 4 focuses on the "private" or individual rights and interests that may warrant restrictions on photographers' and photograph publishers' rights, while Chapter 5 will focus on the more "public" rights or state interests that may also do so. Chapter 4 examines whether or not and the extent to which duties, if any, are being created and placed upon photographers and publishers by the courts through their interpretation of the law on freedom of expression. From a jurisdiction comparison perspective, this chapter focuses on Ireland and the United Kingdom. It also examines the relevant EU law and determinations by the CJEU and the ECtHR.

4.2) Restrictions resulting from the individual's right to privacy

Individuals' right to privacy frequently comes into contention with the freedom of expression rights of photographers and photograph publishers. A number of questions need to be addressed, namely, what is the legal basis of the right to personal privacy? How is it protected and enforced while being balanced with

4 *Müller et al. v Switzerland* App no 10737/84 (ECHR, 24 May 1988)
5 European Convention on Human Rights Act 2003, sch 1, art 10(1)
6 *Müller et al. v Switzerland* App No 10737/84 (ECHR, 24 May 1988), para 27
7 European Convention on Human Rights Act 2003, sch 1, art 10(2)

the rights of photographers and photograph publishers? What restrictions on photographers and publishers result from such a balancing exercise?

4.2.1) Privacy rights under the Constitution of Ireland

The Constitution of Ireland does not contain an expressed general right to personal privacy. In fact, the word "privacy" is not mentioned in the Constitution. However, the Irish Supreme Court in *McGee v Attorney General*[8] held that an individual may invoke the personal rights guaranteed under Art. 40.3.1° of the Constitution to establish an implied right to personal privacy. The balancing by the courts of the implied constitutional right to privacy, as recognised by the Irish Supreme Court in *McGee* as one of the unenumerated personal rights guaranteed under Art. 40.3.1° of the Constitution, with the rights of photographers and photograph publishers will be examined further.

4.2.2) Privacy rights under Irish statutes

Although there have been proposals to create a general statutory right to privacy in Ireland, such has not come into being. While focussing on the protection of the right to privacy from threats resulting from surveillance, the 1998 Law Reform Commission's *Report on Privacy: Surveillance and the Interception of Communications* recommended the creation of a tort of privacy-invasive surveillance to protect a reasonable expectation of privacy from threats from surveillance rather than the creation of a general privacy tort.[9] The Report also stated that one must endure ordinary incidences of everyday life, such as being photographed by a passer-by.[10] Subsequent proposals to enact legislation following the Report of a government-appointed Working Group on Privacy in 2006 were unsuccessful due to concerns about some of the provisions envisaged in the draft Bill.[11] Of primary concern was the need to strike a balance between the prevention of unwarranted intrusions into individuals' personal privacy and the right of freedom of expression.[12] The achievement of such a balance between the competing rights of privacy and freedom of expression is of importance in

8 *McGee v Attorney General and Anor* [1973] IESC 2

9 Law Reform Commission, *Report on Privacy: Surveillance and the Interception of Communications* (LRC 57–1998) (Dublin 1998), 7.04–7.07 <https://publications.lawreform.ie/Portal/External/en-GB/RecordView/Index/30597> accessed 12 May 2018

10 ibid 7.08

11 Department of Justice and Equality, *Report of Working Group on Privacy* (Dublin, 31 March 2006), appendix 1 <www.justice.ie/en/JELR/WkgGrpPrivacy.pdf/Files/WkgGrpPrivacy.pdf> accessed 12 May 2018

12 Minister for Justice and Equality, Alan Shatter, T.D., Seanad Deb 28 March 2012, vol 214, col 581 <http://oireachtasdebates.oireachtas.ie/debates%20authoring/debateswebpack.nsf/takes/seanad2012032800006?opendocument> accessed 12 May 2018

the sphere of photographers and photography as it is in others sectors of society.

A number of statutes, such as the CCRA, the Data Protection Acts 1988–2018 and the Broadcasting Act 2009,[13] provide for the protection of one's right to privacy in respect of specific aspects of one's life. As mentioned in Chapter 3, S.114 of the CRRA grants individuals a moral right to privacy in respect of photographs, which they commission for private or domestic purposes. The making available or the authorising of the making available of such a photograph to the public without the authorisation of its commissioner is an infringement of that right.[14] The CRRA does not define what constitutes 'private or domestic purposes'. However, it may be taken to mean the photography of family-type events such as portraits, weddings, private parties, birthday celebrations, etc. to which family and/or friends are invited, which are not open to the general public and which are not being organised for commercial reasons. When someone commissions a professional photographer to take photographs for private or domestic purposes it involves the payment of a fee to the photographer. It is possible that the right granted under S.114 could also apply in instances where the photographer offered to forgo payment for such work. This right to privacy in such commissioned images is a right possessed by the client and not by the photographer. Consequently, as a photographer does not possess this legal right, he/she does not have any legal right to "reserve" a right to make available any such commissioned images. The S.114 right to privacy may be waived in writing under S.116 of the Act.[15] This right to privacy has the potential to restrict the promotional activities of commercial photographers specialising in wedding and portrait photography, as it curtails their ability to create an up-to-date portfolio, which they may use to promote and advertise their services to prospective new clients. A photographer wishing to have this right to privacy legally waived by a commissioning client via a term contained in a written contract for photographic services would have to expressly explain in such a term, that it is being voluntarily waived by the client in favour of the photographer in respect of specified image(s) for the specified reproduction and making available uses by the photographer. The client would have to expressly agree to such a waiver before it would have any legal effect.

13 Note: Section 42(1) of the Broadcasting Act 2009 places a duty on the Broadcasting Authority of Ireland to implement codes of broadcasting standards and practice and under S.42(2)(d) of the Act such codes must ensure that 'in programmes broadcast by a broadcaster, and in the means employed to make such programmes, the privacy of any individual is not unreasonably encroached upon'. Section 39(1)(e) of the Act places a similar restriction on broadcasters' encroachment on the privacy of individuals.

14 Copyright and Related Rights Act 2000, s 114
Note: This S.114 right to privacy does not apply to photographs taken before the commencement date of Part 2 of the Act (12 December, 2000).
Copyright and Related Rights Act 2000, first sch, para 13.
Copyright and Related Rights Act (Commencement) Order 2000, SI 2000/404.

15 ibid s 116

In the absence of a statute granting a general right to privacy, the Data Protection Acts 1988–2018 have become a surrogate and are relied on in a wide variety of court actions. These Acts offer privacy protections to individuals in respect of their personal data. Among other specified purposes, the Data Protection Act 2018 was introduced to give further effect to Regulation (EU) 2016/679[16] (the General Data Protection Regulation) and Directive (EU) 2016/680;[17] to amend the Data Protection Act 1988 and the Data Protection (Amendment) Act 2003 and to establish the Data Protection Commission.[18] Photographs would come within the meaning of "personal data" as defined by the Data Protection Act 1988–2018 and the 2016 Regulations. Section 2(a)(iv) of the 2003 Act re-defined "personal data" as:

> data relating to a living individual who is or can be identified either from the data or from the data in conjunction with other information that is in, or is likely to come into, the possession of the data controller.[19]

Article 4 of Regulation (EU) 2016/679 defines "personal data" as:

> any information relating to an identified or identifiable natural person ('data subject'); an identifiable natural person is one who can be identified, directly or indirectly, in particular by reference to an identifier such as a name, an identification number, location data, an online identifier or to one or more factors specific to the physical, genetic, mental, economic, cultural or social identity of that natural person;[20]

16 Regulation (EU) 2016/679 of the European Parliament and of the Council of 27 April 2016 on the protection of natural persons with regard to the processing of personal data and on the free movement of such data, and repealing Directive 95/46/EC (General Data Protection Regulation) [2016] OJ L119/1 <http://eur-lex.europa.eu/legal-content/EN/TXT/HTML/?uri=CELEX:32016R0679&from=EN> accessed 12 May 2018

17 Directive (EU) 2016/680 of the European Parliament and of the Council of 27 April 2016 on the protection of natural persons with regard to the processing of personal data by competent authorities for the purposes of the prevention, investigation, detection or prosecution of criminal offences or the execution of criminal penalties, and on the free movement of such data, and repealing Council Framework Decision 2008/977/JHA [2016] OJ L119/89 <https://eur-lex.europa.eu/legal-content/EN/TXT/HTML/?uri=CELEX:32016L0680&from=EN> accessed 13 May 2018

18 Data Protection Act 2018
Note: See the United Kingdom's Data Protection Act 2018.

19 Data Protection (Amendment) Act 2003, s 2(a)(iv)

20 Regulation (EU) 2016/679 of the European Parliament and of the Council of 27 April 2016 on the protection of natural persons with regard to the processing of personal data and on the free movement of such data, and repealing Directive 95/46/EC (General Data Protection Regulation) [2016] OJ L119/1, art 4 <http://eur-lex.europa.eu/legal-content/EN/TXT/HTML/?uri=CELEX:32016R0679&from=EN> accessed 12 May 2018

In relation to personal data, Art. 4 provides a number of other definitions of particular relevance. A "controller" is defined as:

> the natural or legal person, public authority, agency or other body which, alone or jointly with others, determines the purposes and means of the processing of personal data;

A "processor" is:

> a natural or legal person, public authority, agency or other body which processes personal data on behalf of the controller;

The "collecting" or "recording" of personal data comes within the definition of "Processing", which is defined as:

> any operation or set of operations which is performed on personal data or on sets of personal data, whether or not by automated means, such as collection, recording, organisation, structuring, storage, adaptation or alteration, retrieval, consultation, use, disclosure by transmission, dissemination or otherwise making available, alignment or combination, restriction, erasure or destruction.[21]

It is reasonable to assume that the previously mentioned definitions of "personal data", "controller", "processor" and "processing" would encompass the typical activities of photographers and photograph publishers and the subject matter of a significant percentage of created photographs, namely those of people. A photographer could be classified as being either a controller or both a controller and a processor of personal data. For example, where a photographer controls the contents of a photograph containing personal data and how such a photograph is to be used, he/she would fall under the heading of a controller. However, if such a photographer were to undertake any of the functions of a processor, as previously described, then he/she would also act as a data processor. For example, the actual taking of a photograph of an individual, the storing of the image's contents on a computerised photo filing system and the retrieval of the image at a later stage to either view, edit, manipulate, print or send it to a publisher for publication are all activities which would come within the earlier definition of "processing". In effect, virtually all photographers, who photograph people, are both data controllers and data processors. Under Art. 6 of the 2016 Regulations, the processing of personal data is lawfully undertaken only if, among other specified conditions, the data subject has consented to the processing of his/her personal data for one or more specific purposes.[22]

21 ibid
22 ibid art 6

Sections 71 of the 2018 Act prescribes detailed conditions under which personal data may be collected and processed. In particular, personal data must only be collected for specified, explicit and legitimate purposes and it must be processed lawfully and fairly and with the explicit consent of the data subject. Personal data collected and processed must be accurate, adequate, relevant and kept up-to-date.[23] Section 72 of the Act specifies the security measures which a controller must put in place in respect of any personal data collected.[24] The 2018 Act contains provisions concerning the personal data of children (persons under the age of 18 years).[25] In respect of any personal data relating to a child collected by an information society services provider as part of an offer of its services to a child, the Act grants that child a right to be forgotten.[26] A data subject has a right to information[27] of the types specified in S.90 of the Act in relation to the processing of his/her personal data. Subject to some specified exemptions, a data subject, who believes that personal data relating to him/her has been or is being processed by or on behalf of a data controller, has a right to access[28] specified information relating to the processing of his/her personal data. Where a data subject believes that a data controller is processing personal data relating to him/her that is inaccurate or contravenes sub-sections 1–6 of S.71 (on processing of personal data) or S.73(1) (on processing of special categories of personal data) or is required to be erased by another legal obligation, he/she may, as appropriate, request a rectification or an erasure of such personal data.[29] Where the accuracy of such personal data is contested and its accuracy may not be ascertained or the data is required as evidence in a court or tribunal proceeding or in any type of official inquiry, the data controller shall restrict the processing of the data, but shall not rectify or erase it.[30]

The 2016 Regulations recognise the importance of the rights of freedom of expression and of information. As permitted under Art.85 of the Regulations,

23 Data Protection Act 2018, s 70

24 ibid s 72

25 ibid ss 29–33

26 ibid s 33

Note (1): On the relevance of the fair obtaining of personal data to the taking and use of photographs and in particular of school children, see the Data Protection Commissioner's case study on this topic: Data Protection Commissioner, Case Studies, *Case Study 10/98: School Web Site – Personal Data Relating to Children – Issue of Fair Obtaining* <www.dataprotection.ie/docs/EN/Case-Study-10-98-School-Web-Site/m/155.htm> accessed 12 May 2018

Note (2): See also: 'School Children Awarded €62,500 Over Images' *The Irish Times* (Dublin, 30 April 2008) <www.irishtimes.com/news/school-children-awarded-62-500-over-images-1.918406> accessed 12 May 2018

27 ibid s 90

28 ibid s 91

29 ibid s 92(1) and s 92(3)

Note: This right to an erasure of inaccurate personal data is provided in accordance with Art. 17 of Regulation (EU) 2016/679 – the right to be forgotten.

30 ibid s 92(9)

an exemption to the requirement to comply with some specified provisions of the Regulations is provided by S.42 of the 2018 Act in respect of the processing of personal data for the exercise of these rights and particularly for journalistic, academic, artistic and literary expression purposes.[31] Photographers and/or photograph publishers creating and/or publishing photographic images for any of these four purposes would come within this exemption. If they are not able to claim the benefit of this exemption, the possession of a signed model release[32] would be a necessary requirement prior to publishing a photograph featuring identifiable people. A model release would be required for a commercial use of such an image – for example in an advertisement. While it could be argued that print media news publishers should also be required to obtain the consent of every subject featured in their printed news photographs, such a requirement would be an extremely onerous task considering the volume of photographs published by newspapers, the number of individual people featured in them and the likelihood of people refusing to grant consent to the publication of photographs featuring them. If that were to be a legal requirement, it could seriously impact on printed news media outlets' ability to report the news through photographs and possibly on their commercial viability.

A data subject who believes that the processing of his or her personal data infringes a relevant provision or a provision adopted by another Member State which gives effect to the rights of data subjects under the Directive has a right to lodge a complaint with, and have it determined by, the Data Protection Commission.[33] The Act also grants data subjects the right to bring data protection actions, founded on tort, against data controllers and data processors.[34] The 2018 Act specifies a number of offences in respect of the processing of personal data. They relate to the unauthorised disclosure of personal data by data processors or their employees or agents, the disclosure of personal data obtained without authority and offences committed by directors or other persons of corporate bodies.[35]

31 ibid s 43
Note: The provisions of Regulation (EU) 2016/679 to which Article 85 permits this exemption concern: Chapter 2 (Principles) except Article 5(1)(f) concerning the security of personal data; Chapter 3 (Rights of the Data Subject), Chapter 4 (Controller and Processor), Chapter 5 (Transfer of personal data to third countries and international organisations), Chapter 6 (Independent Supervisory Authorities) and Chapter 7 (Co-operation and Consistency).

32 Note: A "model release" is a contract signed by a person featured in a photograph. Normally, a model release stipulates the terms under which a photograph may be published. Frequently, model releases will stipulate that images will not be used in a manner which portrays the featured person in a negative light, involved in illegal activities or endorsing a product/service. Possession by a publisher of a signed model release form relating to a specific image and containing details of expressed uses of the image would assist him in defeating a claim of either defamation or passing-off. The inclusion of a rider with a published image stating that the person featured in the image is a model and does not endorse the product/service would be of additional benefit to its publisher.

33 ibid s 119

34 ibid s 117

35 ibid ss 144–146

Sections 96–100 of the 2018 Act concern the transfer of personal data to third countries or international organisations.[36] In recent years, the transfer of personal data by data controllers from one country to another became a topical issue primarily as a consequence of the 2014 Irish High Court judicial review case of *Schrems v Data Protection Commissioner*.[37] The applicant in *Schrems* claimed that the Data Protection Commissioner's decision to refuse to order the cessation of the transfer of his/her online data from Facebook Ireland to its parent company in the United States was unlawful.[38] The Court referred a question relating to the European Commission's Decision 2000/520[39] to the CJEU for a determination. In the 2015 CJEU case of *Maximillian Schrems v Data Protection Commissioner*, the Grand Chamber held that Decision 2000/520 was invalid.[40] Subsequently, the Office of the Data Protection Commissioner sought and obtained a referral from the Irish High Court to the CJEU for a preliminary ruling on the validity of a number of European Commission decisions relating to the use of standard contract clauses for the transfer of personal data to third countries.[41] This matter is on-going.

4.2.3) Privacy rights under the European Convention for the Protection of Human Rights and Fundamental Freedoms

The European Convention for the Protection of Human Rights and Fundamental Freedoms (hereinafter ECHR), as incorporated into Irish law through the European Convention on Human Rights Act 2003 and into the law of the

36 Data Protection Act 2018, ss 96–100

37 *Schrems v Data Protection Commissioner* [2014] IEHC 310

38 ibid para 1

39 European Commission, Commission Decision of 26 July 2000 pursuant to Directive 95/46/EC of the European Parliament and of the Council on the adequacy of the protection provided by the safe harbour privacy principles and related frequently asked questions issued by the US Department of Commerce (2000/520/EC) <https://eur-lex.europa.eu/legal-content/EN/TXT/HTML/?uri=CELEX:32000D0520&from=EN> accessed 13 May 2018

40 Case C-362/14 *Maximillian Schrems v Data Protection Commissioner* (06 October 2015), para 106 Note: See: Mary Carolan, 'Data Protection Commissioner to Investigate Max Schrems Claims: Student Alleges His Personal Data Was Made Available via Facebook to Intelligence Agencies' *The Irish Times* (Dublin, 20 October 2015) <www.irishtimes.com/news/crime-and-law/courts/high-court/data-protection-commissioner-to-investigate-max-schrems-claims-1.2398728> accessed 13 May 2018

41 *The Data Protection Commissioner v Facebook Ireland and Maximillian Schrems* [2017] IEHC 545

Note: See: Data Protection Commissioner, *Statement by the Office of the Data Protection Commissioner in Respect of Application for Declaratory Relief in the Irish High Court and Referral to the CJEU* (Dublin, 25 May 2016) <www.dataprotection.ie/docs/25-05-2016-Statement-by-this-Office-in-respect-of-application-for-Declaratory-Relief-in-the-Irish-High-Court-and-Referral-to-the-CJEU/1570.htm> accessed 13 May 2018

United Kingdom through the Human Rights Act 1998,[42] recognises a right to privacy. Article 8(1) of the ECHR recognises a right to privacy and states:

> Everyone has the right to respect for his private and family life, his home and his correspondence.[43]

This right to privacy is not an absolute right. However, it should not be interfered with except in accordance with the law and where such an interference is necessary in a democratic society and for one of the reasons specified under the Convention. Article 8(2) states:

> There shall be no interference by a public authority with the exercise of this right except such as is in accordance with the law and is necessary in a democratic society in the interests of national security, public safety or the economic well-being of the country, for the prevention of disorder or crime, for the protection of health or morals, or for the protection of the rights and freedoms of others.[44]

The right to privacy frequently comes into contention with the ECHR's Art. 10 right of freedom of expression.[45] How the courts balance these competing rights in cases concerning the taking and publication of photographs is discussed at Section 4.2.6 of this chapter.

4.2.4) Privacy rights under the Charter of Fundamental Rights of the European Union

The contents of the 2010 Charter of Fundamental Rights of the European Union are broadly similar to those of the Council of Europe's Convention. On privacy, Art. 7 of the Charter states:

> Everyone has the right to respect for his or her private or family life, home and communications.[46]

While the Charter does not define what constitutes "personal data", Art. 8(1) of the Charter states: 'Everyone has the right to the protection of personal data

42 Human Rights Act 1998, sch 1
43 European Convention on Human Rights Act 2003, sch 1, art 8(1)
44 ibid art 8(2)
45 ibid art 10
46 Official Journal of the European Union, *Charter of Fundamental Rights of the European Union* [2010] OJ C83/389, art 7 <www.eur-lex.europa.eu/LexUriServ/LexUriServ.do?uri=OJ:C:2010:083:0389:0403:EN:PDF> accessed 15 May 2018

concerning him or her'.[47] As regards the processing of personal data, Art. 8(2) states:

> Such data must be processed fairly for the specified purposes and on the basis of the consent of the person concerned or some other legitimate basis laid down by law. Everyone has the right of access to data which has been collected concerning him or her, and the right to have it rectified.[48]

The Charter goes on to state that 'Compliance with these rules shall be subject to control by an independent authority'.[49]

Article 52 of the Charter makes provision for the limiting of the rights and freedoms recognised by the Charter. However, any such limitations must be proportionate, necessary and 'genuinely meet the objectives of general interest recognised by the Union or the need to protect the rights and freedoms of others'.[50] Like the European Convention, the Charter also recognises a right of freedom of expression and information. Article 11 of the Charter states: 'Everyone has the right to freedom of expression.'[51] There are a number of significant differences, however, between the right to privacy recognised under the Convention and under the Charter. While the Charter makes specific reference to the protection of one's "personal data", the Convention unsurprisingly does not do so since it was drafted in 1950. Also, the Convention refers to one's "correspondence", whereas the Charter adopts an approach in keeping with modern means of communication and refers to one's "communications". These rights of privacy, the protection of personal data and freedom of expression and information are not absolute and, as is the case with the broadly similar rights granted under the ECHR, they frequently come into contention and have to be balanced by the courts.

47 ibid art 8(1)
48 ibid art 8(2)
49 ibid art 8(3)
Note (1): The European Data Protection Supervisor is charged with ensuring that EU institutions and bodies respect people's privacy rights when they are processing their personal data. It also engages with national authorities to ensure that their application of data protection rules is consistent. European Union, *European Data Protection Supervisor* <https://europa.eu/european-union/about-eu/institutions-bodies/european-data-protection-supervisor_en> accessed 15 May 2018
Note (2): At a national level, the respective EU Member States' Data Protection Commission is responsible for upholding individuals' right to personal data protection.
50 ibid art 52
51 ibid art 11

4.2.5) *Privacy rights under the Universal Declaration of Human Rights, the ICCPR and its Optional Protocol*

Among the rights recognised by the United Nations' Universal Declaration of Human Rights is a right to privacy.[52] While the Universal Declaration is not binding on Member States of the United Nations, the UN's International Covenant on Civil and Political Rights (ICCPR)[53] and its Optional Protocol[54] are binding on States Parties, such as Ireland, that have signed and ratified them. Article 17 of the ICCPR (on the right to privacy) reiterates the wording of the right to privacy as recognised by Art. 12 of the Universal Declaration.[55] The Optional Protocol to the ICCPR deals with the recognition by States Parties to the Protocol of the competence of the United Nations' Human Rights Committee to consider complaints from individuals who have exhausted all domestic remedies concerning claimed violations by a State Party, as opposed to violations by another individual, of the rights granted under the ICCPR.[56] As highlighted by the then Irish Human Rights Commission[57] in its 2014 submission to the UN Human Rights Committee, while the ICCPR and its Optional Protocol have been ratified by Ireland, they have not been incorporated into Irish domestic law.[58] Although the Optional Protocol grants individuals a remedy for a perceived breach by a State Party of their right to privacy, as recognised by the ICCPR, in reality that remedy is of no value to individuals

52 United Nations, *The Universal Declaration of Human Rights*, art 12 <www.un.org/en/universal-declaration-human-rights/index.html> accessed 28 March 2018

53 Office of the High Commissioner for Human Rights, *International Covenant on Civil and Political Rights* <www.ohchr.org/en/professionalinterest/pages/ccpr.aspx> accessed 15 May 2018

54 Office of the High Commissioner for Human Rights, *Optional Protocol to the International Covenant on Civil and Political Rights* <www.ohchr.org/EN/ProfessionalInterest/Pages/OPCCPR1.aspx> accessed 15 May 2018

55 Office of the High Commissioner for Human Rights, *International Covenant on Civil and Political Rights*, art 17 <www.ohchr.org/en/professionalinterest/pages/ccpr.aspx> accessed 15 May 2018

56 Office of the High Commissioner for Human Rights, *Optional Protocol to the International Covenant on Civil and Political Rights*, arts 1–3 <www.ohchr.org/EN/ProfessionalInterest/Pages/OPCCPR1.aspx> accessed 15 May 2018

57 Note: The Irish Human Rights and Equality Commission came into being on 01 November 2014 under the Irish Human Rights and Equality Commission Act 2014

58 Irish Human Rights and Equality Commission, *Irish Human Rights Commission Submission to the UN Human Rights Committee on the Examination of Ireland's Fourth Periodic Report under the International Covenant on Civil and Political Rights*, ch 1, para 5 (Dublin, June 2014) <www.ihrec.ie/download/pdf/20140616113130.pdf> accessed 15 May 2018

Note: See: Office of the High Commissioner for Human Rights, Human Rights Committee, *General Comment No. 16: Article 17 – Right to Respect to Privacy, Family Home or Correspondence, and Protection of Honour and Reputation*, para 2 (Geneva, 28 September 1988) <http://tbinternet.ohchr.org/_layouts/treatybodyexternal/TBSearch.aspx?Lang=en&TreatyID=8&DocTypeID=11> accessed 15 May 2018

who believe that their privacy has been breached by either a photographer or photograph publisher. Under Article 1 of the Optional Protocol, they would not be able to submit a communication to the Committee in respect of such a perceived breach of their right.

4.2.6) Addressing of privacy rights by the courts

In Ireland, the courts have recognised a general right to privacy based on the Constitution. However, that right to privacy is not absolute and the courts, in determining a claim for an infringement of that right, must balance it with any competing right(s), particularly the right of freedom of expression, while also taking public policy considerations into account. In the Irish High Court case of *Kennedy and Arnold v Ireland*,[59] which concerned an invasion of privacy through the tapping by the government of two journalists' private telephones, Hamilton P held that the right to privacy is a fundamental personal right and an unenumerated personal right under Art. 40 of the Constitution. However, Hamilton P also held that one's exercise of this right may be restricted to protect the constitutional rights of other and that it is subject to public order and morality requirements.[60] While there have been many Irish court cases involving various aspects of privacy in one's life, the following sample cases raised specific issues regarding the invasion of the right to privacy either by photographers or through the publication of photographs. The Irish High Court case of *Hanahoe v Hussey*,[61] arose from a leak by a member of An Garda Síochána to the media about a proposed raid on a firm of solicitors' offices, which resulted in the presence of press photographers outside the premises at the time of the raid and subsequent publicity in the media. In *Hanahoe*, Kinlen J held that the deliberate leak to the press amounted to negligence by the state, that it caused harm to the applicant and that there had been a breach of the applicant's right to privacy.[62] A breach of privacy was one of the claims in the Irish High Court case of *Hickey v Sunday Newspapers*[63] following the publication of photographs of the first plaintiff, her partner and their new-born child taken outside the Registry of Births, Marriages and Deaths in Dublin. While balancing the competing rights of privacy and freedom of expression in *Hickey*, Kearns P stated that the right to privacy would outweigh the latter right only in

59 *Kennedy and Arnold v Ireland* [1987] 1 IR 587 (HC)
60 ibid 591–592
61 *Hanahoe v Hussey* [1998] 3 IR 69
62 ibid 107–109
Note: See also: Mary Carolan, 'Court Increases Payout to GAA Player Over Photo' *The Irish Times* (Dublin, 31 July 2008) <www.irishtimes.com/news/court-increases-payout-to-gaa-player-over-photo-1.947718> accessed 15 May 2018
63 *Hickey v Sunday Newspapers* [2010] IEHC 349

exceptional cases.[64] Furthermore, Kearns P held that the right of freedom of expression 'is its own public interest' and that it is not necessary to specify a particular public interest when justifying it.[65] On the right to photograph a person in a public place, Kearns P stated that were the Court to find against the defendant:

> it would have the extraordinary consequence that no public figure could be photographed, for example, attending a funeral or performing any other function in a public place.[66]

Kearns P also held, that the published photographs did not disclose anything which any other person present at the scene could not have seen.[67]

4.2.7) Breach of confidence, misuse of private information and the right to privacy

The approach to the development of privacy law in Ireland has differed to that in the United Kingdom with the former having its basis on the constitutional protection of the right to privacy and the right to privacy under the ECHR, whereas in the UK it has been based on the equitable remedy of breach of confidence and the ECHR right. From this equitable remedy, a cause of action termed the "misuse of private information" has also been developed. Although they are not unknown under Irish law, cases concerning breach of confidence and misuse of private information have arisen mainly in the UK. Breach of confidence was recognised as a cause of action in the 1849 English High Court

64 ibid
Note: In the Irish High Court case *Herrity v Associated Newspapers (Ireland) Ltd.* [2008] IEHC 249, at para 61, Dunne J stated: 'There is a hierarchy of constitutional rights and as a general proposition, I think, that cases in which the right to privacy will prevail over the right to freedom of expression may well be far and few between. However, this may not always be the case and there are circumstances where it seems to me the right to privacy could be such that it would prevail over the right to freedom of expression. One of those circumstances arises on the facts of this case where the freedom of expression asserted is the publication of material obtained unlawfully.' However, in the more recent 2017 Irish Supreme Court case of *Sunday Newspapers Limited and Others v Gilchrist and Rogers* [2017] IESC 18, O'Donnell J, at para 36, stated, 'The Constitution does not itself rank the rights and obligations it provides for, nor does it tell us how to divine any hierarchy. The obligation of a court is to uphold all the provisions of the Constitution . . . In truth the Constitution should not be too readily interpreted to require any hierarchical ranking of rights with the consequent possibility of subordination of one right to another. The Constitution was intended to function harmoniously, and where there were points of potential conflict between the rights and obligations provided for, that should be sought to be resolved without the subordination or nullification of one provision.'

65 ibid

66 ibid

67 ibid

of Chancery case of *Prince Albert v Strange*.[68] *Prince Albert* was applied by that Court in *Pollard v Photographic Company*[69] – a case concerning the unauthorised use of a portrait photograph by its photographer in a Christmas window display at his premises. The doctrine was further developed in the English High Court case of *Coco v A.N. Clark*.[70] In *Coco*, Megarry J stated that three essential elements must be proven for a claim of breach of confidence to succeed, namely: the information communicated must be confidential in nature and not common knowledge; the circumstances under which the information was communicated must have implied an obligation of confidence; and the communicated information must have been used without authorisation and to its communicator's detriment.[71]

In the English High Court case of *Hellewell v Derbyshire Chief Constable*,[72] Laws J equated a breach of confidence to a breach of a right of privacy. In doing so, Laws J stated, as an example, that were a person to use a telephoto lens to take a photograph from a distance of another person engaged in a private act without authority, a subsequent disclosure or publication of the image would be a breach of confidence or as he termed it a breach of privacy.[73] One could wonder whether Laws J was in essence hinting towards the individual's right to have a personal image right, although such a right is not recognised under United Kingdom law. Also, it should be noted that there is no law in either the United Kingdom or Ireland which prohibits the use of any type of camera lens while taking a photograph.

How does an obligation of confidence and its corresponding duty not to disclose information arise for a photographer? How does a photographer become aware of its existence? It will depend upon the circumstances. An obligation of confidence may arise for a photographer through a number of different situations. For example, the contractual terms of engagement of a photographer on a commercial basis may expressly contain a confidentiality requirement in relation to any photographs created under the contract. It could arise where one is an invited guest to a private function and is either pre-advised or advised upon arrival at the event either directly or through generally conveyed, explicit information such as signage, that unauthorised photography would not be permitted at the event. Were one to obtain admittance to such an event without invitation, one could be under a similar obligation of confidence in respect of any photography undertaken at the event. In the English High Court case of *Shelley Films Limited v Rex Features Limited*,[74] Martin Mann QC (sitting as a Deputy High Court Judge) stated that he was not convinced that an express prohibition

68 *Prince Albert v Strange* (1849) 2 De Gex and Smale 652
69 *Pollard v Photographic Company* (1888) 40 ChD 345
70 *Coco v A. N. Clark (Engineers) Ltd.* [1969] RPC 41
71 ibid 47
72 *Hellewell v Chief Constable of Derbyshire* [1995] 1 WLR 804
73 ibid 807
74 *Shelley Films Limited v Rex Features Limited* [1994] EMLR 134

on photography would be required for one to found a breach of confidence claim against a photographer or a photograph publisher.[75] Having placed greater weight on the claimant's assertion that the release of the information contained in the photographs in question would be detrimental to its commercial interests,[76] Mann QC granted the requested injunction[77] and held that it would be for a court trial to determine if the photographer was subject to an obligation of confidence and whether the defendant's knowledge of the circumstances under which the photographs were taken would be enough to place the defendant under an obligation of confidence.[78]

While the English Court of Appeal case of *Douglas and Others v Hello! Ltd.* (No. 1)[79] concerned a claimed breach of confidence, it was more so a claim over the control of publicity. In *Douglas*, Brooke LJ stated that a clear prohibition on photography at a private event, either expressly stated or implied, would bind all those present at the event who are aware of such a prohibition to an obligation of confidence. He also stated that equity may prevent the publication of photographs, which have been taken in breach of an obligation of confidence.[80] Consequently, photographers could leave themselves open to a breach of confidence claim, if they are aware of a prohibition on photography at a private event and proceed to take photographs. The same may also apply in the case of a non-private event, for example a paid entry event to which a prior notice prohibiting photography was a term of the admission payment contract. In *Douglas*, Sedley LJ noted that the appellants had effectively sold most of their privacy and all that remained of their privacy was in the form of an image or publicity right, which he stated had been breached.[81] It would appear that Sedley LJ was equating a control over personal images – effectively a publicity right or a right over the publication of one's personal image – as being an element of one's privacy rights. These are two separate issues. As discussed at Section 4.3, while a claimed personal image publicity right and a claimed privacy right may concern the same individual, the former is not a sub-set of the latter right. On appeal to the House of Lords, the appellants in *Douglas v Hello!*[82] claimed that any photographic information concerning their wedding other than the authorised published images was private and Nicholls L described the unauthorised publication of such private photographic information as a misuse of private information.[83] Nicholls L distinguished between a breach of confidence and the misuse of confidential information as causes of action and stated that

75 ibid 148
76 ibid
77 ibid 151
78 ibid 135
79 *Douglas and Others v Hello! Ltd. (No.1)* [2001] 2 WLR 992
80 ibid para 71
81 ibid para 140
82 *Douglas and Others v Hello! Ltd. and Others* [2007] UKHL 21
83 ibid para 251

while the former protected privacy, the latter protected secret or confidential information. He went on to hold that information may, in some instances, be protectable on both privacy and confidentiality grounds.[84]

The cause of action "misuse of private information" was coined by Nichols L in the 2004 House of Lords case of *Campbell v MGN Ltd.* in which he stated that information concerning a person's private life would in normal parlance be referred to as private information rather than confidential information. He also stated that misuse of private information is a tort.[85] Although Evans LJ determined in the 1994 English Court of Appeal case of *Kitechnology B.V. and Others v Unicor GmbH Plastmaschinen and Others* that the equitable cause of action of breach of confidence was not also a tort,[86] in the 2014 English High Court case of *Judith Vidal-Hall and Others v Google Inc.*, Tugendhat J held that misuse of private information was a tort in its own right for the purpose of serving a civil bill out of the jurisdiction.[87] On appeal to the Court of Appeal, this determination by Tugendhat J was affirmed by McFarlane L and Sharp L.[88]

Due to its visual nature, a published photograph has the ability to convey more information and to have greater impact on its viewers than a written article describing the information conveyed in a photograph. The courts have restrained the publication of photographs while permitting the publication of a description of the information contained within them. While a publisher in the printed media might regard such a restriction as the lesser of two evils, as it would be free to publish a written description of the photograph's contents in a large, attention-grabbing typeface, a photographer who publishes his/her own photographs would in reality be completely restrained by such a court order. The English High Court adopted this approach in the case of *Theakston v MGN*.[89] In *Theakston*, Ouseley J granted an injunction against the publication of photographs of the claimant taken in a brothel without his permission, but not against the publication of the written story by the respondent's newspaper (*The Sunday People*) on the matter.[90] In the English Court of Appeal case of *D v L* [2003],[91] Waller LJ held that the restraining of the publication of an improperly obtained photograph even if its photographer is free to publish a description of the information contained in it would be less of a restriction on the right of freedom of expression.[92] One could argue that such court decisions are essentially

84 ibid para 255
85 *Campbell v MGN Ltd.* [2004] UKHL 22, para 14
Note: See also: *MGN Ltd v United Kingdom* [2011] ECHR 66
86 *Kitechnology B.V. and Others v Unicor GmbH Plastmaschinen and Others* [1995] FSR 765, para 777
87 *Judith Vidal-Hall and Others v Google Inc.* [2014] EWHC 13 (QB), para 70
88 *Google Inc. v Judith Vidal-Hall and Others* [2015] EWCA Civ 311, para 51
89 *Theakston v MGN* [2002] EWHC 137 (QB)
90 ibid para 78
91 *D v L* [2003] EWCA Civ 1169
92 ibid para 23

hair-splitting exercises, so that the courts may partially find for a claimant, while not finding completely against a respondent. If an individual claims in a court that information contained within a photograph is private information and the court deems it to be so and that it should not be communicated to the public, then it would be better if the courts were to completely prohibit such information being made available to the public through any means either visually through the publication of the photograph or through either a written or oral description of the information contained within the photograph rather than cherry-picking an acceptable means of communicating the same information.

4.2.8) (1) ECtHR balancing of competing privacy and freedom of expression claims (2) public figure test in privacy claims

The competing rights of privacy and freedom of expression have been adjudicated by the ECtHR on numerous occasions. The Court has developed a test – *Von Hannover (No. 2)* Test – to be used when balancing of these competing rights. It has also cited Clause 7 of Resolution 1165 (1998) of the Parliamentary Assembly of the Council of Europe, which defines a "public figure". *Von Hannover v Germany*[93] was the first of three separate cases taken by Princess Caroline Von Hannover to the ECtHR in which she claimed breaches of her privacy rights by photographers and publishers. In finding for the applicant, the Court stated that despite the fact the she was well-known to the public, the public did not have a legitimate interest in knowing the whereabouts of the applicant or how she behaves in her private life even if she appears in places that are not secluded.[94] Furthermore, the Court held that even if there is a legitimate public interest or a publisher's commercial interest in publishing photographs of her, such interests must give way to her privacy rights.[95] The Court also held that the national courts did not fairly balance the competing privacy and freedom of expression rights, as the criteria adopted by the courts were not adequate to guarantee the protection of the applicant's private life and that she had a legitimate expectation of such protection.[96]

The central issue in the 2012 ECtHR case of *Von Hannover v Germany (No. 2)*[97] was the alleged inadequacy of the protection offered by the domestic courts to the applicant's right to privacy. The Court stated that it would require compelling reasons to find fault with the decisions of the domestic courts on their balancing of the competing rights of privacy and freedom of expression, provided that they had followed the criteria laid down by the ECtHR case law.[98] Based on the Court's case law, the ECHR in *Von Hannover* (No. 2) stated that

93 *Von Hannover v Germany* [2004] EHRR 294
94 ibid para 77
95 ibid
96 ibid para 78
97 *Von Hannover v Germany (No. 2)* (2012) 55 EHRR 15
98 ibid para 107

the test criteria to be investigated by the Court when balancing these competing rights included: the extent to which an article or photograph contributes to a debate of general interest to the public; the extent to which the individual at the centre of the article or photograph is well-known; the subject matter of the article or photograph; the prior conduct of that individual; the content, form and consequences of the publication of the article or photograph and the circumstances under which the photograph was taken.[99] In finding that there had not been a violation by the national courts of the positive obligations imposed by Art. 8 on the state, the Court stated that the national courts had carefully balanced the competing rights; they had taken explicit account of the ECtHR case law when reaching their decisions on the applicant's claim and the Federal Court of Justice had altered its approach following the previously mentioned *Von Hannover v Germany* judgement.[100] The *Von Hannover (2)* test was applied by the ECtHR in the 2012 case of *Axel Springer AG v Germany*,[101] in which it held that there was not a reasonable proportionality relationship between the restrictions imposed on the applicant's right of freedom of expression and the legitimate aim pursued through such restrictions.[102] It was also applied by the ECtHR in the 2014 case of *Lillo-Stenberg and Saether v Norway*,[103] in which the Court determined that there had not been a violation of the applicants' Art. 8 rights following the publication of unauthorised photographs of their wedding. The applicants, respectively a musician and an actress, were both known to the public in Norway and in an effort to distinguish their claim from *Von Hannover (2)* they claimed that they were not public figures and that the published material did not contribute to a debate of public interest.[104] However, while the Court acknowledged that the applicants did not perform public community functions, it held that they were well-known performing artists and therefore were public figures.[105] While noting that opinions on the outcome of a judgement may differ, the Court determined that, as the Norwegian Supreme Court had carefully followed the ECtHR's case law, particularly *Von Hannover (2)* and *Axel Springer*, it had not failed in its obligations under Art. 8 to protect the applicants' rights to privacy under the Convention.[106] The *Von Hannover (2)* balancing test is now the standard test applied by the ECtHR in cases concerning these competing rights.[107]

99 ibid paras 108–113
100 *Von Hannover v Germany (No. 2)* (2012) 55 EHRR 15, paras 124–125
101 *Axel Springer AG v Germany* [2012] ECHR 227
102 ibid para 110
103 *Lillo-Stenberg and Saether v Norway* [2014] ECHR 59
104 ibid para 21
105 ibid para 37
106 ibid paras 44–45
107 Note: See also: *Von Hannover v Germany (No. 3)* [2013] ECHR 835 and *Couderc and Hachette Filipacchi Associés v France* [2015] ECHR 349

An applicant's raising of a claim of not being a public figure, as featured in *Lillo-Stenberg*, in an effort to prevent a reduction in his or her reasonable expectation of privacy, is an interesting issue. Clause 7 of Resolution 1165 (1998) of the Parliamentary Assembly of the Council of Europe, as cited by the ECtHR in *Von Hannover (No. 2)*,[108] defines public figures as including, among others, individuals who hold public office and those who perform roles in public life in areas such as politics, the economy, the arts, the social sphere and sports.[109] The Assembly's Resolution also states that specific facts concerning the private lives of public figures, particularly in the case of politicians, may be of interest to members of the public, who as voters would have a legitimate interest in being made aware of those facts.[110] This definition of a public figure is fairly broad and it does not impose any minimum threshold level on the extent to which a person must play a role in public life in order to come within its reach. While this Resolution makes particular mention of politicians, its scope is not limited to people involved in political life. It covers any person who is a public figure and the public's right to be made aware of specific matters concerning their private lives. Therefore, well-known individuals could face a difficult challenge in invoking a claim of not being public figures in an effort to convince a court to grant their privacy rights greater weight than the right of freedom of expression.

The Assembly's definition of a public figure was adopted by Tugendhat J in the 2012 English High Court case of *Spelman v Express Newspapers*[111] in which a pre-publication injunction was refused.[112] It has also been applied the 2012 English High Court case of *McClaren v News Group Newspapers Ltd.* in which Lindblom J held that the claimant, a former manager of the England football team, was a public figure within the definition as recognised by Tugendhat J in *Spelman*.[113] In the 2013 English High Court Case of *Edward RocknRoll v News Group Newspapers Ltd.*[114] Briggs J refused to accept the defendant's assertion that the claimant had a reduced expectation of privacy as a result of being a public figure in the social sphere as a consequence of his marriage to actress

108 *Von Hannover v Germany (No. 2)* (2012) 55 EHRR 15, para 71

109 Council of Europe, Parliamentary Assembly, *Resolution 1165 (1998) of the Parliamentary Assembly of the Council of Europe on the Right to Privacy*, clause 7 <http://assembly.coe.int/nw/xml/XRef/Xref-XML2HTML-en.asp?fileid=16641&lang=en> accessed 16 May 2018

110 ibid clause 9

111 *Spelman v Express Newspapers* [2012] EWHC 355 (QB), para 49

112 ibid para 119

Note: See also: Sam Greenhill and Jason Groves, 'Family Secret Cabinet Minister Tried to Hide: Rugby-Playing Teenage Son Exposed as a Drugs Cheat' *Daily Mail* (London, 03 March 2012) <www.dailymail.co.uk/news/article-2109403/Caroline-Spelman-s-Rugby-playing-teenage-son-Jonny-exposed-drugs-cheat.html> accessed 10 May 2018

113 *McClaren v News Group Newspapers Ltd.* [2012] EWHC 2466 (QB), para 34

114 *Edward RocknRoll v News Group Newspapers Ltd.* [2013] EWHC 24 Ch

Kate Winslet.[115] The Court was not persuaded that the defendant would convince a trial court that the proposed publication would add to any public debate on matters of public interest.[116] It is interesting to note, that the Court, in holding for the claimant, took into consideration the potential damaging effect the publication of the photographs could have on the claimant's relationship with Ms. Winslet's children and the latter's risk of being ridiculed at school over the activity of their newly acquired stepfather.[117]

The public's right to be informed was a deciding factor in the English Court of Appeal's refusal of a publication injunction in the 2013 case of *AAA (By her litigation friend BBB) v Associated Newspapers Ltd.*[118] In *AAA*, the Master of the Rolls held that the electorate, when considering at election time the suitability of a senior politician for public office, was entitled to be aware of his adulterous affair and his deception of his wife and AAA's mother's partner. This matter of public interest outweighed the claimant's right to privacy.[119]

4.2.9) Publication of pixelated images

Related to the individual's right to privacy and the media's right to publish photographs of individuals is the practice of pixelating[120] the faces of specific people featured in photographs published either in hardcopy or online formats. While there are statutory prohibitions and restrictions on the visual or other identification of specific types of individuals, such as child defendants in court proceedings and the complainants and the accused in certain sexual offence cases and there are constraints imposed on the use of the personal data contained in photographs of individuals under the Data Protection Acts 1988–2018, there is no explicit general statutory requirement to pixelate the face of any person featured in a published photograph. In the House of Lords case of *Campbell v MGN Ltd.*,[121] the pixelation of the faces of two individuals and not that of the applicant, who were featured in the published photographs, was a central issue.[122] Apart from being ordered by a court to do so, as occurred in the 2009 Belfast

115 ibid paras 14 and 16
116 ibid para 33
117 ibid paras 36 and 39
118 *AAA (By her litigation friend BBB) v Associated Newspapers Ltd.* [2013] EWCA Civ 554
119 ibid para 55
Note: See: Sonia Purnell, 'Boris Johnson: The Flawed Mayor of London' *The Independent* (London, 21 May 2013) <www.independent.co.uk/news/uk/politics/boris-johnson-the-flawed-mayor-of-london-8626198.html> accessed 16 May 2018
120 Note: A "pixel" is a dot or a single point contained within a graphic image and "pixelation" is the process of blurring pixels, so that a portion of an image is not clearly visible to a viewer.
121 *Campbell v MGN Ltd.* [2004] UKHL 22
122 Note: See: *Nolan v Sunday Newspapers t/a The Sunday World* [2017] IEHC 367 – a defamation and breach of privacy case featuring the publication of photographs in which the faces of those other than the plaintiff were pixelated.

High Court case of *Callaghan v Independent News and Media Ltd.*[123] for example, publishers may take an editorial decision to pixelate the faces of individuals featured in their published photographs for a number of practical reasons.

Frequently, one sees published photographs of members of An Garda Síochána, including uniformed members, attending incident scenes or while present at other locations in which some or all of their faces are pixelated.[124] Members of An Garda Síochána do not have a statutory right under which they may object to the taking and/or publication of photographs of them while they are legally performing their duties in either a public or a private place to which the public is freely admitted.[125] Also, there is no statutory prohibition on doing so. However, the identification of certain plain clothes members of An Garda Síochána lawfully involved in under-cover duties could jeopardise their ability to undertake such duties. Aside from such individuals, one posits that the reason the faces of specific, individual members of An Garda Síochána, who are either in uniform or in plain clothes with Garda Síochána insignia clearly visible on their clothing and/or headgear, are pixelated in published photographs is to obtain their co-operation to be included in such photographs.

Newspapers often publish photographs of convicted criminals in the company of other individuals. So as to avoid any likely claims for defamation, the faces of the other individuals featured in such photographs will be pixelated. Frequently, news photographs show individuals present at incidents. Some or all of the individuals may or may not have been involved in the incidents depicted in the images. Again, so as to avoid any potential claims for defamation or to maintain a presumption of innocence and to not prejudice any future criminal trial, the individuals' faces may be pixelated.[126] However, the pixelation of individuals central to criminal investigations is not always undertaken and the

123 *Callaghan v Independent News and Media Ltd.* [2009] NIQB 1

124 Note: See: Dearbhail McDonald, 'Amid the Usual Teen Court Dramas, a Case that Will Shock the Nation' *Irish Independent* (Dublin, 05 December 2015) <www.independent.ie/irish-news/courts/amid-the-usual-teen-court-dramas-a-case-that-will-shock-the-nation-34260969.html> accessed 16 May 2018
Note: This article included a photograph showing four uniformed members of An Garda Síochána with their faces pixelated while casually standing outside Tallaght District Court. No other individuals were featured in the photograph.

125 Note (1): As discussed in Chapter 5, in the United Kingdom the taking and/or publication of a photograph of a police officer could constitute a criminal offence under the Terrorism Act 2000, as amended.
Note (2): See: —— 'Journalists Concerned at Garda Proposal to Criminalise the Photographing of Officers While on Duty' *Irish Examiner* (Cork, 10 April 2017) <www.irishexaminer.com/breakingnews/ireland/journalists-concerned-at-garda-proposal-to-criminalise-the-photographing-of-officers-while-on-duty-785257.html> accessed 15 June 2018

126 Note: See: —— 'Regency Hotel Murder – Astonishing Photos Emerge of "Transvestite" Gunman Fleeing the Scene' *Irish Independent* (Dublin, 7 February 2016) <www.independent.ie/irish-news/regency-hotel-murder-astonishing-photos-emerge-of-transvestite-gunman-fleeing-the-scene-34430698.html> accessed 16 May 2018

identification of suspects in criminal investigations prior to they being charged with a criminal offence could jeopardise their right to a presumption of innocence and of a fair trial.[127]

The registration plates of vehicles featured in published news photographs are frequently pixelated. A possible reason for doing such is to avoid being accused of contravening the Data Protection Acts by the linking of the personal data contained in a photograph of a person with that contained in a photograph of a vehicle's registration number. However, as the personal data relating to any person connected to the number displayed on a vehicle registration plate is only legally accessible by either An Garda Síochána, local authority personnel and any other prescribed bodies, it is questionable as to whether the publication of a photograph clearly showing a vehicle registration plate would be in contravention of the Data Protection Acts. An example of such a pixelated published photograph is that of a marked Garda Síochána Traffic Corps squad car shown in the near foreground of a photograph with its registration plate pixelated. It was obvious from the photograph that the vehicle was a marked squad car, which is state-owned and not personal property.[128] The publication of pixelated images should be done in a manner that is effective in protecting any privacy issues at stake. An example of an ineffective use of pixelation occurred in the case of pixelated front and rear photographs of a personalised Range Rover belonging to Tamara Ecclestone, a daughter of Bernie Ecclestone of Formula One fame. Although the registration plates were pixelated, the name "Tamara" was displayed on its bonnet and tailgate in the place normally occupied by the vehicle's brand name.[129]

Note: The published body copy accompanying a pixelated image of the faces of two armed gunmen stated that the image had been pixelated at the request of An Garda Síochána and due to the nature of the investigation.

127 Note: For an example of such an identification, see: Ralph Riegel, '"I've Just Done a Very Bad Thing" – Young Man After Mother Killed in Knife Attack: Heroic Neighbours Disarm Son as Mother Killed and Dad Stabbed' *Irish Independent* (Dublin, 24 November 2015) <www.independent.ie/irish-news/ive-just-done-a-very-bad-thing-young-man-after-mother-killed-in-knife-attack-34228171.html> accessed 16 May 2018

Note: The individual whose un-pixelated photograph was published with the previously mentioned article concerning his arrest for questioning had not been charged with a criminal offence at the time of publication and was not charged until the following day.

Barry Roche, 'Man (25) Charged With Murder of His Mother in Cork: Paul Horgan Remanded in Custody Over Death of Marian Horgan at Montenotte Home' *The Irish Times* (Dublin, 25 November 2015) <www.irishtimes.com/news/crime-and-law/man-25-charged-with-murder-of-his-mother-in-cork-1.2443000> accessed 16 May 2018

128 Ralph Riegel, 'Garda Injured After Being Rammed By Stolen Van in High Speed Chase' *Irish Independent* (Dublin, 18 April 2014) <www.independent.ie/irish-news/garda-injured-after-being-rammed-by-stolen-van-in-high-speed-chase-30197331.html> accessed 16 May 2018

129 Louise Saunders, 'Tamara Ecclestone Shows Blingy Personalised Car Enjoys Date Night Jay Rutland' *Daily Mail* (London, 22 July 2013) <www.dailymail.co.uk/tvshowbiz/

Occasionally, one sees photographs published in advertisements featuring models, which have been obtained without a model release. In such cases, the model's face may be pixelated so as to lazily get around the problem of not having a model release rather than shooting a model-released image for the advertisement. To give extra legal protection to the privacy rights of children, their faces are frequently pixelated in published news photographs.[130]

4.2.10) Children and their right to privacy

Due to their vulnerability and lack of maturity and for the protection of their security, safety and well-being, children may be offered additional protection of their rights, and in particular their right to privacy, over and above that offered by the law to an adult. They are also afforded a statutory protection to their identity in specific circumstances, such as in court-related matters. Although the Constitution of Ireland guarantees the rights of children,[131] it does not offer children a specific protection to their right to privacy purely on the basis of their age. At an international level, a right of privacy is offered to children through Art. 16 of the United Nations' Convention on the Rights of the Child.[132] However, that right is not absolute. At an EU level, the Charter of Fundamental Rights provides for the protection of children.[133] While the Charter does not make any specific reference to children's privacy, they do have a right to privacy under Art. 7 of the Charter, as that right applies to everyone. Likewise, they have protection under the ECHR's Art. 8 right to privacy. The protection of children's privacy has been an issue in a number of court cases which concerned the taking and publication of photographs. Not all court applications grounded on a claim to protect the privacy of a child will result in the granting of an order restraining publication. For such applications to succeed, the courts have taken a wide range of factors into consideration including whether the applicant (on the behalf of the child) has challenged the veracity of the proposed publication material; the expressed guarantee of freedom of expression in the Constitution; the test of a reasonable expectation of privacy; the child's age; the balancing of competing rights; the potential personal dam-

article-2373149/Tamara-Ecclestone-shows-blingy-personalised-car-enjoys-date-night-Jay-Rutland.html> accessed 16 May 2018

130 Note: For example, see: Sara Stack, 'Bringing Adrian's Killers to Justice Will Be Difficult But We Will Find Them, Says Garda Chief' *Irish Independent* (Dublin, 31 January 2013) <www.independent.ie/irish-news/bringing-adrians-killers-to-justice-will-be-difficult-but-we-will-find-them-says-garda-chief-29025452.html> accessed 16 May 2018

131 Constitution of Ireland (*Art. 42A*) (on Children)

132 United Nations, Office of the High Commissioner for Human Rights, *Convention on the Rights of the Child*, art 16 <www.ohchr.org/en/professionalinterest/pages/crc.aspx> accessed 17 May 2018

133 Official Journal of the European Union, *Charter of Fundamental Rights of the European Union* [2010] OJ C83/389, art 24(1) <www.eur-lex.europa.eu/LexUriServ/LexUriServ.do?uri=OJ:C:2010:083:0389:0403:EN:PDF> accessed 17 May 2018

age or harm resulting from its publication; and the safety of the child. The following sample cases illustrate each of these factors in turn.

Veracity of the allegations and the constitutional guarantee of freedom of expression

In the Irish High Court case of *M.M. v Drury*,[134] following an in-court application the plaintiff's children were joined as parties to her application to the court for an interim injunction to prevent the publication of photographs and other material concerning her family life. The plaintiff claimed that such publication could potentially result in psychological damage to her children and that the Constitution entitled them to protection from such damage.[135] In *M.M.*, O'Hanlon J pointed out that the material in question actually concerned the plaintiff's alleged extra-marital affair and not her marital life as claimed by her.[136] O'Hanlon J stated that the plaintiff had not disputed the veracity of the allegations contained in the material to be published and taking into account the constitutionally expressed guaranteed right of freedom of expression, he could not identify either legal precedent or a basis within the Constitution upon which he could, in such circumstances, grant the requested publication restraint for the purpose of preventing distress to the children.[137] Had the truth of the allegations been challenged, the Court would have intervened.[138]

Reasonable expectation of privacy

In the English Court of Appeal in *Murray v Big Pictures*,[139] Sir Anthony Clarke MR focussed on one of the key tests in a privacy action, namely a reasonable expectation of privacy, and stated that the existence of such depended upon all the circumstances pertaining to any particular case.[140] Due to a child's lack of appreciation that his privacy may be invaded by a photographer and the publication of a photograph, Clarke MR stated that there is a difference between a case concerning a child's privacy and that of an adult.[141] He went on to hold that just as the child of non-famous parents could reasonably expect that he would not be targeted by the press and have his photograph published, the

134 *M.M. v Drury* [1994] 2 IR 8
135 ibid 9
Note: This case pre-dated the amendment of the Constitution to insert Article 42A on Rights of Children.
136 ibid 14
137 ibid 17
138 ibid 36
139 *Murray (by his litigation friends Murray and Another) v Big Pictures (UK) Ltd.* [2008] EWCA Civ 446
140 ibid para 36
141 ibid para 37

child of a famous person could have an equal expectation to privacy.[142] Sir Anthony stated that the central issue in *Murray* should be on the publication of the photograph rather than on the actual taking of it and in the absence of any distress having been caused to the child by the taking of a photograph of the child, its taking may not be completely objectionable.[143] Sir Anthony held that the child had a reasonable expectation of not being the focus of a photographer in a public place to obtain photographs for a future publication, where the photographer or the publisher was aware that such would be objected to on the child's behalf. Having found that the child had a reasonable expectation of privacy, Sir Anthony stated that it was not a guaranteed right and that it must be balanced with the competing right of freedom of expression.[144]

The child's age

The child applicant's age was a central issue in the determination of the 2011 English High Court case of *Spelman v Express Newspapers*.[145] *Spelman* concerned an application for the continuation of a pre-publication injunction by a 17-year-old boy who had played rugby for England until he was injured. Activities (detailed in a Closed Judgement)[146] central to the injunction application occurred subsequent to that injury and were claimed to be of a private information nature.[147] The Court had been told that a proposed newspaper article against which the injunction was being sought had not, as yet, been written.[148] In *Spelman*, Tugendhat J stated that children do not have a general right to privacy purely on the basis of their age, but that in specific circumstances a child may be entitled to protection by the law from publicity, whereas an adult would not.[149] Tugendhat J differentiated *Murray*, which concerned an infant, from *Spelman*, which concerned a 17-year-old who possessed his own personality and public profile.[150] As required under the Human Rights Act 1998,[151] Tugendhat J referred to the then in-force Press Complaints Commission's Code of Practice[152] and specifically to its clause on children and to the permitted public interest exceptions to the Code. While refusing to grant a continuation of the injunction, Tugendhat J concluded that if the respondent were to publish the

142 ibid para 46
143 ibid para 54
144 ibid paras 57–58
145 *Spelman v Express Newspapers* [2012] EWHC 355 (QB)
146 ibid para 79
147 ibid para 1
148 ibid para 2
149 ibid para 53
150 ibid para 55
151 Human Rights Act 1998, s 12(4)
152 *Spelman v Express Newspapers* [2012] EWHC 355 (QB), para 35

information which the applicant sought to have prohibited, the respondent would have a good possibility of establishing a public interest defence.[153]

Balancing competing rights

The 2011 English Court of Appeal case of *ETK v News Group Newspapers Ltd.*[154] was one of a number of cases which became known as "super-injunction"[155] cases; the appellant was a married man who had been in a sexual relationship with another married woman "X" with whom he worked in the entertainment industry. Having been confronted by his wife, the appellant admitted to the affair and agreed with his wife to end it so as to rebuild their marriage and for the sake of their teenage children. The applicant had sought an injunction to restrain the *News of the World* newspaper from publishing information concerning the relationship.[156] In *ETK*, Ward LJ noted the requirements of S.12 of the Human Rights Act 1998[157] while balancing the competing Art. 8 and Art. 10 rights and he determined that any harmful effect on the children due to negative publicity concerning their father's behaviour could, even when having taken such behaviour into account, outbalance the right of freedom of expression.[158]

153 *Spelman v Express Newspapers* [2012] EWHC 355(QB), para 102

154 *ETK v News Group Newspapers Ltd.* [2011] EWCA Civ 439

155 Note: Definition of "super-injunction": 'The term has been used to describe interim injunctions: which provide for party anonymity; which contain a prohibition on publishing or disclosing the fact of the substantive order and proceedings; which provide both for party anonymity, a prohibition on publishing or disclosing the fact of the substantive order and proceedings, as well as, for instance, restricting access to documents on the court file.'

Courts and Tribunals Judiciary, *The Report of the Committee on Super-Injunctions: Super-Injunctions, Anonymised Injunctions and Open Justice*, page 16 (London, 20 May 2011) <www.judiciary.gov.uk/wp-content/uploads/JCO/Documents/Reports/super-injunction-report-20052011.pdf> accessed 15 May 2018

156 *ETK v News Group Newspapers Ltd.* [2011] EWCA Civ 439, para 1

157 Note (1): Under S.12 of the Human Rights Act 1998, which incorporated the European Convention for the Protection of Human Rights and Fundamental Freedoms into the domestic law of the United Kingdom, 'If a court is considering whether to grant any relief which, if granted, might affect the exercise of the Convention right to freedom of expression . . . No such relief is to be granted so as to restrain publication before trial unless the court is satisfied that the applicant is likely to establish that publication should not be allowed.' Human Rights Act 1998, ss12(1) and 12(3)

Note (2): It is noted that the European Convention on Human Rights Act 2003, which transposed the Convention into domestic Irish law, does not contain a similar statutory protection of the right of freedom of expression when it is being balanced with the right to privacy.

158 *ETK v News Group Newspapers Ltd.* [2011] EWCA Civ, para 18

Potential damage or harm

In the 2015 English Court of Appeal case of *Weller and Others v Associated Newspapers Limited*,[159] Tomlinson LJ stated that a court's finding that a child has a reasonable expectation of privacy does not equate to a guarantee of privacy and as in cases concerning the privacy of an adult a balancing exercise must be undertaken in those concerning a child's privacy.[160] He went on to state: 'although the best interests of a child is not a trump card in the balancing exercise, the primacy of the best interests of a child means that, where a child's interests would be adversely affected, they must be given considerable weight'.[161] On the harm to a child resulting from an invasion of his privacy through the publication of photographs, Tomlinson LJ stated that evidence of actual harm is not required by the Court, which will make its own decision on such based on 'common sense and its own experience'.[162] Finding that Dingemans J was right in determining in the High Court case of *Weller and Others v Associated Newspapers Ltd.*[163] that the claimants had a reasonable expectation of privacy and that the photographs should not be published,[164] he implemented the previously mentioned *Von Hannover (No. 2)* balancing test and concluded that the claimants' Art. 8 rights outweighed the defendant's Art. 10 right.[165]

Safety of the child

The safety of a child will be considered in privacy cases involving either the taking or publication of photographs of a child. For example, the 2013 ECtHR case of *Soderman v Sweden*[166] concerned the covert filming of a 14-year-old child in a shower by her stepfather. Holding that the filming violated the applicant's integrity and Art. 8 right to privacy, the Court in *Soderman* stated that the aggravating factors included the fact that she was a minor, that the filming was undertaken in her home (a place where she should feel safe) and by her stepfather – someone she had an entitlement and an expectation to trust.[167]

4.3) Personal image rights and publicity rights

Closely related to, and often confused with, privacy are two other types of rights, namely personal image and publicity rights. Respectively, they may be

159 *Weller and Others v Associated Newspapers Limited* [2015] EWCA Civ 1176
160 ibid para 39
161 ibid para 40
162 ibid para 41
163 *Weller and Others v Associated Newspapers Ltd. [2014] EWHC 1163 (QB)*
164 *Weller and Others v Associated Newspapers Limited* [2015] EWCA Civ 1176, para 59
165 ibid paras 72–80
166 *Soderman v Sweden* App No 5786/08 (ECtHR November 2013)
167 ibid para 117

defined as a right to control the use of one's personal image and to command a controlling right over one's own publicity.[168] The Constitution of Ireland does not expressly guarantee such rights. In Ireland, as in the United Kingdom, these rights are not provided through legislation and they are not recognised by the courts, although, as mentioned, some courts have made reference to them.[169] In the absence of both image and publicity rights in Ireland, court cases concerning what are essentially claims to such rights have been taken under claims of passing-off through the use of photographs.[170] In the United Kingdom, the courts have differentiated between the existing legal right to privacy, an obligation of confidence and the absence of a legal right over the use of one's image and of a publicity right. In the 2004 House of Lords case of *Campbell v MGN*, Hale B stated that an image right was not recognised under United Kingdom law.[171] In the 2007 House of Lords case of *Douglas and Others v Hello*,[172] Hoffmann L stated that it was not a matter of creating an image right, but that by having enough control over information which had a commercial value, namely the personal images contained in the photographs at issue, the appellants would be able to impose an obligation of confidence.[173] One could take the view that Hoffman L was actually indirectly acknowledging the existence of a publicity right under the guise of an obligation of confidence. The 2015 English Court of Appeal case of *Robyn Rihanna Fenty and Others v Arcadia Group Brands and Topshop*, Kitchin LJ re-affirmed that no image right existed under English law.[174]

In *Reklos v Greece*, the ECtHR recognised a person's image as being an element of one's personality and that one has the right to protect and control the use of one's image. The Court also held, that these rights included a right of

168 Note: See: (1) *Proactive Sports Management v Wayne Rooney and Others* [2011] EWCA Civ 1444
(2) Gillian Black, *Publicity Rights and Image: Exploitation and Legal Control* (Hart Publishing 2011)

169 Note (1): See: Donnchadh Boyle, 'Farrell Calls for Image Rights Issue to be Tackled' *Irish Independent* (Dublin, 02 May 2008) <www.independent.ie/sport/gaelic-games/gaelic-football/farrell-calls-for-image-rights-issue-to-be-tackled-26443561.html> accessed 23 May 2018
Note (2): Technically, it may be possible to register a photograph of an individual as a trademark under the Trade Marks Act 1966, as amended. However, doing so would not protect an individual's personal image, as only the registered photograph and no other photographs of that individual would be protected through such a registration.

170 Note: For example, see: Joe Leogue and Ed Carty, 'Keane Latest Celebrity to Sue Paddy Power Over Image Rights' *Irish Examiner* (Cork, 11 July 2015) <www.irishexaminer.com/ireland/keane-latest-celebrity-to-sue-paddy-power-over-image-rights-341915.html> accessed 17 May 2018

171 *Campbell v MGN Ltd.* [2004] UKHL 22, para 154

172 *Douglas and Others v Hello! Ltd. and Others* [2007] UKHL 21

173 ibid para 124

174 *Robyn Rihanna Fenty and Others v Arcadia Group Brands and Topshop* [2015] EWCA Civ 3, para 29

consent over whether or not a person may be photographed by a third party.[175] Effectively, the Court in *Reklos* coupled a publicity right with an image right. As the domestic courts had not taken into account that the applicants had not consented to their son being photographed or to the photographer's retention of the negatives of the photographs of their son, the ECtHR held that the applicants' son's Art. 8 right had been violated.[176] The *Reklos* decision was adopted by the ECtHR in the 2012 case of *Von Hannover v Germany (No. 2)*.[177] This is an important development by the ECtHR, as it appears to have expanded the reach of the wording of the Art. 8 right to privacy beyond any notion of privacy. While there is neither a constitutional nor statutory personal image or publicity right in Ireland or the United Kingdom, their courts will have to take cognisance of this ECtHR decision when determining cases in which image and publicity rights are being claimed. A recognition of these rights by the courts in Ireland and the United Kingdom could result in a disproportionate restriction on the right of freedom of expression and in individuals cherry-picking which images of themselves they will object to being published in order to create a public visual profile of themselves, which is either fabricated or at best one-sided.[178]

4.4) Right against harassment, stalking, revenge porn and voyeurism

Individuals have a legal right not to be harassed. Harassment may take place through a variety of forms and it may be undertaken by, among others, photographers and publishers of photographs. Closely related to harassment are a range of other activities including stalking, voyeurism and the publication of what is commonly referred to as revenge porn.[179]

175 *Reklos and Another v Greece* (2009) 27 BHRC (App No 1234/05), para 40
176 ibid para 43
177 *Von Hannover v Germany (No. 2)* (2012) 55 EHRR 15, para 96
178 Note: See (1): Gordon Rayner, 'Kate Middleton Won't Sue Over Privacy Invasion of Prince George Holiday Photos' *The Independent* (London, 04 February 2014) <www.independent.ie/style/celebrity/celebrity-news/kate-middleton-wont-sue-over-privacy-invasion-of-prince-george-holiday-photos-29978354.html> accessed 25 May 2018 (2): Darryn Lyons, *Mr. Paparazzi: My Life as the World's Most Outrageous Celebrity Photographer* (John Blake Publishing, 2008)
179 Note (1): See: Law Reform Commission, *Report on Harmful Communications and Digital Safety* (LRC 116–2016) Dublin 2016 <https://publications.lawreform.ie/Portal/External/en-GB/RecordView/Index/37669> accessed 20 May 2018
Note (2): See: Sarah Bardon, '"Upskirting", Cyberstalking, and Revenge Porn to be Criminal Offences: Tánaiste Says Acts "Can Cause Serious and Lasting Harm to Young People"' *The Irish Times* (Dublin, 15 May 2017) <www.irishtimes.com/news/politics/upskirting-cyberstalking-and-revenge-porn-to-be-criminal-offences-1.3082855> accessed 20 May 2018

4.4.1) Harassment

One has a right not to be harassed. In Ireland, the harassment of an individual by another is a criminal offence under the Non-Fatal Offences Against the Persons Act 1997. Under S.10(1) of the Act:

> Any person who, without lawful authority or reasonable excuse, by any means including by use of the telephone, harasses another by persistently following, watching, pestering, besetting or communicating with him or her, shall be guilty of an offence.[180]

While S.10 of the Act focuses on harassment through the use of a telephone, the inclusion of the words "by any means" would embrace harassment through the use of a camera. Also, through the use of the word "persistently" in S.10(1), it would appear, that a one-off incident could not be construed as harassment. More than one incident would need to occur for it to be persistent. Section 10(2) of the Act defines "harassment" and states:

> a person harasses another where (a) he or she, by his or her acts intentionally or recklessly, seriously interferes with the other's peace and privacy or causes alarm, distress or harm to the other, and (b) his or her acts are such that a reasonable person would realise that the acts would seriously interfere with the other's peace and privacy or cause alarm, distress or harm to the other.[181]

In addition to the previously mentioned offence, the Defamation Act 2009, which provided for the recognition of an independent Press Council in Ireland,[182] placed an onus on the Press Council to implement a code of standards for its members which specifically would ensure, among other things, 'that intimidation and harassment of persons does not occur and that the privacy, integrity and dignity of the person is respected'.[183] The *Editors' Code of Practice* of the United Kingdom's Independent Press Standards Organisation[184] and the IMPRESS *Standards Code*[185] prohibit, subject to public interest exemptions, the harassment of individuals by their members. In comparison to the statutory offence of harassment in Ireland, the United Kingdom's Protection from Harassment Act

180 Non-Fatal Offences Against the Persons Act 1997, s 10(1)
181 ibid s 10(2)
182 Defamation Act 2009, s 44 and sch 2, s 3
183 ibid sch 2, s 10
184 Independent Press Standards Organisation, *Editors' Code of Practice*, clause 3 <www.ipso.co.uk/IPSO/cop.html> accessed 19 May 2018
Note: The IPSO Code states that there is a public interest in freedom of expression itself.
185 IMPRESS, *The IMPRESS Standards Code*, clause 5 <www.impress.press/downloads/file/code/the-impress-standards-code.pdf> accessed 19 May 2018

1997 does not define the term "harassment".[186] However, in the 2010 English High Court case of *Dowson and Others v Chief Constable of Northumbria Police*, Simon J stated that for a claim of harassment to succeed, the claimant must prove as a matter of law that the conduct in question occurred on a minimum of two occasions; that it was targeted at the claimant; that on an objective view it was calculated to cause alarm or distress and it is objectively judged to be oppressive and unacceptable conduct. Simon J also stated, that the social or working context in which the conduct occurred could have a bearing on what constitutes oppressive and unacceptable conduct.[187]

Court cases concerning claims of harassment against photographers are not a regular occurrence in the Irish courts, particularly the superior courts. In the 2011 Irish High Court case of *Hickey v Sunday Newspapers*,[188] harassment featured indirectly through the claimant's reliance on *Von Hannover v Germany*.[189] However, Kearns P stated that such reliance was of no benefit to the claimant, as in *Von Hannover*, unlike in *Hickey*, the photographs were central to a harassment campaign targeted at a public figure.[190] A number of individuals have been convicted of the offence of harassment in respect of conduct involving photography by the lower Irish courts. Due to the absence of an offence of voyeurism in Ireland, it would appear that the S.10(1) offence of harassment is used as a means to prosecute such cases.[191] While infrequent, a number of court cases in the United Kingdom concerning harassment by photographers resulted from the interaction of members of the paparazzi with celebrities and public figures.[192] In other court cases, matters such as harassment resulting from the unauthorised

186 Protection from Harassment Act 1997

187 *Dowson and Others v Chief Constable of Northumbria Police* [2010] EWHC 2612 (QB), para 142

188 *Hickey v Sunday Newspapers* [2011] 1 IR 228

189 *Von Hannover v Germany* [2004] ECHR 294

190 *Hickey v Sunday Newspapers* [2011] 1 IR 228, para 37
Note: See also: *Collins & Another v Griffiths & Another* [2017] IEHC 658 – a case involving, among other matters, harassment through repetitive videoing of plaintiff in public places.

191 Note (1): See (1): Ann Healy, 'Landlord Convicted of Spying on Tenants' *The Irish Times* (Dublin, 8 April 2003) <www.irishtimes.com/news/landlord-convicted-of-spying-on-tenants-1.470727> accessed 19 May 2018 (2): Katheryn Hayes, 'Paramedic to Pay Colleague €5,000 After Harassment' *The Irish Times* (Dublin, 9 March 2013) <www.irishtimes.com/news/paramedic-to-pay-colleague-5-000-after-harassment-1.1320292> accessed 19 May 2018
Note (2): See: Law Reform Commission, *Report on Harmful Communications and Digital Safety* (LRC 116–2016) Dublin 2016 <https://publications.lawreform.ie/Portal/External/en-GB/RecordView/Index/37669> accessed 19 May 2018
Note (3): Two separate Bills currently before the Oireachtas, namely the Harassment, Harmful Communications and Related Offences Bill 2017 and the Harmful Communications and Digital Safety Bill 2017, each contain proposals to reform the law on harassment, harmful communications and related offences.

192 For example, see: *Ting Lan Hong and KLM v XYZ and Others* [2011] EWHC 2995 (QB)

distribution of explicit sexual photographs of a claimant over the Internet[193] and claims of harassment following the disclosure of extra-marital affairs and the publication of photographs relating to same were the central issues.[194]

Although a right against being harassed is not expressly conferred in the ECHR, in cases before the ECtHR the issue of harassment has been raised by the Court. For example, in the 2004 case of *Von Hannover v Germany*,[195] which centred on a claim of a breach of privacy, the Court noted that photographs published in the tabloid press are frequently taken under conditions of continual harassment, which causes the individuals concerned to feel that their private lives have been invaded.[196] The harassment of a subject by a photographer could have a bearing on whether or not a published image would be deemed by the ECtHR as a contributing factor to the violation of a person's privacy rights. The applicants in the ECtHR case of *Von Hannover v Germany (No. 2)* had claimed that the photographs complained of had been taken under conditions of general harassment and that they were constantly being confronted by photographers. However, the Court stated that the German Federal Court of Justice had concluded that the complainant had not complained that the photographs had been taken under conditions that were unfavourable to her. The Court held that the photographs of the complainant taken in a street were not in themselves offensive to an extent that would warrant them being prohibited.[197]

4.4.2) Stalking

Related to the offence of harassment is the activity known as stalking. It is not an offence in Ireland. In the United Kingdom, two new offences of stalking were created by the Protection of Freedoms Act 2012[198] through its insertion of S.2A and S.4A in the Protection from Harassment Act 1997. These new offences are of relevance to photographers, particularly paparazzi-style photographers, and to publishers of their photographs. Section 2A(1) of the 1997 Act states:

> A person is guilty of an offence if (a) the person pursues a course of conduct in breach of section 1(1), and (b) the course of conduct amounts to stalking.[199]

193 For example, see: *AMP v Persons Unknown* [2011] EWHC 3454 (TCC)
194 For example, see (1): *Carina Trimingham v Associated Newspapers Limited* [2012] EWHC 1296 (QB). (2): *ABK v KDT and FGH* [2013] EWHC 1192 (QB)
195 *Von Hannover v Germany* [2004] ECHR 294
196 ibid para 59
197 *Von Hannover v Germany (No. 2)* (2012) 55 EHRR 15, paras 121–123
198 Protection of Freedoms Act 2012, s 111(1)
199 Protection from Harassment Act 1997, s 2A(1)

Section 2A(2) of the 1997 Act states:

> a person's course of conduct amounts to stalking of another person if (a) it amounts to harassment of that person, (b) the acts or omissions involved are ones associated with stalking, and (c) the person whose course of conduct it is knows or ought to know that the course of conduct amounts to harassment of the other person.[200]

The Act does not define the term "stalking", but it does provide examples of the types of acts and omissions, which are associated with stalking. Such acts include "following", "watching", "spying" on a person and "publishing" material relating to a person.[201] Section 4A of the Act deals with stalking which involves the additional element of the creation of fear of violence, serious alarm or distress within another person.[202] For the "fear" element under S.4A of the Act to be engaged, such fear must be caused on more than one occasion. Although infrequent, a number of individuals have been convicted of stalking offences under the Act.[203] A statutory offence of stalking should be introduced in Ireland.

4.4.3) Revenge porn

What is colloquially termed as "revenge porn" is closely related to harassment. It involves the unauthorised publication of private, sexual photographs of individuals on the Internet or through other means of publication with the intention of either harassing or causing distress to such individuals. Due to the widespread access to, and use of, the Internet and a range of communications technologies, including smartphones, revenge porn has become a current issue. Although many victims of revenge porn may have consented to the taking of the images concerned, it is unlikely that they would have consented to their publication either on the Internet or elsewhere.[204] To protect individuals' privacy and to

200 ibid s 2A(2)

201 ibid s 2A(3)

202 ibid s 4A(1)

203 For example, see: Steve Morris, 'Man Jailed After Using Explicit Images of Ex-Wife in £2m Blackmail Bid: James Casbolt Posted Sexually Explicit Images of Haley Meijer, Daughter of a US Hypermarket Tycoon, Online and Threatened Her Family After Split' *The Guardian* (London, 28 July 2015) <www.theguardian.com/uk-news/2015/jul/28/man-jailed-blackmail-sexually-explicit-images-ex-wife-haley-meijer> accessed 20 May 2018

204 Note: See (1): David Barrett, 'What Is the Law on Revenge Porn? What Is Revenge Porn and What Is the Law on It?' *The Telegraph* (London, 13 April 2015) <www.telegraph.co.uk/news/uknews/law-and-order/11531954/What-is-the-law-on-revenge-porn.html> accessed 20 May 2018 (2): Conor Lally, 'Gardaí Have "Limited Scope" on "Revenge Porn"' *The Irish Times* (Dublin, 22 April 2015) <www.irishtimes.com/news/crime-and-law/garda%C3%AD-have-limited-scope-on-revenge-porn-1.2185457> accessed 20 May 2018

assist in preventing and/or reducing the cause of online or offline harassment of, and distress to, individuals through revenge porn, specific legislation creating offences in relation to revenge porn should be enacted in Ireland. Also, offences should be created in respect of the unauthorised taking and/or publication of what are colloquially known as "up-skirt" and "down-blouse" photographs. In addition, the publication of images of individuals without their permission on pornographic websites or with captions of a highly sexual or pornographic nature on social media sites with the intention of causing distress to the individuals featured in the published images should be made an offence.[205]

In the United Kingdom, the disclosure of private sexual photographs of an individual without that person's consent and with the intent to cause distress is an offence under S.33(1) of the Criminal Justice and Courts Act 2015.[206] Section 33 of the Act does provide a number of defences against a charge of such an offence including the defence that the disclosure was made in the course of the publication of journalistic material.[207] Schedule 8 of the Act deals with the liability of information society service providers in respect of an offence committed under S.33 of the Act and the terms of the liability exemption available to them.[208] Although few in number, there have been some convictions for this offence.[209]

4.4.4) Voyeurism

Unlike the legal position in Ireland, in the United Kingdom voyeurism is an offence under the Sexual Offences Act 2003, as amended.[210] It would be appropriate for a statutory offence of voyeurism to be introduced in Ireland rather than using the previously mentioned S.10 of the 1997 Act, the wording of which is not appropriate for the prosecution of cases of voyeurism. Depending upon the circumstances of each case, an act of voyeurism may or may not constitute a S.10 offence of harassment (as previously defined above) and for a S.10 offence of harassment to be established the activity complained of must, under S.10(1), be persistent – on more than one occasion. [211]

205 Note: See: Law Reform Commission, *Report on Harmful Communications and Digital Safety* (LRC 116–2016) Dublin 2016 <https://publications.lawreform.ie/Portal/External/en-GB/RecordView/Index/37669> accessed 20 May 2018

206 Criminal Justice and Courts Act 2015, s 33

207 ibid s 33(4)

208 ibid sch 8

209 Note: For example, see: —— '"Revenge Porn" Man Jason Asagba Sentenced' (*BBC News*, 01 September 2015) <www.bbc.com/news/uk-england berkshire-33819264> accessed 18 May 2018

210 Sexual Offences Act 2003, s 67

211 Note: See: Law Reform Commission, *Report on Harmful Communications and Digital Safety* (LRC 116–2016) Dublin 2016 <https://publications.lawreform.ie/Portal/External/en-GB/RecordView/Index/37669> accessed 20 May 2018

4.5) The right to a good name

All citizens have a right to a good name guaranteed under Article 40.3.2° of the Constitution.[212] This right, which may also be referred to as the right to one's reputation, is primarily protected through the law of defamation, although other areas of both substantive and procedural law offer some protection in specific circumstances. The publication of photographs has the potential to infringe this right. Section 6(2) of the Defamation Act 2009 states that the tort of defamation consists of 'the publication, by any means, of a defamatory statement concerning a person to one or more than one person (other than the first-mentioned person), and "defamation" shall be construed accordingly'.[213] Under S.6(3) of the Act, a defamatory statement concerns a person 'if it could reasonably be understood as referring to him or her'.[214] Section 2 of the Act defines a "defamatory statement" as 'a statement that tends to injure a person's reputation in the eyes of reasonable members of society, and "defamatory" shall be construed accordingly'.[215] In contrast, under the United Kingdom's Defamation Act 2013, a statement is not defamatory 'unless its publication causes or is likely to cause serious harm to the reputation of the claimant'.[216] While the word "photograph" is not specifically mentioned in the 2009 Act, photographs are covered by it through the inclusion of the words "visual images" in the Act's definitions of both a "statement" and an "electronic communication". The Act's definition of a "statement" includes the "internet" as a medium of communication in relation to the publication of defamatory statements.[217]

Anyone who claims to be the subject of a statement which he alleges to be defamatory may, as a remedy, seek a court order certifying that the statement is false or defamatory.[218] However, a defamation action may not be brought after the expiration of one year or such longer period as a court may direct, but not exceeding two years from the date on which the cause of action accrued.[219] Where defamation has been proven, the court may award damages to the plaintiff.[220] A court may also, subject to freedom of expression considerations, make an interim, interlocutory or permanent order prohibiting the publication or further publication of a statement if it believes that it is defamatory and the defendant has no defence 'to an action that is reasonably likely to succeed'.[221] The Act does offer a number of defences to a claim of defamation, namely: truth, absolute privilege, qualified privilege, honest opinion, offer to

212 Constitution of Ireland *(Art. 40.3.2°)* (on Personal Rights)
213 Defamation Act 2009, s 6(2)
214 ibid s 6(3)
215 ibid s 2
216 Defamation Act 2013, s 1
217 Defamation Act 2009, s 2
218 ibid s 28(1)
219 ibid s 38
220 ibid ss 31–32
221 ibid s 33

make amends, apology, consent to publish, fair and reasonable publication on a matter of public interest and innocent publication.[222]

The publication of photographs may have the potential to result in defamation claims. Such a claim may arise, for example, following the publication of an article which includes named, or reasonably identifiable, individuals and which is accompanied by a photograph of other people who are totally unrelated to, or not the subject of, the particular content that is claimed to be defamatory. It could also arise from the publication of a photograph of an individual printed juxtaposed with another unrelated article. On viewing the photograph and article as printed, a reader could form the opinion that the individual featured in the photograph had been involved in the activity detailed in the unrelated article. Defamation claims may result from the publication of photographs of individuals mis-identified as other people[223] or from the use of photographs cropped to suit the storyline of an article.[224] The 2012 Irish High Court case of *McKeogh v John Doe 1 and Others*[225] embraced a number of related issues relating to the right to one's good name: the right not to be falsely accused of a crime; mis-identification; a request for anonymity, photography and the Internet. In *McKeogh*, Peart J held that the publication of a video on YouTube by a taxi driver of a person alighting from his taxi without paying the fare did not of itself defame the plaintiff, but doing so created a risk that someone else could, and did, wrongly identify the plaintiff and that the latter had caused the damage to the plaintiff's reputation.[226]

Defamation law applies to all forms of publication including on the Internet. As the Internet is a global medium, there may be problems locating the source of the defamation and problems of appropriate jurisdiction for bringing a case to court. At an EU level, there are a number of Directives and court decisions dealing with such matters. For instance, the European Communities Directive

222 ibid ss 16–27

223 Note (1): For examples of defamation cases resulting from mis-identification of individuals in photographs, see: (1) *Hill v Cork Examiner Publications Limited* [2001] IESC 95. (2) *Patrick McGarth v Independent Newspapers (Ireland) Limited* [2004] IEHC 157. (3) *Dwek v Macmillan Publishers Limited* [1999] EWCA Civ J0728–11. (4) *David Christie v TV3 Television Network Limited* [2015] IEHC 694
Note (2): Book publishers may have to defend defamation claims as a direct result of their non-possession of model releases in respect of the inclusion of photographs of people in their published works. For example, see: Gordan Deegan, 'Singer Sues Historian Diarmuid Ferriter Over Alcoholic Book Cover Photo' *Irish Independent* (Dublin, 20 July 2012) <www.independent.ie/irish-news-singer-sues-historian-diarmuid-ferriter-over-alcoholic-book-cover-photo-26877786.html> accessed 21 May 2018

224 See: *Monica Leech v Independent Newspapers (Ireland) Limited* [2014] IESC 79 and *Independent Newspapers (Ireland) Limited v Ireland* App No 28199/15 (ECHR, 15 June 2017)

225 *McKeogh v John Doe 1 and Others* [2012] IEHC 95

226 ibid

2000/31/EC,[227] which applies to civil actions including defamation, concerns certain legal aspects of information society services, particularly the Internet. The Directive was transposed into Irish law by the European Communities (Directive 2000/31/EC) Regulations 2003.[228] Regulation 3 of the Regulations offers a number of definitions which are of relevance at this juncture. A "relevant service provider" is defined as 'any natural or legal person providing a relevant service' and a "relevant service" is defined as 'an information society service within the meaning of Article 1.2 of Directive 98/34/EC as amended by Directive 98/48/EC, that is to say, any service normally provided for remuneration, at a distance, by electronic means and at the individual request of a recipient of the service, other than a service specified in Schedule 1 to the Regulations'.[229] The categories of services excluded from this definition under Schedule 1 include services that either are not provided at a distance or by electronic means and services that are not supplied at the individual request of a recipient of services.[230] The Regulations define "caching" as 'the automatic intermediate and temporary storage of information which is performed for the sole purpose of making more efficient that information's onward transmission to other users of the service upon their request'.[231] Under Regulation 15 and Regulation 18 of the Regulations, an exemption from liability for damages is respectively available to relevant service providers[232] and intermediary service providers[233] in certain specified circumstances. If the provider of a website chatroom, forum or blog can prove that it is both a "relevant service provider" and an "intermediary service provider", it may be able to benefit from this exemption in respect of claims for damages resulting from publication of alleged defamatory materials on such platforms.

The Irish High Court case of *Mulvaney and Others v The Sporting Exchange Ltd. trading as Betfair*[234] was a preliminary hearing resulting from a claim for defamation following the posting of comments in a chatroom known as the "Betfair Forum", which was hosted on *Betfair's* website.[235] *Mulvaney* dealt with the question of whether or not the defendant could meet the requirements of the previously mentioned Regulation 18 and thus be able to claim the exemp-

227 Directive 2000/31/EC of the European Parliament and of the Council of 8 June 2000 on certain legal aspects of information society services, in particular electronic commerce, in the Internal Market ('Directive on electronic commerce') [2000] OJ L178 <http://eur-lex.europa.eu/LexUriServ/LexUriServ.do?uri=CELEX:32000L0031:en:HTML> accessed 21 May 2018
Note: This Directive is frequently referred to as the "e-Commerce Directive".

228 European Communities (Directive 2000/31/EC) Regulations 2003, SI 2003/68

229 ibid regulation 3

230 ibid sch 1

231 ibid regulation 17

232 ibid regulation 15

233 ibid regulation 18

234 *Mulvaney and Others v The Sporting Exchange Ltd. trading as Betfair* [2009] IEHC 133

235 ibid para 1

tion granted under Directive 2000/31/EC. Although *Mulvaney* did not involve the publication of photographs in the alleged defamatory material, it is of relevance to publishers of photographs on the "Comments" or "Forum" sections of websites and on social media sites. In *Mulvaney*, Clarke J stated:

> It is clear, therefore, that if Betfair come within the provisions of Article 14/ Regulation 18 [of Directive 200/31/EC], then there can be no liability for information stored provided it can be shown that Betfair:
>
> a) did not have actual knowledge of the unlawful activities, i.e. the allegedly defamatory comments posted on the Chatroom;
> b) were not aware of the allegedly defamatory comments; and/or
> c) on being made aware of the potentially defamatory comments, acted expeditiously to remove or disable access to the comments.[236]

Applying that test, Clarke J found in favour of *Betfair*.[237] More recently, the ECtHR has addressed this issue of third-party comments on news portals – see *Delfi v Estonia*.[238]

The United Kingdom's Defamation Act 2013 offers a defence to website operators in respect of statements posted on their websites. Under S.5(2) of the Act, 'It is a defence for the operator to show that it was not the operator who posted the statement on the website.'[239] However, under S.5(3) of the Act this defence is defeated

> if the claimant shows that (a) it was not possible for the claimant to identify the person who posted the statement, (b) the claimant gave the operator a notice of complaint in relation to the statement, and (c) the operator failed to respond to the notice of complaint in accordance with any provision contained in regulations.[240]

A court, having found in favour of a claimant, may order the operator of a website to remove a defamatory statement.[241] It is noted that the term "operators of websites" is not defined by the Act.

The ECtHR case of *Delfi AS v Estonia*[242] arose from anonymous defamatory comments concerning SLK (AS Saaremaa Laevakompanii) which were posted

236 ibid para 3.5
237 ibid para 5.14
238 Note: The requirement of a service provider having "actual knowledge of unlawful activity" was also a central issue in the Northern Ireland High Court case of *CG V Facebook Ireland Limited and Joseph McCloskey* 2015 NIQB 11
239 Defamation Act 2013, s 5(2)
240 ibid s 5(3)
241 ibid s 13(1)(a)
242 *Delfi AS v Estonia* (App No 64569/09) (Grand Chamber ECHR, 16 June 2015)

by users of a news portal website operated by Delfi.[243] The Estonian Court of Appeal held that Delfi was not a technical intermediary in respect of the comments and that its activity was not of a merely technical, automatic and passive nature as it invited users to add comments. As a consequence, Delfi was held to be a provider of content services rather than of technical services and therefore could not claim a liability exclusion. The Estonian Supreme Court upheld that decision.[244] On application to the ECtHR for a determination of a claimed violation of Art. 10, the Court held that the applicant's rights under Art. 10 had not been violated and that the restriction of such rights was prescribed for in law, it had been proportionate to its aims and it was pursued with the legitimate aim of protecting the reputation and rights of others.[245] *Delfi* was subsequently referred to the Grand Chamber of the ECtHR. Of particular note was the Court's differentiation between the applicant's professionally managed, commercially operated news portal website on which it published its own news articles and permitted its readers to comment on such articles and that of other online fora on which their operators did not publish their own content, but did permit others to post their own content or commentary without it being monitored by the operators of such fora.[246] The ECtHR held that the interference imposed on the applicant's Art. 10 rights was prescribed for in law and that the relevant legal provisions would, in principle, have made it predictable to a media publisher operating a commercial Internet news portal that it could be held liable under the domestic law for permitting the uploading of comments, which were obviously unlawful.[247] The unlawfulness of the posted comments was not disputed. After the comments were disclosed the applicant had failed to remove them of its own volition, but the applicant had done so once it was notified about them.[248] However, the Supreme Court had held that such initial inaction was unlawful, as the applicant had not proven an absence of culpability.[249] Holding that there had not been a violation of the applicant's Art. 10 right of freedom of expression, the ECtHR determined that the Supreme Court's decision was based on relevant and sufficient grounds and that the restriction of the applicant's Art. 10 right was not disproportionate.[250]

243 ibid paras 12–13
244 ibid paras 29 and 31
245 ibid paras 62–65
246 ibid paras 115–116
247 ibid para 128
248 ibid para 140
249 ibid para 141
250 ibid para 162
Note (1): *Delphi* was the ECtHR's first determination on the relatively new issue of commentary online by third parties.
Note (2): See also: (1) *Payam Tamiz v Google Inc.* [2013] EWCA Civ 68 and (2) *Tamiz v The United Kingdom* App No 3877/14 (ECHR, 19 September 2017).
Note (3): Another issue to emerge that is related to individuals' right to a good name and their online privacy is an online activity colloquially called "fraping". "The term

4.6) The right to be forgotten

The right to privacy concerns the protection of personal information that is not in the public domain from entering it without one's authorisation. Conversely, the "right to be forgotten" signifies the right to have personal information that is in the public domain via the Internet, or a link to such information, removed. The basis of this right is the right to erasure and blocking of personal data and the right to object to the processing of personal data as respectively provided for under Art. 12(b) and Art. 14(b) of EC Directive 95/46, as amended.[251] This Directive has been repealed by Regulation (EU) 2016/679[252] and Art. 17 of the Regulation provides a right to erasure (right to be forgotten).[253] Publicity surrounding the 2014 CJEU case of *Google Spain SL and Google Inc. v Agencia Espanola de Proteccion de Datos and Gonzalez*[254] brought the right to be forgotten to the attention of the public in general. This right applies to material published on the Internet and there is no equivalent right in respect of the deletion or removal of offline sources of information, such as newspapers' hard-copy archives or library collections. *Google Spain* resulted from a complaint by the second defendant Costeja González to the Spanish Data Protection Agency (AEPD), in which he sought the removal from the website of a Spanish newspaper *La Vanguardia* of information concerning a real estate auction related to attachment proceedings against him for the recovery of social security debts. He also sought the removal or concealment of such information in Google's search engine results and links from them to the relevant webpages of *La*

"fraping" is a portmanteau of "Facebook" and "raping" and refers to when someone alters the profile or other contents on another person's Facebook or a similar type of social media page without the latter's consent. Fraping was the basis of a successful claim of defamation in the English High Court case of *Applause Store Productions and Firsht v Raphael* [2008] EWCH 1781 (QB). In *Applause*, the defendant created a false Facebook profile which contained false allegations regarding the complainant's creditworthiness and his sexual preferences. The false Facebook profile also included a photograph of the claimant, who claimed defamation and misuse of private information. The photograph had been lifted by the defendant from the claimant's Facebook profile and placed into the false Facebook profile.

251 Directive 95/46/EC of the European Parliament and of the Council of 24 October 1995 on the protection of individuals with regard to the processing of personal data and on the free movement of such data [1995] OJ L281/31, art 12(b) and art 14(b) <http://eur-lex.europa.eu/LexUriServ/LexUriServ.do?uri=CELEX:31995L0046:en:HTML> accessed 22 May 2018

252 Regulation (EU) 2016/679 of the European Parliament and of the Council of 27 April 2016 on the protection of natural persons with regard to the processing of personal data and on the free movement of such data, and repealing Directive 95/46/EC (General Data Protection Regulation) [2016] OJ L119/1 <http://eur-lex.europa.eu/legal-content/EN/TXT/HTML/?uri=CELEX:32016R0679&from=EN> accessed 21 May 2018

253 ibid art 17

254 Case C-131/12 *Google Spain SL and Google Inc. v Agencia Espanola de Proteccion de Datos and Gonzalez* [2014]

Vanguardia. The AEPD rejected the complaint against *La Vanguardia*, as the publication of the material was legally justified. However, it upheld the complaint against Google on the grounds that Google, as the operator of a search engine, was subject to data protection legislation.[255] Google Spain and Google Inc. appealed this decision to the Spanish High Court, which referred a number of questions to the CJEU, in particular in relation to the scope of the right of erasure.[256] The CJEU held that a search engine was a data processor and that the operator of a search engine was a data controller within the meaning of Directive 95/46/EC, as amended.[257] The CJEU stated that in order for a search engine to comply with a data subject's right of access to his/her personal data under Art. 12 of Directive 95/46 and his/her right to object to the processing of his/her personal data under Art. 14 of the Directive, a search engine was required to remove his/her personal data from search engine results, even when the publication of such data on the webpages listed in the search results is lawful.[258] The CJEU also determined that one's right to be forgotten overrides both the economic interests of a search engine operator and the interest of the general public in having access to the information that a person may be seeking to have deleted.[259] The right to be forgotten is not absolute and the CJEU held the superiority of that right would not prevail

> if it appeared, for particular reasons, such as the role played by the data subject in public life, that the interference with his fundamental rights is justified by the preponderant interest of the general public in having, on account of its inclusion in the list of results, access to the information in question.[260]

One could argue, that the *Google Spain* decision is a step towards permitting a free-for-all type of censorship of the Internet by individuals for their own personal motives while an equivalent offline right does not legally exist. However, it does assist in removing search engine links to defamatory and other material, such as revenge porn from the Internet. It should be noted that the CJEU's finding in *Google Spain* applies solely to the removal of search engine links and does not extend to the removal of any material from original source websites listed in search engine search results.[261] In theory, the *Google Spain* decision could be of benefit to photographers who have had their images illegally copied

255 paras 14–17
256 ibid para 20
257 ibid para 100
258 ibid
259 ibid
260 ibid
261 Note: On the topic of the courts ordering the deletion of publications' online and offline archives, see the ECtHR case of *Wegrzynowski and Smolczewski v Poland* [2013] ECHR 690 in which the Court, at para. 65, stated that it was not its role to rewrite history.

from their own or their clients' websites and re-posted on other websites, as they could have search engine links to those latter websites removed from search engine results.

The European Commission's Article 29 Data Protection Working Party adopted a set of guidelines on the implementation of the decision in *Google Spain*. Among other matters, the Guidelines state that there is no requirement on individuals to contact an original website in order to exercise their rights against search engines.[262] The associated issue of getting original material which had been referenced by a search engine removed from its original publisher website is a totally different matter. Such as task is not without its own problems, including tracing and obtaining usable contact details for the actual owner(s) and operator(s) of the websites and successfully getting them to either remove the infringing images or to pay a licence fee for their use online, without having to resort to initiating court proceedings. In many instances, court costs would totally outweigh the licence fees involved.

Subsequent to *Google Spain*, the English High Court determined the 2015 case of *Mosley v Google Inc. and Anor*,[263] in which the claimant claimed damages and injunctive relief against Google Inc. and Google UK over the appearance in its search engine results of postings by persons other than Newsgroup of the images and video footage of him, which were central to the case of *Mosley v Newsgroup Newspapers*.[264] The claimant stated that even though a number of websites containing the images were blocked from search engine results, some still appeared or reappeared in such results.[265] Having reviewed S.10 of the UK Data Protection Act 1998 on the right to prevent the processing of data that is likely to cause damage or distress, Mitting J held that if a claimant can prove that he is suffering or has suffered unwarranted damage or distress as a consequence of Google's processing of his personal data and that he has provided written notice of such to Google and the latter has not provided any reasons

262 European Commission, Article 29 Data Protection Working Party, *Guidelines on the Implementation of the Court of Justice of the European Union Judgment on "Google Spain and Inc. v Agencia Espanola de Proteccion de Datos (AEPD) and Mario Costeja Gonzalez" C-131/12* (14/ENWP 225) (Brussels, 26 November 2014), para 11 <http://ec.europa.eu/justice/article-29/documentation/opinion-recommendation/files/2014/wp225_en.pdf> accessed 22 May 2018

Note: The Article 29 Data Protection Working Party ceased to exist on 25 May 2018 and was replaced by the European Data Protection Board.

263 *Mosley v Google Inc. and Anor* [2015] EWHC 59 (QB)

264 *Mosley v Newsgroup Newspapers* [2008] EWHC 1777 QB

Note: Subsequent to this case, *Mosley* claimed in the ECtHR case of *Mosley v United Kingdom* [2011] ECHR 774 that there had a violation of his Art. 8 right to privacy due to the absence of a legal, pre-publication, notification requirement in the domestic law. However, the Court (at para. 132) held that Art. 8 did not require a pre-notification of the applicant of any impending publications, which would have alerted him to a possible need to seek a pre-publication injunction.

265 *Mosley v Google Inc. and Anor* [2015] EWHC 59 (QB), paras 1–6

for holding that that notice is unjustified, then the claimant is entitled to request the Court to order Google to take such measures as the court deems necessary to comply with that notice and the court may so order.[266] The issues of general and specific monitoring by service providers, such as search engines, were central to *Mosley*. The defendants claimed that Art. 15 of the E-Commerce Directive prohibited the making of the court orders sought because what the claimant required amounted to general monitoring as opposed to specific monitoring. From his analysis of the jurisprudence of the CJEU on the application of Art. 15, Mitting J stated that it seemed to suggest that the CJEU held the view that Art. 15 did not prevent specific monitoring.[267] On the blocking of individual images by search engines, Mitting J also stated that it was accepted that existing technology permitted search engines to block individual images without going to any disproportionate effort or expense.[268] Therefore, for photographers seeking the blocking of links from search engines to infringing copies of their images, it should not be an onerous task for search engines.

4.7) Photography and the property rights of others

The taking and publication of photographs are separate, but related, issues. The property rights of the owners of privately owned properties may restrict the rights of photographers to take photographs of their property while they are either on or outside of such property and to publish such images. Also, the property rights attached to publicly owned property may lead to similar restrictions. This section of the chapter examines the extent to which property rights may impact on photographers' and photograph publishers' rights.

4.7.1) Private property rights and photography

The right to the ownership of private property is guaranteed under the Constitution and Article 43.1.1° states: 'The State acknowledges that man, in virtue of his rational being, has the natural right, antecedent to positive law, to the private ownership of external goods.'[269] Also, the ownership of private property is specified as one of the personal rights guaranteed under the Constitution. Article 40.3.2° states: 'The State shall, in particular, by its laws protect as best it may from unjust attack and, in the case of injustice done, vindicate the life, person, good name, and property rights of every citizen.'[270] In addition, Article 40.5 the Constitution guarantees the inviolability of the home and states: 'The

266 ibid para 24
267 ibid paras 50–52
268 ibid para 54–55
Note: See *Savage v Data Protection Commissioner and Another* [2018] IEHC 122 – the Irish High Court's first take-down case under the Right to be Forgotten.
269 Constitution of Ireland *(Art. 43.1.1°)* (on Private Property)
270 ibid (*Art. 40.3.2°*) (on Personal Rights)

dwelling of every citizen is inviolable and shall not be forcibly entered save in accordance with the law.'[271] Property rights are also enshrined in the Protocol to the ECHR. Article 1 of the Protocol states:

> Every natural or legal person is entitled to the peaceful enjoyment of his possessions. No one shall be deprived of his possessions except in the public interest and subject to the conditions provided for by law and by the general principles of international law.[272]

Any restriction on a photographer's rights should therefore be justified by reference to the public interest and be provided for by law. The legality of the taking of photographs of privately owned property while not physically on such property was raised in *Atherton v DPP*,[273] a case stated to the Irish High Court in 2005. *Atherton* concerned a complaint from a complainant that a neighbour (the "accused") had cut his hedge without his permission and caused damage to it. In response, the complainant had arranged for a fixed video camera to be set up in an upstairs front window of a house across the road from the complainant's house, which was attached to the accused's house. There was video evidence before the court that apart from the hedge there was incidental video footage of the front of the accused's house. Evidence from a garda stated 'everything that is seen on the video camera was capable of being seen from the street itself, albeit that one might have to stand up on a step-ladder to do so'.[274] There had not been any trespass on the accused's property. In *Atherton*, Peart J held that the video recording of the accused's house and his next-door neighbour's hedge by the latter from an upstairs window of another neighbour's property across the road, in circumstances which did not constitute a trespass to the complainant's private property, did not breach the accused's constitutional right to privacy attached to the right to the inviolability of his dwelling as contained in Article 40.5 of the Constitution.[275] Peart J also stated:

> In my view there is no meaningful distinction between the evidence of what was happening to the hedge in the garden opposite that house being given in the form of video footage, and that very same evidence being given by the owner of the house opposite if he arranged things so that he was standing at the same window as the camera was set up at and observing himself what was happening. He would undoubtedly be permitted to give evidence viva voce of anything which he observed happening in the garden into which he was looking, and it could not possibly be seriously contended

271 ibid (*Art. 40.5*) (on Personal Rights)
272 European Convention on Human Rights Act 2003, sch 2, art 1
273 *Atherton v DPP* [2005] IEHC 429
274 ibid para 5
275 ibid para 21

> that if that person also saw the accused re-entering his house through the front door, and while the door was open saw also into the hallway, that in some way that person had breached the accused's right to privacy by seeing what he saw. The camera has done no more and no less than that.[276]

In the earlier 1978 English High Court case of *Bernstein of Leigh (Baron) v Skyviews and General Ltd.*,[277] Griffiths J had held that provided one does not cross the boundary from one piece of adjoining land to another, one may take a photograph of the exterior of a property which is located on the latter adjoining land.[278] The taking of photographs while on privately owned property may be either prohibited or restricted by the owner of such property, even where one is granted access to the property by its owner or licensee. For example, members of the public are granted access to the Aviva Stadium in Dublin. However, such access is granted subject to the Aviva Stadium Ground Rules, which prohibit the unauthorised use of certain types of cameras and lenses within the Stadium.[279]

4.7.2) Publicly owned property and restrictions on photography

Frequently, members of the public are permitted to have relatively unhindered access to publicly owned properties and locations such as beaches, parks, open spaces, streets, airports, sea ports and harbours, railway systems and recreational playing fields. However, photographers proposing to undertake photography at these types of locations may be subject to either restrictions or prohibitions on photography. Such restrictions and/or prohibitions are put in place through bye-laws. The following are a number of examples. Under the Local Government Act 2001, as amended, local authorities have the legal power to make bye-laws in respect of the regulation or management of land under their control or management.[280] A number of local authorities have implemented bye-laws which include a prohibition on commercial photography being undertaken without having obtained a licence from the local authority. For example, Dublin City Council controls commercial photography within its functional area through its Parks and Open Spaces Bye-Laws 2002.[281] In accordance with these Bye-Laws, permits from Dublin City Council are required by anyone wishing to undertake commercial photography, photo calls or fashion shoots. A permit fee

276 ibid para 19
277 *Bernstein of Leigh (Baron) v Skyviews and General Ltd.* [1978] QB 479
278 ibid 488
279 Aviva Stadium, FAQs and *Ground Rules* <www.avivastadium.ie/faqs-ground-rules> accessed 22 May 2018
280 Local Government Act 2001, s 199(1)
281 Dublin City Council, Parks and Open Spaces Bye-Laws 2002 s 4(13)(a) and s 4(13)(f) <www.dublincity.ie/sites/default/files/content//RecreationandCulture/DublinCityParks/Documents/ParksBye-Laws2D.pdf> accessed 22 May 2018

exemption is offered in respect of, among others, wedding photography.[282] Wedding photography and fashion photography are two types of photography undertaken by commercial photographers. One would have to question why the former but not the latter is granted a fee exemption? Kerry County Council's Playground Bye-Laws 2008 prohibit the use of a camera in a Council-controlled playground by anyone other than a family member without the Council's authorisation.[283] In Co. Clare, photography is prohibited inside any burial ground that comes within the scope of Clare County Council's Burial Ground Bye-Laws 2015 unless a prior consent has been received from the next of kin or their undertaker during an internment or from the Council at any other time.[284] The Office of Public Works manages a number of national monuments and historical properties throughout the state, such as Dún Aonghasa on Inis Mór, Aran Islands and St. Stephen's Green in Dublin. While photography is permitted at both of these locations, permits are required for commercial photography at them.[285] The Luas light railway system in Dublin comes under the Light Railway (Regulation of Travel and Use) Bye-Laws 2012, which prohibit the use of a camera on a light rail vehicle or a light railway without permission.[286] Bye-laws may prohibit or restrict photography at airports. For example, the Shannon Airport Bye-Laws 2015 regulate the use of photographic equipment within the Airport's area.[287]

Should one wish to commercially publish photographs of the exterior of a privately owned property which were taken without having entered the property, the prior obtaining of a signed property release would be an advised necessity. Photographing the interior of a building may be either prohibited or permitted subject to conditions laid down by the owner of the building, irrespective of whether the building is a publicly or privately owned building to which the public may or may not have either paid or have free access. Again, it would be advisable to obtain a signed property release form prior to the commercial publication of any such photographs. A similar word of caution would apply in respect of the photography of any movable property owned by third parties, if the intention is to use any created photographs of such movable property for

282 Dublin City Council, *Applications for Activities in Dublin City Parks* <www.dublincity.ie/main-menu-services-recreation-culture-dublin-city-parks/commercial-activities-dublin-city-parks> accessed 22 May 2018

283 Kerry County Council, *Playground Bye-Laws 2008*, s 4(m) <www.kerryplay.ie/byelawseng.asp> accessed 22 May 2018

284 Clare County Council, *Burial Ground Bye-Laws 2015 – County Clare*, s 35 <www.clarecoco.ie/community/burial-grounds/burial-ground-bye-laws-2015-county-clare-21961.pdf> accessed 22 May 2018

285 Heritage Ireland, *Dún Aonghasa* <www.heritageireland.ie/en/west/dunaonghasa/> accessed 22 May 2018 and Heritage Ireland, *St. Stephen's Green* <www.heritageireland.ie/en/dublin/ststephensgreen/> accessed 22 May 2018

286 Light Railway (Regulation of Travel and Use) Bye-Laws 2015, SI 2015/322, s 6(1)(f) <www.luas.ie/luas-byelaws.html> accessed 22 May 2018

287 Shannon Airport Bye-Laws 2015, SI 2015/69, s 6(1)(32)

commercial purposes. A photographer may be prevented from publishing a photograph featuring a product that shows a legally protected trademark or a product, the design of which is protected under copyright law as an artistic work. To do so without authorisation may constitute an infringement of the trademark or copyright holder's rights. If a photographer is in doubt as to whether a product which he/she proposes to photograph and publish for commercial-use purposes is trademark or copyright protected, it would be advisable for him to ask the product's owner or producer prior to taking the photograph. Possession of a signed product release would be appropriate prior to a commercial publication of such images.

4.7.3) Photographers and trespass and nuisance

Trespass to land comes within both criminal and tort law in Ireland. Under the Criminal Justice (Public Order) Act 1994, as amended, it is 'an offence for a person, without reasonable excuse, to trespass on any building or the curtilage thereof in such a manner as causes or is likely to cause fear in another person'.[288] A member of An Garda Síochána, with reasonable cause, may order a person found acting in such a manner to leave the vicinity of such a place.[289] Also, the torts of trespass and nuisance may be applied against photographers. The tort of trespass comprises a number of individual torts of which trespass to land and trespass to chattels are of the most relevance to the activities of photographers, when they are seeking to take photographs. If one enters another person's land or property for an unlawful purpose or having been granted permitted to enter the land or property, but with a restriction or prohibition on the taking of photographs while thereon, and then abuses that permission by taking photographs thereon, one be will a trespasser *ab initio.* Also, if one enters land or property with permission and then undertakes photography thereon without permission, it is possible that one could be found by a court to have committed a trespass to the property. In the 2005 Irish High Court case of *Cogley v RTÉ* and *Aherne and Others v RTÉ*,[290] at the request of RTÉ, a care worker obtained employment at a nursing home and subsequently used a hidden camera to shoot footage inside the home for a proposed programme on the standard of care provided to patients in nursing homes in general and specifically at that home. On the claim of trespass, Clarke J stated that 'the plaintiffs in the Aherne proceedings have made out an arguable case that such trespass occurred'.[291] Based on the possibility that RTÉ might adopt a similar covert approach at a future date to carry-out further filming at the nursing home, on the balance of

288 Criminal Justice (Public Order) Act 1994, s 13(1)
289 ibid s 13(2)(2)
290 *Cogley v Radio Telefis Eireann* and *Aherne and Others v Radio Telefis Eireann* [2005] IEHC 181
291 ibid

convenience, Clarke J granted an interlocutory injunction preventing RTÉ from undertaking any future trespass at the property.[292]

The tort of trespass to land may not be used as a cause of action in order to obtain an injunction to prevent the publication of photographs and thus to protect one's good name, where a defendant intends to plead a defence of justification. The English High Court case of *Service Corporation International Plc and Another v Channel Four Television Corporation and Another*[293] concerned the secret filming of malpractices at a funeral home by an employee of the funeral home for a documentary to be aired by the defendants. In seeking an injunction against the publication of the filmed material, the plaintiffs' statement of claim included a claim of trespass. In refusing to grant an injunction, Lightman J stated that where there is a claim of defamation an interlocutory injunction may not be granted if the defendant intends to plead a defence of justification and that that rule did not extend to claims founded on other causes of action. He further stated that if a claim founded on some other cause of action was in reality being used to get around this rule to protect one's reputation, then the more important requirement to protect the right of freedom of expression necessitated that the same rule would be applicable.[294] Lightman J held that the protection of the plaintiffs' reputation was the basis of the application[295] and he went on to hold that whether or not the defendants were trespassers *ab initio* did not grant the plaintiffs a right to prevent the defendants from publishing the film.[296] Also, Lightman J determined that the plaintiffs' claim that the malpractices alleged in the film was a single incidence, which they were now addressing, did not mean that there was not a substantial public interest in the film's contents.[297]

In addition to the tort of trespass, the tort of nuisance can provide some limited protection for landowners. The tort consists of two types of nuisance, namely private nuisance and public nuisance. The former consists of an interference with a person's use and/or enjoyment of his property in the absence of a lawful justification for doing so,[298] while the latter consists of an act or omission resulting in either an injury to or having an affect on the reasonable comfort and convenience of members of the public. A public nuisance is only actionable by an individual if the damage he/she has suffered is greater than that suffered

292 ibid
Note: See also: Tom Shiel, 'Judge Rules Áras Attracta Care Home Video Footage Admissible' *The Irish Times* (Dublin, 09 October 2015) <www.irishtimes.com/news/crime-and-law/courts/district-court/judge-rules-%C3%A1ras-attracta-care-home-video-footage-admissible-1.2385662> accessed 22 May 2018

293 *Service Corporation International Plc and Another v Channel Four Television Corporation and Another* [1999] EMLR 83

294 ibid 84

295 ibid 89

296 ibid 90

297 ibid 91

298 *Royal Dublin Society v Yates* [1997] IEHC 144, para 73

by other members of the public.[299] In the 1978 English High Court case of *Bernstein of Leigh (Baron) v Skyviews and General Ltd.*,[300] the court considered the tort of nuisance even though *Bernstein* was not founded in nuisance. In *Bernstein*, Griffiths J stated that a court would not find the taking of a single photograph from an aircraft as constituting a nuisance, but if a plaintiff were to suffer harassment through a repetitive surveillance and photography of his home and his movements from the air, it is possible that a court would regard such behaviour as an actionable nuisance.[301] Griffiths J noted that under S.40(1) of the Civil Aviation Act 1949, and subject to specified provisions, no action lies in trespass or nuisance by reason only of the flight of an aircraft over a property.[302] In Ireland, the Irish Air Navigation and Transport Act 1936, as amended contains a similar provision.[303]

4.8) Passing-off: misrepresentation through the use of photographs

Advertisers and publishers may be the respondents to claims of passing-off through misrepresentation by their use of misleading photographs in their works. Legislative provisions and both statutorily required and self-regulated business sector codes of practice are used to regulate the contents of advertising materials.[304] While some legislative provisions are of a general application, others focus on specific industries, trades, products or services. For example, advertisements published through the broadcast media are covered under the Broadcasting Act 2009. Section 41(3) of the Act prohibits a broadcaster from broadcasting politically aimed advertisements or advertisements relating to industrial disputes,[305] while S.41(4) of the Act prohibits the broadcasting of an advertisement which 'addresses the issue of the merits or otherwise of adhering to any religious faith or belief or of becoming a member of any religion or religious organisation'.[306] The Act also places a statutory requirement on the Broadcasting Authority of Ireland to implement codes of standards and practice to be observed by broadcasters.[307] The Authority operates and regularly updates a range of broadcasting codes of standards and practice by which broadcasters and their advertisers must abide.[308] A number of statutes contain provisions that restrict

299 *Convery v The County Council of the County of Dublin* [1996] 3 IR 153, 168
300 *Bernstein of Leigh (Baron) v Skyviews and General Ltd.* [1978] QB 479
301 ibid 489
302 ibid 488
303 Air Navigation and Transport Act 1936, s 55
304 Note: See Chapter Five on codes of advertising practice.
305 Broadcasting Act 2009, s 41(3)
306 ibid s 41(4)
307 Broadcasting Act 2009, s 42
308 Broadcasting Authority of Ireland, *Codes and Standards* <www.bai.ie/en/codes-standards/> accessed 11 June 2018

the advertising for certain products. These include the Misuse of Drugs Act 1984, as amended, which provides for offences relating to the advertising and promotion of controlled drugs,[309] while the Criminal Justice (Psychoactive Substances) Act 2010 contains a prohibition on the advertising of psychoactive substances.[310] However, under S.6 of the Act it is not an offence for certain specified types of people, such as registered general practitioners, dentists and pharmacists, to do so for the purpose of their profession.[311] An example of trade specific statutory prohibition on advertising is the Taxi Regulation Act 2013, as amended, which prohibits the promotion and advertising of unlicensed small public service vehicle services.[312] At a product specific level, the Public Health (Tobacco) Act 2002, as amended, prohibits the advertising of tobacco products.[313] The previously mentioned and other similar legislative restrictions may affect photographers from the perspective of the contents of photographs used as elements of advertisements.

The misleading of an advertisement's viewers through its contents is prohibited under the Consumer Protection Act 2007, as amended.[314] Section 43(1) of the Act states that a commercial practice is misleading if

> it includes the provision of false information in relation to any matter set out in subsection (3) and that information would be likely to cause the average consumer to make a transactional decision that the average consumer would not otherwise make.[315]

Among the matters included under S.43(3) is "the main characteristics of a product".[316] The benefit or fitness for purpose of a product is included in S.43(3) as one of the specified main characteristics of a product.[317] It is an offence for a trader to engage in a misleading commercial practice specified under S.43 of the Act.[318] In addition to the previously mentioned statutory prohibition on

309 Misuse of Drugs Act 1984, s 5(1)
310 Criminal Justice (Psychoactive Substances) Act 2010, s 5
311 ibid s 6
312 Taxi Regulation Act 2013, s 27(1)
313 Public Health (Tobacco) Act 2002, s 33
314 Consumer Protection Act 2007, s 42
Note: The 2007 Act gives effect to the Unfair Commercial Practices Directive – Directive 2005/29/EC of the European Parliament and of the Council of 11 May 2005 concerning unfair business-to-consumer commercial practices in the internal market and amending Council Directive 84/450/EEC, Directives 97/7/EC, 98/27/EC and 2002/65/EC of the European Parliament and of the Council and Regulation (EC) No. 2006/2004 of the European Parliament and of the Council [2005] OJ L149/22 <https://eur-lex.europa.eu/legal-content/EN/TXT/HTML/?uri=CELEX:32005L0029&from=EN> accessed 23 May 2018
315 ibid s 43(1)
316 ibid s 43(3)
317 ibid
318 ibid s 47(1)

misleading commercial practices involving advertisements, advertisers are also subject to the provisions of the European Communities (Misleading and Comparative Communications) Regulations 2007, which prohibits traders from engaging in misleading marketing communications.[319] The Regulations define a "marketing communication" as 'any form of representation made by a trader in connection with a trade, business or profession in order to promote the supply of a product' and a "representation" as, among other items, 'any oral, written, visual, descriptive, or other representation by a trader, including any commercial communication, marketing or advertising'.[320] Regulations 3(2) and 4 of the Regulations specify the various circumstances under which a marketing communication will be considered "misleading".[321]

Passing-off is a tort at common law. In the 1990 English House of Lords case of *Reckitt & Coleman Products Limited v Borden Inc.* Oliver J stated that for a claimant to establish a claim of passing-off he must prove that a goodwill or reputation attached to his goods or services was recognised by the public through the get-up of his goods or services, that the defendant misrepresented to the public that his goods or services were that of the claimant and that he had suffered or was likely to suffer damage as a consequence of the defendant's misrepresentation.[322] *Reckitt & Coleman* was affirmed by MacMenamin J in the Irish Supreme Court case of *McCambridge Limited v Joseph Brennan Bakeries.*[323] Although very infrequent, a few claims for passing-off by misrepresentation through photographs have featured in cases in the Irish courts.[324] In the 2003 English Court of Appeal case of *Irvine v Talksport*,[325] the former Formula One racing driver Eddie Irvine claimed that a doctored photograph of him used on

319 European Communities (Misleading and Comparative Communications) Regulations 2007, SI 2007/774, reg 3(1)

320 ibid reg 2(1)

321 ibid reg 3(2) and reg 4

322 *Reckitt & Coleman Products Limited v Borden Inc* [1990] RPC 341, 406

323 *McCambridge Limited v Joseph Brennan Bakeries* [2012] IESC 46, para 19

324 Note: See (1): Aoife Finneran, 'McEvoy Gets €80,000 Libel Award From Impresario' *Irish Independent* (Dublin, 17 November 2011) <www.independent.ie/irish-news/courts/mcevoy-gets-80000-libel-award-from-impresario-26792885.html> accessed 23 May 2018
(2): —— 'GAA Star Sues Newspaper Over Use of His Image' *Irish Independent* (Dublin, 25 January 2008) <www.independent.ie/irish-news/gaa-star-sues-newspaper-over-use-of-his-image-26347077.html> accessed 23 May 2018
(3): Donnchadh Boyle, 'Farrell Calls for Image Rights Issue to be Tackled' *Irish Independent* (Dublin, 02 May 2008) <www.independent.ie/sport/gaelic-games/gaelic-football/farrell-calls-for-image-rights-issue-to-be-tackled-26443561.html> accessed 23 May 2018
(4): Ray Managh, 'Father Sues Doonbeg Lodge After His Three Young Kids Appeared on Promotional Brochures Without Consent' *Irish Independent* (Dublin 07 February 2017) <www.independent.ie/irish-news/courts/father-sues-doonbeg-lodge-after-his-three-young-kids-appeared-on-promotional-brochures-without-consent-35430940.html> accessed 23 May 2018

325 *Irvine v Talksport* [2003] EWCA Civ 423

the front cover of the defendant's promotional literature without his consent would have led a viewer of the literature to conclude that he had endorsed *Talksport*, when in fact he had not. Parker LJ accepted that at the time of the alleged passing-off, the plaintiff had generated valuable goodwill and reputation in his name and his image, which he was entitled to protect from unauthorised misuse by third parties for commercial gain and which had been damaged by the defendant's actions. Parker LJ allowed the plaintiff's appeal and increased the previously awarded damages of £2,000 for passing-off to £25,000, as he felt that that would have been the minimum amount that the defendant would have had to pay the plaintiff as an endorsement fee.[326]

More recently, the 2013 English High Court case of *Robyn Rihanna Fenty and Others v Arcadia Group Brands and Topshop*[327] concerned a claim of passing-off resulting from the sale by Topshop of t-shirts which featured an image based on a photograph of the pop star Rihanna without her approval. In *Fenty*, Birss J implemented the previously mentioned *Reckitt & Colman Products* test and stated that the selling of a garment featuring a recognisable photographic image of a well-known person was not of itself an act of passing-off. For it to constitute passing-off, there is a requirement that a purchaser's decision to buy the product must be influenced by a false belief communicated by the seller to the purchaser.[328] Having reviewed the image on the garment and in view of a previous joint marketing campaign between the claimant and Topshop, Birss J held that the sale of the garment constituted an act of passing-off.[329] On appeal to the English Court of Appeal, Kitchin LJ confirmed this decision.[330]

The incorporation of altered photographs in advertisements may leave advertisers open to accusations of misrepresentation or the misleading of viewers. The use of post-production software to retouch or alter a created image featured in an advertisement may be the basis of such a claim. Rather than initiating court proceedings, a claimant may opt to make a complaint to a relevant advertising standards authority – in Ireland the Advertising Standards Authority of Ireland and in the United Kingdom the Advertising Standards Authority.[331] While incidences of claimed misrepresentation through the publication of photographs may not result in legal actions or complaints to advertising

326 ibid para 114

327 *Robyn Rihanna Fenty and Others v Arcadia Group Brands and Topshop* [2013] EWCH 2310 (ch)

328 ibid para 36

329 ibid para 75

330 *Robyn Rihanna Fenty and Others v Arcadia Group Brands and Topshop* [2015] EWCA Civ 3, para 62

331 For example, see: Advertising Standards Authority, *ASA Adjudication on Parfums Christian Dior (UK) Ltd. Complaint Ref: A12–196932* (24 October 2012) <www.asa.org.uk/Rulings/Adjudications/2012/10/Parfums-Christian-Dior-UK-Ltd/SHP_ADJ_196932.aspx> accessed 23 May 2018

standards authorities being instigated, they may generate negative media coverage for the parties concerned.[332]

Photographers and publishers of photographs owe a general duty of care to any models or other individuals featured in their photographs to ensure that they are not portrayed in a negative, defamatory or misrepresentative fashion. While it is not a legal requirement,[333] it is prudent for photographers to obtain and keep safe signed model releases from models and/or other individuals participating in photographic shoots for commercial advertisements, so as to protect both themselves and their clients from any potential claims of misrepresentation by those individuals. A signed model release form should contain an explicit consent of the person being photographed to the specified commercial usage and/or non-usage of the created photographs.[334] As virtually all created photographic images require some form of post-production work varying from basic changes to brightness and contrast levels to extensive manipulation of an image, a model release form should stipulate the model's consent to such work being undertaken on the proviso that the model would not be negatively or otherwise adversely portrayed in any resulting, published image. If any proposed photographs are to be used in the promotion of a specific "sensitive" subject, then the model release form should contain details of the intended use of the photograph and an explicit consent signed by the model and/or any other individual featured in the photograph approving such usage. Also, when publishing such a photograph, the published photograph should contain a caption stating that the person shown in the photograph is a model.

332 Note: For examples of such negative media coverage, see:

(1) Kitty Holland, 'Borg Serves Fine Gael Notice of His Displeasure' *The Irish Times* (Dublin, 21 September 2013) <www.irishtimes.com/news/politics/borg-serves-fine-gael-notice-of-his-displeasure-1.1536199> accessed 23 May 2018

(2) Melanie Finn, 'BOD Gets Landed in a Political Scrum Over Election Snap' *Irish Independent* (Dublin, 13 May 2014) <www.independent.ie/irish-news-bod-gets-landed-in-a-political-scrum-over-election-snap-30269441.html> accessed 23 May 2018

333 Note: See model release requirement for advertisers under Code 3.27 of the *Code of Standards for Advertising and Marketing Communications in Ireland*. Advertising Standards Authority of Ireland, *Code of Standards for Advertising and Marketing Communications in Ireland* (7th edn) <www.asai.ie/asaicode/> accessed 23 May 2018

334 Note (1): For an example of a misrepresentation through the publication of a stock photo library image in an advertisement without an appropriate model release, see: Peter Murtagh, 'Couple Denounce Use of their Image on NO Campaign Posters: Man and Woman "Completely" Support Same Sex Marriage' *The Irish Times* (Dublin, 07 May 2015) <www.irishtimes.com/news/ireland/irish-news/couple-denounce-use-of-their-image-on-no-campaign-posters-1.2203515> accessed 23 May 2018

Note (2): See also: Ray Managh, '"Guinness"' Actors Settle Action Over Image Rights' *Irish Independent* (Dublin, 23 April 2013) <www.independent.ie/irish-news/courts/guinness-actors-settle-action-over-image-rights-29214139.html> accessed 23 May 2018

4.9) Contractual and accreditation scheme restrictions

When photographers contract to undertake photography for clients, they are legally bound by the terms of any agreed contracts. The extent to which a contract for services may or may not restrict a photographer will largely depend upon the terms of the contract. Normally, a commercial photographer would not include terms disadvantageous to themself in either their own normal contract or in one drafted by them for a specific client's proposed photographic work, unless they had to do so in order to obtain the work. However, if the contract is drafted by the client, it is likely to be on terms in their favour. In any event, if a contract includes terms dealing with for example, exclusive usage rights to the created photographs or non-disclosure, the photographer is contract bound to honour such terms. As mentioned in Chapter 3, there has been an increase in the trend for clients' contracts and tender request documentation to include terms under which the contracting photographer must transfer his/her copyright and moral rights in any work created to the client.

Such terms restrict a photographer's existing legal rights under copyright law including, among others, the right to reproduction and moral rights (the paternity right, the integrity right and the right against false attribution). For example, if a photographer were to be contracted under such restrictive contract terms to either shoot fresh or to supply existing general urban landscape photographs from his/her photographic library as part of a package of photographs on a client's property, he/she would not be able to use those images again for either his/her own use or for another future client.

Many photographer accreditation schemes are contractually based. The United Nations' Human Rights Committee's General Comment No. 34 of 2011 on Article 19 of the ICCPR concerns the right of freedom of expression.[335] On limited accreditation schemes for journalists, the General Comment states that such schemes should be implemented through the use of objective criteria and in a non-discriminatory fashion.[336] In reality, the operation of accreditation schemes is often somewhat different to the General Comment's aspirations. The organisers of events such as trade fairs, conferences, music concerts and sports events to which members of the public are admitted may either prohibit or restrict photography within the events' venues. Such a prohibition or restriction may be stipulated as a term within the purchase contract for an admission ticket to the event. If an admission ticket is provided on a non-payment basis, it may state that admission to the venue is granted subject to one's acceptance of a specified prohibition or restriction on photography. Venues, event promoters, sports organisations and associations, performers and sports people may also wish to control and/or limit the admission of commercial and/or press

335 United Nations Human Rights Committee, *General Comment No. 34 on Article 19: Freedoms of Opinion and Expression, International Covenant on Civil and Political Rights* <www2.ohchr.org/english/bodies/hrc/docs/gc34.pdf> accessed 23 May 2018

336 ibid para 44

photographers to their events and the reproduction[337] of photographs taken at events. Accreditation of photographers is used to achieve such required control and limitation. Accreditation in respect of individual venues or events will differ. For example, in respect of a performance by an entertainer accreditation may be granted by the venue, the promoter, the performer's management or by a combination of such groupings. The accreditation process may range from just simply presenting one's credentials to signing a contract, which would detail what may and may not be photographed at the event, the manner in which any created photographs may or may not be published or used commercially and whether or not any specified fees or royalties will be payable to the photographed performers or sports people by the photographer to either take and/or commercially use any created photographs.

The CRRA, as amended, grants qualifying performers, among other rights, a range of exclusive rights relating to the recording and reproduction of either the whole or a substantial part of their qualifying performances.[338] On the basis of the definition of the word "recording" in S.204[339] of the Act and of the words "photograph", "film" and "fixation" in S.2 of the Act, while the unauthorised filming of a performance would be in breach of a performer's rights under the Act, it is questionable whether the taking of still photographs of a performance would infringe these rights of a performer. Furthermore, the word "substantial", as used in S.203 and S.204 of the Act, is not defined. Therefore, it is also questionable whether the taking of a "single" still image of a performance would amount to a recording of a "substantial part of a qualifying performance". However, it would be prudent for photographers and publishers of photographs proposing to either photograph performers during a performance and/or to publish such photographs for commercial purposes to seek the express prior approval of any and all performers participating in a live performance prior to photographing it. Performers, particularly music performers, often attempt to control media coverage of their personal images through the accreditation of commercial and press photographers for their live public performances.[340] In some instances, press photographers and media organisations may refuse to sign performers' accreditation contracts, as their terms are too restrictive.[341] The

337 See: *Ashby Donald and Others v France* [2013] ECHR 28

338 Copyright and Related Rights Act 2000, s 203 and s 204

339 Section 202(4) of the CRRA, as amended, defines a "*recording*" in relation to a performance as 'any fixation (a) made directly or indirectly from the live performance, (b) made from a broadcast of, or cable programme including, the performance, or (c) made directly or indirectly from another recording of the performance'.

340 Note: For example see: Eleanor Gower, 'Beyonce Bans Press Photographers From Her Mrs Carter Show Tour After those Unflattering Super Bowl Snaps' *Daily Mail* (London, 25 April 2013) <www.dailymail.co.uk/tvshowbiz/article-2314100/Beyonce-bans-press-photographers-Mrs-Carter-Show-tour-those-unflattering-Super-Bowl-snaps.html> accessed 23 May 2018

341 Note: For example, see (1): Jim Carroll, 'Why There's No Photo of Taylor Swift's Gig in Today's "Irish Times": Terms of Photographic Contract "Too Restrictive" for a

accreditation of photographers may also be used at other types of events, such as sports events.[342] At some political and economic events, where security may be a primary concern, it is likely that accreditation would be granted by the event organiser in conjunction with An Garda Síochána. If overseas politicians are involved, other police forces may also be parties to the event's accreditation process.

4.10) Brief conclusions

None of the rights pertaining to the taking or publishing of photographs is absolute. Rather, they may be restricted in support of other interests, in particular the "private" rights of individuals. Chapter 4 examined the range of private rights of individuals that either may come into contention with or restrict the legal rights of photographers and publishers of photographs. In general, these private rights do not place onerous restrictions on photographers and photograph publishers who act responsibly. However, some of these private rights, particularly the right to privacy, the right against harassment and the right to be forgotten, may be, and are being, invoked by individuals in an attempt to prevent personal information from becoming public knowledge. Such practice may result in a restriction on the rights of press photographers to report matters of public interest. Also, the right to privacy and the right against being harassed have been invoked by individuals in an attempt to create and manage a personal image right and a right to publicity, rather than actually wishing to protect their privacy. The courts place a significant weight on the freedom of expression rights of photographers and photograph publishers. The chapter examined a number of tests that have been implemented by the courts when they are balancing the right of freedom of expression with any competing private rights of individuals. It also raises a number of important issues which could benefit from the enactment of legislation and Chapter 6 discusses a number of recommendations in this regard.

Working Newspaper-and-Website' *The Irish Times* (Dublin, 30 June 2015) <www.irishtimes.com/culture/music/why-there-s-no-photo-of-taylor-swift-s-gig-in-today-s-irish-times-1.2267332> accessed 23 May 2018
(2): 'NPPA Helps Revise Taylor Swift Credential Agreement' *National Press Photographers' Association* (21 July 2015) <https://nppa.org/news/nppa-helps-revise-taylor-swift-credential-agreement> accessed 23 May 2018

342 Note: For example see: Football DataCo, *Media Accreditation* <www.football-dataco.com/?page_id=12> accessed 22 May 2018

References

Books

Black G, *Publicity Rights and Image: Exploitation and Legal Control* (Hart Publishing 2011)

Delany H and Carolan E, *The Right to Privacy: A Doctrinal and Comparative Analysis* (Thomson Round Hall 2008)

Kelleher D, *Privacy and Data Protection in Ireland* (Tottel 2006)

Lyons D, *Mr. Paparazzi: My Life as the World's Most Outrageous Celebrity Photographer* (John Blake Publishing 2008)

McMahon B and Binchy W, *Law of Torts* (4th edn, Bloomsbury Professional 2013)

Michalos C, *The Law of Photography and Digital Images* (Sweet and Maxwell 2004)

Quill E, *Torts in Ireland* (Gill and Macmillan 1999)

Warby M, Moreham N, Christie I and Tugendhat M, *Tugendhat and Christie: The Law of Privacy and the Media* (2nd edn, Oxford University Press 2011)

Journal articles

Barendt E, 'An Overlap of Defamation and Privacy?' (2015) 7(1) *Journal of Media Law* 85

Diggelmann O and Cleis M, 'How the Right to Privacy Became a Human Right' (2014) 14(3) *Human Rights Law Review* 441

Foster S, 'Press Photographers: Protecting the Privacy of Celebrities and Their Children' (2014) 19(3) *Commercial Law* 86

Hughes K, 'Photographs in Public Places and Privacy' (2009) 2 *Journal of Media Law* 159–171

—— 'Publishing Photographs Without Consent' (2014) 6(2) *Journal of Media Law* 180–192

Mills A, 'The Law Applicable to Cross-Border Defamation on Social Media: Whose Law Governs Free Speech in "Facebookistan"?' (2015) 7(1) *Journal of Media Law* 1

Stallard H, 'The Right of Publicity in the United Kingdom' (1998) 18 *Loyola of Los Angeles Entertainment Law Review* 565

Thomson M and McCann N, 'Harassment and the Media' (2009) 2 *Journal of Media Law* 149

Warren S and Brandeis L, 'The Right to Privacy' (1890) 4(5) *Harvard Law Review* 193

Newspaper articles and other online articles and press releases

—— 'Former Police Officer Convicted of Voyeurism' *Lancashire Police* (Lancashire, 21 September 2017) <www.lancashire.police.uk/news/2017/september/former-police-officer-convicted-of-voyeurism/> accessed 20 May 2018

—— 'GAA Star Sues Newspaper Over Use of His Image' *Irish Independent* (Dublin, 25 January 2008) <www.independent.ie/irish-news/gaa-star-sues-newspaper-over-use-of-his-image-26347077.html> accessed 23 May 2018

—— 'Journalists Concerned at Garda Proposal to Criminalise the Photographing of Officers While on Duty' *Irish Examiner* (Cork, 10 April 2017) <www.irishexaminer.

com/breakingnews/ireland/journalists-concerned-at-garda-proposal-to-criminalise-the-photographing of officers while-on-duty-785257 html> accessed 15 June 2018

—— 'NPPA Helps Revise Taylor Swift Credential Agreement' *National Press Photographers' Association* (21 July 2015) <https://nppa.org/news/nppa-helps-revise-taylor-swift-credential-agreement> accessed 23 May 2018

—— 'Regency Hotel Murder – Astonishing Photos Emerge of "Transvestite" Gunman Fleeing the Scene' *Irish Independent* (Dublin, 07 February 2016) <www.independent.ie/irish-news/regency-hotel-murder-astonishing-photos-emerge-of-transvestite-gunman-fleeing-the-scene-34430698.html> accessed 16 May 2018

—— '"Revenge Porn" Man Jason Asagba Sentenced' *BBC News* (01 September 2015) <www.bbc.com/news/uk-england-berkshire-33819264> accessed 18 May 2018

—— 'School Children Awarded €62,500 Over Images' *The Irish Times* (Dublin, 30 April 2008) <www.irishtimes.com/news/school-children-awarded-62-500-over-images-1.918406> accessed 12 May 2018

Bardon S, '"Upskirting", Cyberstalking, and Revenge Porn to Be Criminal Offences: Tánaiste Says Acts "Can Cause Serious and Lasting Harm to Young People"' *The Irish Times* (Dublin, 15 May 2017) <www.irishtimes.com/news/politics/upskirting-cyberstalking-and-revenge-porn-to-be-criminal-offences-1.3082855> accessed 20 May 2018

Barrett D, 'What Is the Law on Revenge Porn? What Is Revenge Porn and What Is the Law on It?' *The Telegraph* (London, 13 April 2015) <www.telegraph.co.uk/news/uknews/law-and-order/11531954/What-is-the-law-on-revenge-porn.html> accessed 20 May 2018

Boyle D,— 'Farrell Calls for Image Rights Issue to Be Tackled' *Irish Independent* (Dublin, 02 May 2008) <www.independent.ie/sport/gaelic-games/gaelic-football/farrell-calls-for-image-rights-issue-to-be-tackled-26443561.html> accessed 23 May 2018

Carolan M, 'Court Increases Payout to GAA Player Over Photo' *The Irish Times* (Dublin, 31 July 2008) <www.irishtimes.com/news/court-increases-payout-to-gaa-player-over-photo-1.947718> accessed 15 May 2018

—— 'Data Protection Commissioner to Investigate Max Schrems Claims: Student Alleges His Personal Data Was Made Available Via Facebook to Intelligence Agencies' *The Irish Times* (Dublin, 20 October 2015) <www.irishtimes.com/news/crime-and-law/courts/high-court/data-protection-commissioner-to-investigate-max-schrems-claims-1.2398728> accessed 13 May 2018

Carroll J, 'Why There's No Photo of Taylor Swift's Gig in Today's "Irish Times": Terms of Photographic Contract "Too Restrictive" for a Working Newspaper-and-Website' *The Irish Times* (Dublin, 30 June 2015) <www.irishtimes.com/culture/music/why-there-s-no-photo-of-taylor-swift-s-gig-in-today-s-irish-times-1.2267332> accessed 23 May 2018

Data Protection Commissioner, 'Case Study 10/98: School Web Site – Personal Data Relating to Children – Issue of Fair Obtaining' *Data Protection Commissioner* <www.dataprotection.ie/docs/EN/Case-Study-10-98-School-Web-Site/m/155.htm> accessed 12 May 2018

—— 'Statement by the Office of the Data Protection Commissioner in Respect of Application for Declaratory Relief in the Irish High Court and Referral to the CJEU' (Dublin, 25 May 2016) <www.dataprotection.ie/docs/25-05-2016-Statement-by-this-Office-in-respect-of-application-for-Declaratory-Relief-in-the-Irish-High-Court-and-Referral to the CJEU/1570.htm> accessed 26 May 2018

Deegan G, 'Singer Sues Historian Diarmuid Ferriter Over Alcoholic Book Cover Photo' *Irish Independent* (Dublin, 20 July 2012) <www.independent.ie/irish-news-singer-sues-historian-diarmuid-ferriter-over-alcoholic-book-cover-photo-26877786.html> accessed 21 May 2018

Finn M, 'BOD Gets Landed in a Political Scrum Over Election Snap' *Irish Independent* (Dublin, 13 May 2011) <www.independent.ie/irish-news-bod-gets-landed-in-a-political-scrum-over-election-snap-30269441.html> accessed 23 May 2018

Finneran A, 'McEvoy Gets €80,000 Libel Award From Impresario' *Irish Independent* (Dublin, 17 November 2011) <www.independent.ie/irish-news/courts/mcevoy-gets-80000-libel-award-from-impresario-26792885.html> accessed 23 May 2018

Girvin S, 'Man Guilty of Putting Spy-Cam in Ulster Folk Museum's Disabled Toilets' *Belfast Telegraph* (Belfast, 18 June 2013) <www.belfasttelegraph.co.uk/sunday-life/man-guilty-of-putting-spycam-in-ulster-folk-museums-disabled-toilets-29353681.html> accessed 24 May 2018

Gower E, 'Beyonce Bans Press Photographers From Her Mrs Carter Show Tour After Those Unflattering Super Bowl Snaps' *Daily Mail* (London, 25 April 2013) <www.dailymail.co.uk/tvshowbiz/article-2314100/Beyonce-bans-press-photographers-Mrs-Carter-Show-tour-those-unflattering-Super-Bowl-snaps.html> accessed 23 May 2018

Greenhill S and Groves J, 'Family Secret Cabinet Minister Tried to Hide: Rugby-Playing Teenage Son Exposed as a Drugs Cheat' *Daily Mail* (London, 03 March 2012) <www.dailymail.co.uk/news/article-2109403/Caroline-Spelman-s-Rugby-playing-teenage-son-Jonny-exposed-drugs-cheat.html> accessed 10 May 2018

Hayes K, 'Paramedic to Pay Colleague €5,000 After Harassment' *The Irish Times* (Dublin, 9 March 2013) <www.irishtimes.com/news/paramedic-to-pay-colleague-5-000-after-harassment-1.1320292> accessed 19 May 2018

Healy A, 'Landlord Convicted of Spying on Tenants' *The Irish Times* (Dublin, 8 April 2003) <www.irishtimes.com/news/landlord-convicted-of-spying-on-tenants-1.470727> accessed 19 May 2018

Holland K, 'Borg Serves Fine Gael Notice of His Displeasure' *The Irish Times* (Dublin, 21 September 2013) <www.irishtimes.com/news/politics/borg-serves-fine-gael-notice-of-his-displeasure-1.1536199> accessed 23 May 2018

Lally C, 'Gardaí Have "Limited Scope" on "Revenge Porn"' *The Irish Times* (Dublin, 22 April 2015) <www.irishtimes.com/news/crime-and-law/garda%C3%AD-have-limited-scope-on-revenge-porn-1.2185457> accessed 20 May 2018

Leogue J and Carty E, 'Keane Latest Celebrity to Sue Paddy Power Over Image Rights' *Irish Examiner* (Cork, 11 July 2015) <www.irishexaminer.com/ireland/keane-latest-celebrity-to-sue-paddy-power-over-image-rights-341915.html> accessed 17 May 2018

Managh R, '"Guinness"' Actors Settle Action Over Image Rights' *Irish Independent* (Dublin, 23 April 2013) <www.independent.ie/irish-news/courts/guinness-actors-settle-action-over-image-rights-29214139.html> accessed 23 May 2018

—— 'Father Sues Doonbeg Lodge After His Three Young Kids Appeared on Promotional Brochures Without Consent' *Irish Independent* (Dublin 07 February 2017) <www.independent.ie/irish-news/courts/father-sues-doonbeg-lodge-after-his-three-young-kids-appeared-on-promotional-brochures-without-consent-35430940.html> accessed 23 May 2018

McDonald D, 'Amid the Usual Teen Court Dramas, a Case that Will Shock the Nation' *Irish Independent* (Dublin, 05 December 2015) <www.independent.ie/

irish-news/courts/amid-the-usual-teen-court-dramas-a-case-that-will-shock-the-nation-34260969.html> accessed 16 May 2018

Morris S, 'Man Jailed After Using Explicit Images of Ex-wife in £2m Blackmail Bid: James Casbolt Posted Sexually Explicit Images of Haley Meijer, Daughter of a US Hypermarket Tycoon, Online and Threatened Her Family After Split' *The Guardian* (London, 28 July 2015) <www.theguardian.com/uk-news/2015/jul/28/man-jailed-blackmail-sexually-explicit-images-ex-wife-haley-meijer> accessed 20 May 2018

Murtagh P, 'Couple Denounce Use of Their Image on NO Campaign Posters: Man and Woman "Completely" Support Same Sex Marriage' *The Irish Times* (Dublin, 07 May 2015) <www.irishtimes.com/news/ireland/irish-news/couple-denounce-use-of-their-image-on-no-campaign-posters-1.2203515> accessed 23 May 2018

Purnell S, 'Boris Johnson: The Flawed Mayor of London' *The Independent* (London, 21 May 2013) <www.independent.co.uk/news/uk/politics/boris-johnson-the-flawed-mayor-of-london-8626198.html> accessed 16 May 2018

Rayner G, 'Kate Middleton Won't Sue Over Privacy Invasion of Prince George Holiday Photos' *The Independent* (London, 04 February 2014) <www.independent.ie/style/celebrity/celebrity-news/kate-middleton-wont-sue-over-privacy-invasion-of-prince-george-holiday-photos-29978354.html> accessed 25 May 2018

Riegel R, 'Garda Injured After Being Rammed by Stolen Van in High Speed Chase' *Irish Independent* (Dublin, 18 April 2014) <www.independent.ie/irish-news/garda-injured-after-being-rammed-by-stolen-van-in-high-speed-chase-30197331.html> accessed 16 May 2018

—— '"I've Just Done a Very Bad Thing" – Young Man After Mother Killed in Knife Attack: Heroic Neighbours Disarm Son as Mother Killed and Dad Stabbed' *Irish Independent* (Dublin, 24 November 2015) <www.independent.ie/irish-news/ive-just-done-a-very-bad-thing-young-man-after-mother-killed-in-knife-attack-34228171.html> accessed 16 May 2018

Roche B, 'Man (25) Charged With Murder of His Mother in Cork: Paul Horgan Remanded in Custody Over Death of Marian Horgan at Montenotte Home' *The Irish Times* (Dublin, 25 November 2015) <www.irishtimes.com/news/crime-and-law/man-25-charged-with-murder-of-his-mother-in-cork-1.2443000> accessed 16 May 2018

Saunders L, 'Tamara Ecclestone Shows Blingy Personalised Car Enjoys Date Night Jay Rutland' *Daily Mail* (London, 22 July 2013) <www.dailymail.co.uk/tvshowbiz/article-2373149/Tamara-Ecclestone-shows-blingy-personalised-car-enjoys-date-night-Jay-Rutland.html> accessed 16 May 2018

Shiel T, 'Judge Rules Áras Attracta Care Home Video Footage Admissible' *The Irish Times* (Dublin, 09 October 2015) <www.irishtimes.com/news/crime-and-law/courts/district-court/judge-rules-%C3%A1ras-attracta-care-home-video-footage-admissible-1.2385662> accessed 22 May 2018

Stack S, 'Bringing Adrian's Killers to Justice Will Be Difficult But We Will Find Them, Says Garda Chief' *Irish Independent* (Dublin, 31 January 2013) <www.independent.ie/irish-news/bringing-adrians-killers-to-justice-will-be-difficult-but-we-will-find-them-says-garda-chief-29025452.html> accessed 16 May 2018

Sweeney M, 'Miller Settles With Big Pictures' *The Guardian* (London, 21 November 2008) <www.theguardian.com/media/2008/nov/21/sienna-miller-big-pictures-privacy> 08 May 2018

Official reports and publications

Advertising Standards Authority, *ASA Adjudication on Parfums Christian Dior (UK) Ltd. Complaint Ref: A12–196932* (24 October 2012) <www.asa.org.uk/Rulings/Adjudications/2012/10/Parfums-Christian-Dior-UKLtd/SHP_ADJ_196932.aspx> accessed 23 May 2018

Council of Europe, Parliamentary Assembly, *Resolution 1165 (1998) of the Parliamentary Assembly of the Council of Europe on the Right to Privacy* (Strasbourg, 26 June 1998) <http://assembly.coe.int/nw/xml/XRef/Xref-XML2HTML-en.asp?fileid=16641&lang=en> accessed 16 May 2018

Courts and Tribunals Judiciary, *The Report of the Committee on Super-Injunctions: Super-Injunctions, Anonymised Injunctions and Open Justice* (London, 20 May 2011) <www.judiciary.gov.uk/wp-content/uploads/JCO/Documents/Reports/super-injunction-report-20052011.pdf> accessed 15 May 2018

Department of Communications, Climate Action and Environment, *Report of the Internet Content Governance Advisory Group* (Dublin, May 2014) <www.dccae.gov.ie/en-ie/communications/publications/Documents/70/InternetContentGovernanceAdvisoryGroupReport.pdf> accessed 29 May 2018

Department of Justice and Equality, *Report of Working Group on Privacy* (Dublin, 31 March 2006) <www.justice.ie/en/JELR/WkgGrpPrivacy.pdf/Files/WkgGrpPrivacy.pdf> accessed 12 May 2018

Dublin City Council, *Applications for Activities in Dublin City Parks* <www.dublincity.ie/main-menu-services-recreation-culture-dublin-city-parks/commercial-activities-dublin-city-parks> accessed 22 May 2018

—— *Parks and Open Spaces Bye-Laws 2002* <www.dublincity.ie/sites/default/files/content//RecreationandCulture/DublinCityParks/Documents/ParksBye-Laws2D.pdf> accessed 22 May 2018

European Commission, *Commission Decision of 26 July 2000 Pursuant to Directive 95/46/EC of the European Parliament and of the Council on the Adequacy of the Protection Provided By the Safe Harbour Privacy Principles and Related Frequently Asked Questions Issued by the US Department of Commerce (2000/520/EC)* <https://eur-lex.europa.eu/legal-content/EN/TXT/HTML/?uri=CELEX:32000D0520&from=EN> accessed 13 May 2018

—— Article 29 Data Protection Working Party, *Guidelines on the Implementation of the Court of Justice of the European Union Judgment on "Google Spain and Inc. v Agencia Espanola de Proteccion de Datos (AEPD) and Mario Costeja Gonzalez" C-131/12* (14/ENWP 225) (Brussels, 26 November 2014) <http://ec.europa.eu/justice/article-29/documentation/opinion-recommendation/files/2014/wp225_en.pdf> accessed 22 May 2018

Irish Human Rights and Equality Commission, *Irish Human Rights Commission Submission to the UN Human Rights Committee on the Examination of Ireland's Fourth Periodic Report Under the International Covenant on Civil and Political Rights* (Dublin, June 2014) <www.ihrec.ie/download/pdf/20140616113130.pdf> accessed 15 May 2018

Law Reform Commission, *Report on Harmful Communications and Digital Safety* (LRC 116–2016) Dublin 2016 <https://publications.lawreform.ie/Portal/External/en-GB/RecordView/Index/37669> accessed 20 May 2018

—— *Report on Privacy: Surveillance and the Interception of Communications* (LRC 57–1998) (Dublin 1998) <https://publications.lawreform.ie/Portal/External/

en-GB/RecordView/Index/30597> accessed 12 May 2018Seanad Éireann Debate 28 March 2012, vol 214, col 581 Privacy Bill 2012 <http://oireachtasdebates.oireachtas.ie/debates%20authoring/debateswebpack.nsf/takes/seanad2012032800006?opendocument> accessed 25 May 2018

United Nations, *The Universal Declaration of Human Rights* <www.un.org/en/universal-declaration-human-rights/index.html> accessed 10 May 2018

—— Human Rights Committee, *General Comment No. 34 on Article 19 of the International Covenant on Civil and Political Rights* (on Freedom of Expression) CCPR/C/GC/34 (Geneva, 12 September 2011) <www2.ohchr.org/english/bodies/hrc/docs/gc34.pdf> accessed 23 May 2018

—— Office of the High Commissioner for Human Rights, Human Rights Committee, *General Comment No. 16: Article 17 – Right to Respect to Privacy, Family Home or Correspondence, and Protection of Honour and Reputation*, para 2 (Geneva, 28 September 1988) <http://tbinternet.ohchr.org/_layouts/treatybodyexternal/TBSearch.aspx?Lang=en&TreatyID=8&DocTypeID=11> accessed 15 May 2018

Codes of behavioural standards

Advertising Standards Authority of Ireland, *Code of Standards for Advertising and Marketing Communications in Ireland* (7th edn) <www.asai.ie/asaicode/> accessed 23 May 2018

Aviva Stadium, *FAQs and Ground Rules* <www.avivastadium.ie/faqs-ground-rules> accessed 14 May 2018

Broadcasting Authority of Ireland, *Codes and Standards* <www.bai.ie/en/codes-standards/> accessed 11 June 2018

IMPRESS, *The IMPRESS Standards Code* <www.impress.press/downloads/file/code/the-impress-standards-code.pdf> accessed 19 May 2018

Independent Press Standards Organisation, *Editors' Code of Practice* <www.ipso.co.uk/IPSO/cop.html> accessed 19 May 2018

Websites of interest

European Union, *European Data Protection Supervisor* <https://europa.eu/european-union/about-eu/institutions-bodies/european-data-protection-supervisor_en> accessed 15 May 2018

Football DataCo, *Media Accreditation* <www.football-dataco.com/?page_id=12> accessed 22 May 2018

Heritage Ireland, *Dún Aonghasa* <www.heritageireland.ie/en/west/dunaonghasa/> accessed 22 May 2018

—— *St. Stephen's Green* <www.heritageireland.ie/en/dublin/ststephensgreen/> accessed 22 May 2018

5 Legal restrictions on the taking and publishing of photographs in support of public interests, through statutory provisions, on public morality grounds and under ethical codes of behaviour

5.1) Introduction

In addition to the restrictions that may be placed on photographers' and photograph publishers' freedom of expression rights in order to protect and enforce the personal rights of individuals, their rights may also be either restricted or prohibited in support of public interests, including the protection of public order, the security and defence of the state and the administration of justice. They may also be restricted as a consequence of a variety of miscellaneous statutory provisions or on public morality grounds. Also, ethical codes of behaviour may place restrictions on the legal rights of certain classes of photographers and photograph publishers. The effect of the previously mentioned classes of restrictions may range from a limitation to, in certain circumstances, a total prohibition on the exercise of photographers' and photograph publishers' legal rights. This chapter examine these issues.

5.2) Restrictions on photographers and publishers on the basis of public order, security and defence of the state and crime prevention and investigation

The right of freedom of expression guaranteed by Article 40.6.1°(i) of the Constitution is not an absolute right and it is subject to public order and morality.[1] Also, the right of freedom of expression guaranteed under Art. 10(1) of the ECHR is not an absolute right and it may be restricted, as prescribed by law, to protect national security, territorial integrity and public safety interests and health and morals; to prevent disorder and crime; to protect the reputation or the rights of other people; to prevent the disclosure of information received in confidence; and to maintain the authority and impartiality of the judiciary.[2]

1 Constitution of Ireland *(Art. 40.6.1°)* (on Personal Rights)
2 European Convention on Human Rights Act 2003, sch 1, art 10(2)

Statutes dealing with public order, the security and defence of the state and crime prevention and investigation contain provisions which may be used to either restrict or prohibit photographers from taking, possessing and/or publishing photographs. This section of the chapter discusses such statutory restrictions and how they either do or could impinge on the rights of photographers and publishers of photographs. It also discusses the statutory provisions that could be used by the police against journalists, including press photographers, in order to acquire possession of their journalistic materials.

5.2.1) Public order

Members of An Garda Síochána have a range of statutory powers which, if used by them, could result in photographers being prevented from taking photographs in public places. A number of provisions under the Criminal Justice (Public Order) Act 1994, as amended, are of particular relevance to photographers. Section 3 of the Act specifies a range of places that come within its definition of "public place" including highways; outdoor areas, cemeteries, graveyards and premises to which members of the public are permitted access and trains, vessels and vehicles used for the carriage of people for reward.[3] Under Section 6 of the Act it is an offence for a person in a public place to 'use or engage in any threatening, abusive or insulting words or behaviour with intent to provoke a breach of the peace or being reckless as to whether a breach of the peace may be occasioned'.[4] Either "intention" or "recklessness" must be present in order to constitute an offence of breach of the peace and that would have to be proven in a court before someone could be convicted of a S.6 offence. The fault standard is high, intention and recklessness requiring a higher standard of proof than negligence, for example. The Act does not define what actually constitutes a breach of the peace. However, in the 1932 Irish Court of Criminal Appeal case of *The Attorney General v Cunningham*, O'Byrne J held that for an act to amount to a breach of the peace it must be such that it would cause reasonable alarm and apprehension to members of the public.[5] Were a photographer to be in the process of taking photographs in a public place, for example on a street or a beach, and if a third party were to object, a potential breach of the peace could become an issue for the photographer. Whether or not it was the action of the photographer or of the objecting third party that would be the cause of provoking a possible breach of the peace would depend upon the specific circumstances of the case and a court's interpretation of the evidence presented relating to that event. Coverage of a lawful, peaceful protest or demonstrations that turned violent could be another example. A person's dislike of or objection to either being photographed or seeing a photograph

3 Criminal Justice (Public Order) Act 1994, s 3
4 ibid s 6(1)
5 *The Attorney General v Cunningham* [1932] IR 28, 33

being taken in a public place, such as on a street, neither makes that activity illegal nor does it equate to reasonable alarm and apprehension to members of the public. In the 2004 House of Lords case of *Campbell v MGN Ltd.*, Hope L stated that the photographing of people in public streets must be accepted as being an ordinary activity of everyday living. He further stated that consideration must be given to whether the publication of such photographs could be offensive.[6]

The public interest in journalists and photographers covering public events on behalf of the public is important. Were a member of An Garda Síochána to become involved in such a situation, it is quite possible he/she may attempt to encourage the photographer to desist from taking the photographs,[7] which the photographer would have a legal right to take, in order to diffuse rather than to exacerbate the situation. From the photographer's perspective, the importance of taking the photograph would have to be weighed against the possibility of exacerbating an on-street scene with the third-party objector. Section 8(1) of the 1994 Act gives a member of An Garda Síochána with reasonable cause the power to instruct a person, in specified circumstances including loitering,[8] to move away from a particular public place and under S.8(2) of the Act one's failure to follow such an instruction is an offence. It would be for the prosecution to prove that a photographer standing on a street was actually "loitering" – standing around with no apparent legal purpose and thus

6 *Campbell v MGN Ltd.* [2004] UKHL 22, para 122

7 Note (1): See: Dan Griffin, 'Garda Stops Journalists Photographing "Slab" Murphy at Polling Station: Associate of Murphy's Tells Photographers Not to Take Pictures Outside Co Louth School' *The Irish Times* (Dublin, 26 February 2016) <www.irishtimes.com/news/politics/garda-stops-journalists-photographing-slab-murphy-at-polling-station-1.2549485> accessed 06 June 2018

Note (2): See: Shane Phelan, 'Gardaí Criticised for Hampering Photographers' *Irish Independent* (Dublin, 27 February 2016) <www.independent.ie/irish-news/news/garda-criticised-for-hampering-photographers-34490957.html> accessed 06 June 2018

Note (3): See: 'Intimidation of Media at Polling Station "Affront to Democracy"' *National Union of Journalists* (Dublin, 26 February 2016) <www.nuj.org.uk/news/intimidation-of-media-at-polling-station-affront-to-democracy/> accessed 06 June 2018

Note (4): Notes (1)–(3) concerned a number of press photographers who were waiting in vicinity of the exterior of a polling station for Thomas "Slab" Murphy to emerge from it. Murphy was due to appear later that day in the Special Criminal Court for sentencing in relation to revenue offences. The photographers were reportedly ordered to leave the area by a garda, who claimed that they were interfering with the voting process. Section 147(1) of the Electoral Act 1992, as amended, states: 'A person shall not interfere with or obstruct or impede an elector going to or coming from or in the vicinity of or in a polling station.' In any court case concerning an incident involving a photographer at or near a polling station, the actual physical distance between the photographer and a person which the photographer might be alleged to have "interfered with, obstructed or impeded" would have to be taken into account by the court when it would be determining whether the photographer had actually committed an offence under S.147 of the Act.

8 Criminal Justice (Public Order) Act 1994, s 8(1)

acting illegally. The 2014 ECtHR case of *Pentikainen v Finland*[9] is of relevance to the previously mentioned powers of members of An Garda Síochána under S.8 of the Act. In *Pentikainen*, the applicant was a photographer and journalist for a weekly magazine who had been photographing a demonstration which turned into a riot. A separate area had been reserved for media representatives from which they could photograph the demonstration. The police had sealed off the demonstration area and ordered it to be cleared. A number of people, including the applicant, remained in the sealed-off demonstration area until the demonstration ended and he was then arrested and detained by the police for failing to obey a police instruction to leave the demonstration area.[10] The applicant was found guilty by Helsinki District Court of disobeying the police order. However, no penalty was imposed on him. The applicant had not informed the arresting officer that he was a journalist and the arresting officer was not aware that he was a journalist prior to the applicant's arrest. The applicant appealed his conviction to the Helsinki Court of Appeal on the grounds that his arrest contravened his Art. 10 rights and that the District Court had not determined why his arrest and conviction was necessary in a democratic society and that it consequently failed to justify the State's interference with his Art. 10 rights. The Court of Appeal dismissed his appeal without giving any reason and the Supreme Court refused the applicant leave of appeal.[11] The ECtHR held that the applicant was not technically prevented from expressing his Art. 10 rights and reporting the event and the fact that he was a journalist did not grant him a right greater than anyone else to remain in the secured area.[12] The Court determined that the criminal sanction imposed on the applicant was as a consequence of his refusal to obey a police order and was not a sanction on his journalistic activity.[13] As to the necessity of the restriction placed upon the applicant, the ECtHR held that the state had acknowledged the public interest in having the event reported on by the press by creating a separate area outside of the secured area from which journalists could report the event.[14] Furthermore, the ECtHR noted that the Helsinki District Court had not imposed a penalty or a criminal conviction on the applicant. In finding that there had not been a violation of the applicant's Art. 10 rights, the Court held that the reasons relied on by domestic courts were relevant and sufficient, that the domestic courts had fairly balanced the competing rights and that they were entitled to determine that the interference complained of by the applicant was necessary in a democratic society.[15]

9 *Pentikinen v Finland* [2014] ECHR 106
10 ibid paras 8–12
11 ibid para 14–17
12 ibid para 47
13 ibid para 49
14 ibid para 51
15 ibid paras 54–56

Returning to Irish law, under S.9 of the 1994 Act, 'Any person who, without lawful authority or reasonable excuse, wilfully prevents or interrupts the free passage of any person or vehicle in any public place shall be liable on summary conviction to a fine not exceeding £200 [€254].'[16] Depending upon the particular location and the circumstances in question, a member of An Garda Síochána could, under S.9 of the Act, instruct a photographer taking photographs on a street to desist from doing so and to leave the public place in question. The extent to which free passage may or may not be obstructed by an individual photographer would depend upon the ground area dimensions at any specific location. If a group of photographers were to congregate at the location, a different situation could arise. The wilful obstruction of a "peace officer" performing his/her duty is an offence under S.19 of the Act.[17] A "peace officer" is defined as 'a member of the Garda Síochána, a prison officer or a member of the Defence Forces'.[18] The Act does not define what would actually constitute an obstruction of a peace officer. If a photographer happened to be quietly photographing a peace officer exercising his/her duties from a distance of say 20 metres, such action by the photographer, if seen by the peace officer, could possibly be to the latter's displeasure or even regarded by the latter as some type of a distraction. Peace officers performing their duties in public places are surrounded by all kinds of distractions on a daily basis. A distraction is not an obstruction. For such action by the photographer to constitute a "wilful" obstruction, the prosecution would have to prove that the photographer "intended" to "obstruct" the peace officer exercising his/her duties by taking the photographs. It is unlikely that a court could reasonably hold that the photographer in the previous scenario was guilty of an offence under S.19 of the Act. Also, under S.24 of the Act, where a member of An Garda Síochána finds a person committing an offence under a relevant provision of the Act, they may arrest such a person without a warrant.[19] The Act's definition of a "relevant provision" includes, among other Sections, Sections 6, 8 and 19 of the Act, as previously mentioned.[20] While the 1994 Act, as amended, is not frequently used against photographers, it could be.

5.2.2) Security and defence of the state

With regard to the security and defence of the State, a number of statutes, particularly the Official Secrets Act 1963, as amended; the Defence Act 1954, as amended; and the Offences Against the State Act 1939, as amended, contain

16 Criminal Justice (Public Order) Act 1994, s 9
Note: Under S.8(3) of the Fines Act 2010, this maximum fine upon summary conviction would now be a Class "E" fine of not greater than €346.

17 ibid s 19(3)

18 ibid s 19(6)

19 ibid s 24(1)

20 ibid s 24 (5)

provisions of relevance to photographers and publishers of photographs. Of particular relevance to people working in the media is the Official Secrets Act 1963, which prohibits the unauthorised disclosure and obtaining of official information.[21] The Act defines an "official document" as

> any secret official code word or password, and any sketch, plan, model, article, note, document or information which is secret or confidential or is expressed to be either and which is or has been in the possession, custody or control of a holder of a public office, or to which he has or had access, by virtue of his office, and includes information recorded by film or magnetic tape or by any other recording medium.[22]

Also, the Act defines a "sketch" as including 'a photograph or other mode of representing any place or thing'.[23] Under the Act, it is an offence for a person to 'retain any official document or anything which constitutes or contains official information when he has no right to retain it or when not required by his duty as the holder of a public office to retain it'.[24] Section 9 of the Act prohibits the obtaining, recording and/or communication of information which may prejudice the safety or the preservation of the state.[25] So as to avoid a possible breach of the Act, photographers and publishers should seek to obtain the appropriate prior authorisation if they are planning to photograph and/or publish photographs of any structure or any item of the type specified under S.9 of the Act. However, it is quite possible that such permission would be refused. Court cases concerning breaches of the Official Secrets Act are rare. The Freedom of Information Acts 1997–2014[26] considerably changed the culture of secrecy in Government and government agencies. The Acts enable members of the public to access information in the possession of public bodies and other specified bodies in keeping with the public interest. The 2014 Act, among other issues, amended the Official Secrets Act 1963[27] and it provides for the possible refusal to disclose certain

21 Official Secrets Act 1963, s 4

22 ibid s 2(1)

23 ibid

24 ibid s 6(1)

25 ibid s 9

26 Note: The Freedom of Information Act 2014 entirely repealed the Freedom of Information Act 1997 and the Freedom of Information (Amendment) Act 2003.

27 Section 51 of the 2014 Act states: '(1) A person who is, or reasonably believes that he or she is, authorised by this Act to communicate official information to another person shall be deemed for the purposes of section 4 of the Official Secrets Act 1963 to be duly authorised to communicate this information. (2) In a prosecution for an offence under section 5 or 9 of that Act, it shall be a defence to prove that the act to which the charge of the offence relates is authorised, or is reasonably believed by the person charged to be authorised, by this Act.'
Note: Section 5 of the Official Secrets Act 1963 concerns the disclosure of confidential information in official contracts.

records[28] likely to prejudice or impair law enforcement and public safety[29] or that could reasonably be expected to affect adversely security, defence and international relations.[30] Journalists are one of the primary groups that use and benefit from the provisions of freedom of information legislation. The 2014 Act does not have a restrictive application to photographers wishing to take photographs. However, the previously mentioned grounds for refusing to disclose records, which may include photographs, could be regarded as a restriction on the publication of existing photographs held by government agencies that may be in the public interest. The Freedom of Information Act is premised on the public's right of access to official information ("records") and there is a strong presumption that information will be released in the public interest.

Under the Defence Act 1954, as amended, it is an offence to make or attempt to make photographs, without lawful authority, of 'any fort, battery, field work, fortification or any military work of defence, aerodrome, barracks, post, magazine, munition factory, stores depot or any other Government property occupied or partly occupied by the Defence Forces'.[31] Any unauthorised photographs taken of such locations and any photographic equipment found in the possession of an offender are liable to be forfeited.[32] It is also an offence if one approaches or enters, without authority, any of these types of locations with photographic equipment in one's possession with the intention of committing an offence under S.268(1) and any photographic equipment found in one's possession will be forfeited and may be disposed of.[33] It is an offence for one to trespass on the previously mentioned types of locations or on a military vessel.[34] The State Group of Buildings on Dublin's Merrion Street, which include, among others, Government Buildings, Leinster House, the National Arts and Antiquities Museum, the Natural Museum and the National Library, are occupied on a 24-hours basis for security and fire picket purposes by a permanent detachment of military personnel (Military Police).[35] From a photographer's perspective, these buildings and also Portlaoise Prison, at which the Defence Forces have a permanent security presence,[36] would come within the meaning of the previously mentioned S.268(1) of the Act. Should a photographer propose to

28 Section 2 of the Freedom of Information Act 2014 contains a broad definition of the term "records" which includes "visual images".

29 Freedom of Information Act 2014, s 32

30 ibid s 33

31 Defence Act 1954, s 268(1)

32 ibid

33 ibid s 268(2)

34 ibid s 268(3)

35 Signal Magazine, *Military Police at Government Buildings* (Dublin, 19 May 2005), vol Summer 2005, 49–51 <www.raco.ie/attachments/082_4_1_militarypolice.pdf> accessed 06 June 2018

36 Department of Defence and Defence Forces, *Annual Report 2016* (Newbridge, 2016), 49 <www.military.ie/fileadmin/user_upload/images/Info_Centre/documents/Annual_Reports/Annual_Report_2016__English_.pdf> accessed 06 June 2018

legally create and/or publish photographs of any of the previously mentioned types of locations, prior authorisation would be required.

Under the Offences Against the State Act 1939, as amended, it is not lawful 'for any person to have any treasonable document, seditious document, or incriminating document in his possession or on any lands or premises owned or occupied by him or under his control'.[37] Section 2 of the Act defines a "document" as:

> a book and also a newspaper, magazine, or other periodical publication, and also a pamphlet leaflet, circular, or advertisement.[38]

Section 5 of the Offences Against the State (Amendment) Act 1972 amended the Section 2 definition of a "document" through its inclusion, among other things, of all types of visual images and specifically "photographs".[39] Furthermore, Section 8(1) of the Offences Against the State Act (Amendment) Act 1998, which deals with the unlawful collection of information, states:

> It shall be an offence for a person to collect, record or possess information which is of such a nature that it is likely to be useful in the commission by members of any unlawful organisation of serious offences generally or any particular kind of serious offence.[40]

The 1998 Act offers a defence to such a charge and it is for an accused to prove that such information was not being collected or recorded or in his/her possession for the purpose of it being used in the commission of the types of offences mentioned under S.8 of the Act.[41] The Offences Against the State Acts have rarely been invoked in recent times against journalists and, in particular, photographers. However, their provisions hang over them as a threat.

5.2.3) (1) Unlawful disclosure of confidential information by An Garda Síochána (police) (2) retention of, and access to, communications data

Journalists obtain information from a variety of sources,[42] including members of An Garda Síochána. The Garda Síochána Act 2005, as amended, imposes a

37 Offences Against the State Act 1939, s 12(1)

38 ibid s 2
Note: Section 2 also defines what individually constitute "treasonable", "seditious" and "incriminating" documents.

39 Offences Against the State Act (Amendment) Act 1972, s 5

40 Offences Against the State Act (Amendment) Act 1998, s 8(1)

41 ibid s 8(2)

42 Note: For a discussion on, and definitions of, the terms of the terms "journalist", "information" and "sources" see: Council of Europe, Committee of Ministers, *Recommendation*

legal obligation on current and former members and on civilian employees of the force not to unlawfully disclose confidential information while knowing that such a disclosure is likely to have a harmful effect.[43] Section 62(2) of the Act contains detailed specifics of what types of disclosures will or will not have a harmful effect.[44] Also, S.62(4) of the Act contains a number of specified exceptions to the previously mentioned S.61(1) prohibition, including for example disclosures made to the Director of Public Prosecutions or in a court.[45] Journalists and photographers working on the production of news stories for the print media, television and radio stations rely on receiving information from a variety of sources including members of An Garda Síochána. It is without doubt that sources of information frequently disclose information to journalists to suit their own agendas. Some investigative journalists look upon S.62 of the Act as a gagging of their Garda Síochána information sources. They also believe that sections within An Garda Síochána are more interested in identifying journalists' sources of information within the force than in taking action against criminal gangs, who, following the publication of articles on them, have made personal threats to journalists' lives.[46] The 2005 Act, as amended, established the Garda Síochána Ombudsman Commission.[47] The Ombudsman may

> if it appears desirable in the public interest to do so and without receiving a complaint, investigate any matter that appears to indicate that a member of the Garda Síochána may have – (a) committed an offence, or (b) behaved in a manner that would justify disciplinary proceedings.[48]

Also, under the S.102 of the Act, as amended by S.6 of the Garda Síochána (Amendment) Act 2015, it may do so even where

---

No. R (2000) 7 of the Committee of Ministers to Member States on the Right of Journalists Not to Disclose their Sources of Information (Strasbourg, 08 March 2000), Appendix. <www.coe.int/en/web/freedom-expression/committee-of-ministers-adopted-texts/-/asset_publisher/aDXmrol0vvsU/content/recommendation-no-r-2000-7-of-the-committee-of-ministers-to-member-states-on-the-right-of-journalists-not-to-disclose-their-sources-of-information?inheritRedirect=false&desktop=true> accessed 06 June 2018

43 Garda Síochána Act 2005, s 62(1)
Note: See: Gerry McLaughlin, 'Garda Admits Passing Information to Criminals Known as "The Child" and "The Pharmacy"' *Irish Independent* (Dublin, 30 May, 2018) <www.independent.ie/irish-news/courts/garda-admits-passing-information-to-criminals-known-as-the-child-and-the-pharmacy-36960048.html> accessed 14 June 2018

44 ibid s 62(2)

45 ibid s 62(4)

46 Henry McDonald, 'Irish Journalists Accuse Police of "Stasi-like" Monitoring: Garda Síochána Alleged to be Monitoring Phone Calls and Threatening Reporters With Arrest in Attempt to Reveal Sources' *The Guardian* (London, 11 May 2012) <www.guardian.co.uk/media/2012/may/11/irish-journalists-police-monitoring> accessed 06 June 2018

47 Garda Síochána Act 2005, s 64

48 ibid s 102(4)

(a) the identity of the member of the Garda Síochána concerned may not be known when the investigation is undertaken, or (b) the offence or behaviour concerned may also involve or have involved a person who is not a member of the Garda Síochána.[49]

In relation to the protection of their sources, the Communications (Retention of Data) Act 2011, as amended, is of relevance to journalists. Among other matters, this Act gives effect to the provisions of Directive 2006/24/EC.[50] Under Section 6(1) of the Act:

> A member of the Garda Síochána not below the rank of chief superintendent may request a service provider to disclose to that member data retained by the service provider in accordance with *section 3* where the member is satisfied that the data are required for –
>
> (a) the prevention, detection, investigation or prosecution of a serious offence,
> (b) the safeguarding of the security of the State,
> (c) the saving of human life.[51]

A "service provider" is defined by the Act as 'a person who is engaged in the provision of a publicly available electronic communications service or a public communications network by means of fixed line or mobile telephones or the Internet'.[52] A service provider may not refuse to comply with an authorised request for communications data.[53] Schedule 2 of the Act specifies the type of

49 ibid s 102(5A)

50 Directive 2006/24/EC of the European Parliament and of the Council of 15 March 2006 on the retention of data generated or processed in connection with the provision of publicly available electronic communications services or of public communications networks and amending Directive 2002/58/EC [2006] OJ L105/54 <http://eur-lex.europa.eu/legal-content/EN/TXT/HTML/?uri=CELEX:32006L0024&from=EN> accessed 06 June 2018
Note: The CJEU held in Case C-293/12 *Digital Rights Ireland v Minister for Communications and Others* [2014], at paras 65–71, that Directive 2006/24/EC was invalid, as, among other reasons, it does not prescribe clear, specific rules controlling the extent of the permitted interference with fundamental rights and particularly the right to privacy.

51 Communications (Retention of Data) Act 2011, s 6(1)
Note: Sections 6(2), 6(3) and 6(3A) of the Act also provide for disclosure requests from specified members of the Permanent Defence Force, officers of the Revenue Commissioners and members of the Competition and Consumer Protection Commission respectively in respect of the security of the State; the prevention, detection, investigation or prosecution of revenue offences; and the prevention, detection, investigation or prosecution of competition offences.

52 ibid s 1(1)

53 ibid s 7

data, namely traffic and location data, to be retained by service providers in respect of fixed network and mobile telephony data[54] and Internet access, Internet email and Internet telephony data.[55] However, the Act does not apply to the content of communications made by users of such communications networks.[56] *The Irish Times* reported that the text messages and call details of a number of journalists were accessed by An Garda Síochána while it investigated a possible unlawful disclosure of confidential information by a member of An Garda Síochána to members of the media. However, in that instance such data had been obtained by An Garda Síochána from the mobile phone of the Garda under investigation and not through its acquisition of the journalists' communications data.[57] Following a Review of the Law on the Retention of and Access to Communications Data by Mr. Justice John L. Murray,[58] a general scheme for a proposed Communications (Retention of Data) Bill 2017[59] has been published.

The Interception of Postal Packets and Telecommunications Messages (Regulation) Act 1993 was amended by the Garda Síochána (Amendment) Act 2015.[60] For the purposes of a criminal investigation or for the protection of the security of the state, under the 1993 Act, as amended, the Commissioner of An Garda Síochána or the chairperson of the Garda Síochána Ombudsman Commission and the Chief of Staff of the Defence Forces may respectively apply to the Minister for Justice for an authorisation to intercept either a postal packet or a telecommunications message.[61] Section 2 of the 1993 Act grants the Minister the power to grant such a requested authorisation.[62] An authorisation under

54 ibid sch 2, part 1
55 ibid sch 2, part 2
56 ibid s 2
57 Conor Lally, 'Journalists' Texts Form Part of Garda Leak Inquiry: Messages and Call Details Accessed From Phone of Officer Who Is Under Investigation' *The Irish Times* (Dublin, 25 July 2015) <www.irishtimes.com/news/crime-and-law/journalists-texts-form-part-of-garda-leak-inquiry-1.2296482> accessed 06 June 2018
58 Department of Justice and Equality, *Review of the Law on the Retention of and Access to Communications Data* (April 2017) (Dublin, 03 October 2017) <http://justice.ie/en/JELR/Review_of_the_Law_on_Retention_of_and_Access_to_Communications_Data.pdf/Files/Review_of_the_Law_on_Retention_of_and_Access_to_Communications_Data.pdf> accessed 08 June 2018
59 Department of Justice and Equality, *General Scheme Communications (Retention of Data) Bill 2017* (Dublin, 03 October 2017) <http://justice.ie/en/JELR/General_Scheme_-_Communications_(Retention_of_Data)_Bill.pdf/Files/General_Scheme_-_Communications_(Retention_of_Data)_Bill.pdf> accessed 08 June 2018
Note: Head 8 of the General Scheme of the Bill provides for an authorising judge to authorise the disclosure of communications traffic and location data.
60 Garda Síochána (Amendment) Act 2015, s 12
61 Interception of Postal Packets and Telecommunications Messages (Regulation) Act 1993, s 6(1)
62 ibid s 2

the 1993 Act should not be decided by a politician.[63] Access to anybody's postal packets or telecommunications messages under the 1993 Act should only be permitted with the prior approval of an external, impartial third party, namely a High Court judge, and on a case by case basis. Where a judge would be considering an application for access to a journalist's postal packets or telecommunications messages under the Act, it should be a requirement for the party seeking such access to prove to the satisfaction of the judge that there is an overriding public interest in being granted such access for a specific and stated legal purpose and not as a fishing exercise.

The Criminal Justice (Surveillance) Act 2009, as amended by the Garda Síochána (Amendment) Act 2015,[64] provides for a judge of the District Court to grant on an ex-parte basis and otherwise than in public an authorisation for surveillance to a superior officer of either An Garda Síochána, the Defence Forces or the Revenue Commissioners or a member of the Garda Síochána Ombudsman Commission other than its chairperson for specified purposes including the investigation or prevention of arrestable offences, the security of the State and revenue offences.[65] The Act states that an authorisation may not be issued if the judge is satisfied that the 'surveillance being sought to be authorised is likely to relate primarily to communications protected by privilege'.[66] The Act does not define "privileged communications" and as applications are on an ex-parte basis, the judge is at the mercy of the information provided to him by the applicant. Section 7 of the Act provides for the issuing of an authorisation (for a short term duration) by a superior officer rather than a judge in the case of an application of an urgent nature.[67] An overriding public interest test should apply in respect of the granting of an authorisation under this Act for the surveillance of journalists. The author recommends that such surveillance authorisations should only be granted by a senior judge, who would be independent of any investigation, and not by a superior officer as defined by Section 1 of the Act.

63 Note: For an example of the misuse by government ministers of similar powers to authorise the interception of individuals' telephone communications, see: *Kennedy and Arnold v Ireland* [1987] 1 IR 587 (HC).

64 Garda Síochána (Amendment) Act 2015, s 13

65 Criminal Justice (Surveillance) Act 2009, s 4
Note (1): Section 1 of the Act, as amended, defines "surveillance" as: '(a) monitoring, observing, listening to or making a recording of a particular person or group of persons or their movements, activities and communications, or (b) monitoring or making a recording of places or things, by or with the assistance of surveillance devices'.
Note (2): Section 13(d) of the Garda Síochána (Amendment) Act 2015 amended Section 4 of the Criminal Justice (Surveillance) Act 2009 and granted the right to seek a surveillance authorisation under the 2009 Act to a superior officer of the Garda Síochána Ombudsman Commission.

66 ibid s 5(4)

67 ibid s 7

In the United Kingdom, the Regulation of Investigatory Powers Act 2000 (RIPA), as amended, provides for both the interception[68] and the accessing[69] of communications data. A wide grouping of designated state bodies ranging from the police to local authorities are granted such powers under the Act.[70] Section 22(2) of the Act specifies the grounds for which communications data may be accessed and disclosed by a designated person. Such grounds include, among others, in the interest of national security, the prevention or detection of crime, in the interest of the economic well-being of the United Kingdom and the protection of public health.[71]

Following the publication of the Interception of Communications Commissioner's Office's report on its inquiry into the use of the Act by police forces in the United Kingdom to identify journalists' sources,[72] the United Kingdom's Home Office published a new code of practice on the acquisition and disclosure of communications data under RIPA.[73] The Code specifically excludes, on an interim basis, the use of RIPA for the acquisition of journalists' communications data in order to identify their sources of journalistic information. The Data Retention and Investigatory Powers Act 2014 (DRIPA) amended RIPA. Section 1 of the 2014 Act made provision for the Secretary of State to require, by notice, telecommunications operators to retain relevant communications data 'if the Secretary of State considers that the requirement is necessary and proportionate for one or more purposes falling within paragraphs (a) to (h) of Section 22(2) of the Regulation of Investigatory Powers Act 2000'.[74] The 2015 English High Court case of *David Davis MP and Others v The Secretary of State for the Home Department*[75] concerned a challenge that DRIPA was in contravention of EU Charter of Fundamental Rights' Art. 7 right to privacy and Art. 8 right to protection of personal data. In *Davis*, Bean LJ referred to the

68 Regulation of Investigatory Powers Act 2000, part 1 ch 1
69 ibid part 1 ch 2
70 ibid sch 1
71 ibid s 22(2)
72 Interception of Communications Commissioner's Office, *IOCCO Inquiry into the Use of Chapter 2 of Part 1 of the Regulation of Investigatory Powers Act (RIPA) to Identify Journalistic Sources* (February 2015) <http://webarchive.nationalarchives.gov.uk/20170914105829/www.iocco-uk.info/sections.asp?sectionID=1&type=top> accessed 07 June 2018
73 United Kingdom Home Office, *Acquisition and Disclosure of Communications Data: Code of Practice* (March 2015) <https://assets.publishing.service.gov.uk/government/uploads/system/uploads/attachment_data/file/426248/Acquisition_and_Disclosure_of_Communications_Data_Code_of_Practice_March_2015.pdf> accessed 06 June 2018 Note: Under Principle 3.78 of this Code, a court order is required to permit access by law enforcement agencies with powers under the Police and Criminal Evidence Act 1984 (PACE) to communications data in order to identify journalists' sources.
74 Data Retention and Investigatory Powers Act 2014, s 1(1)
75 *David Davis MP and Others v The Secretary of State for the Home Department* [2015] EWHC 2092 (Admin)

CJEU decision in *Digital Rights Ireland* and he held that Section 1 of DRIPA was inconsistent with European Union law as:

(a) it does not lay down clear and precise rules providing for access to and use of communications data retained pursuant to a retention notice to be strictly restricted to the purpose of preventing and detecting precisely defined serious offences or of conducting criminal prosecutions relating to such offences; and
(b) access to the data is not made dependent on a prior review by a court or an independent administrative body whose decision limits access to and use of the data to what is strictly necessary for the purpose of attaining the objective pursued.[76]

Following *Davis*, the Investigatory Powers Act 2016 was introduced. The Act offers a number of safeguards relating to the use of powers under the Act to identify or confirm journalists' sources of information. They include a requirement that a Judicial Commissioner must approve an authorisation to access a journalist's communication data to identify or confirm his/her sources of information.[77] However, in the 2018 High Court case of *Liberty v Home Office*[78] Singh LJ held that Part 4 of the Act, which deals with the retention of communications data, was incompatible with fundamental rights in EU law, as '(1) access to retained data is not limited to the purpose of combating "serious crime"; and (2) access to retained data is not subject to prior review by a court or an independent administrative body'.[79]

5.2.4) *Stop, search and seizure powers of An Garda Síochána (police)*

An Garda Síochána is responsible for the prevention and investigation of criminal offences. Various statutes including the Offences Against the State Act 1939, as amended; the Criminal Law Act 1976, as amended; and the Misuse of Drugs Act 1977, as amended, provide members of An Garda Síochána with stop, search and seizure powers in specific instances without the need for a court-issued warrant.[80] Aside from such provisions, members of An Garda Sío-

76 ibid para 114
77 Investigatory Powers Act 2016, s 77
78 *The Queen on the application of the National Council for Civil Liberties (Liberty) v Secretary of State for the Home Department and Others* [2018] EWHC 975 (Admin)
Note: See also the CJEU decision in the joint cases of Case C-203/15 *Tele2 Sverige AB v Post- och telestyrelsen* [2016] and Case C-698/15 *Secretary of State for the Home Department v Tom Watson and Others* [2016]
79 ibid para 186
80 Note: The relevant statutory provisions are Section 30 of the Offences Against the State Act 1939, as amended; Section 8(2) of the Criminal Law Act 1976, as amended; and

chána and also other authorised persons, such as members of the Defence Forces, may exercise search and seizures powers through their use of court-issued warrants granted under a range of other statutory provisions. For example, having entered a place named on a search warrant issued under S.29[81] of the Offences Against the State Act 1939, as amended, a member of An Garda Síochána may under S.29(6)(c):

> seize anything found at that place, or anything found in the possession of a person present at that place at the time of the search, that that member reasonably believes to be evidence of, or relating to, the commission of an offence to which this section applies.[82]

The Official Secrets Act 1963 provides for the issuing of search warrants to members of An Garda Síochána to authorise their entry to and search of any premises, place, vessel or aircraft named on the warrant and 'to seize any document or thing found therein or on such person which such member reasonably believes to be evidence of or to relate, directly or indirectly, to a contravention or intended contravention of section 9'.[83] The wording of the two previously mentioned statutory provisions gives An Garda Síochána very wide seizure powers. In the case of a search of a photographer's premises, the result could mean the removal by An Garda Síochána of the photographer's complete library of still film photographs, computers, hard disk drives, digital cameras and their memory cards for examination. Under the Criminal Law Act 1976, as amended, where a member of the Garda Síochána is exercising powers under that Act or is involved in a search under any other power and:

> finds or comes into possession of anything which he believes to be evidence of any offence or suspected offence, it may be seized and retained for use as evidence in any criminal proceedings, . . . for such period from the date of seizure as is reasonable or, if proceedings are commenced in which the thing so seized is required for use in evidence, until the conclusion of the proceedings, and thereafter the Police (Property) Act, 1897, shall apply to the thing so seized in the same manner as that Act applies to property which has come into the possession of the Garda Síochána in the circumstances mentioned in that Act.[84]

Section 23 of the Misuse of Drugs Act 1977, as amended by S.12 of the Misuse of Drugs Act 1984.

81 Note: Section 1 of the Criminal Justice (Search Warrants) Act 2012 inserted a new S.29 in the 1939 Act.

82 Offences Against the State Act 1939, s 29(6)(c)

83 Official Secrets Act 1963, s 16(3)
Note: Section 9 of the Act concerns acts which are contrary to the safety or preservation of the State.

84 Criminal Law Act 1976, s 9(1)

Section 7(1) of the Criminal Justice Act 2006 concerns the powers of An Garda Síochána to seize and retain evidence and it states:

> Where a member of the Garda Síochána who is in: (a) a public place, or (b) any other place under a power of entry authorised by law or to which or in which he or she was expressly or impliedly invited or permitted to be, finds or comes into possession of any thing, and he or she has reasonable grounds for believing that it is evidence of, or relating to, the commission of an arrestable offence, he or she may seize and retain the thing for use as evidence in any criminal proceedings.[85]

The Police (Property) Act 1897 also applies to anything seized under S.7 of the 2006 Act.[86] In relation to S.7(1) of the 2006 Act, were a photographer to photograph, for example, either the commissioning of a crime or a crime scene and a member of An Garda Síochána either observed or became aware of such photography, a number of possible events could unfold. If the photographer had been using a digital camera, the member could seek the photographer's permission to view the images stored in the camera's memory card(s). If the photographer were to accede to such a request and in doing so he handed the camera to the member to view the images, the camera and its memory card(s) would then technically come into the member's possession for the purposes of the previously mentioned S.7(1) of the 2006 Act. The member could then attempt to seize the camera and its memory card(s) as evidence and to retain them until the conclusion of any court proceedings. If the photographer were to refuse the member's request to view the images stored in the camera memory card(s), the member could seek a search warrant to search the photographer's home or business premises under S.10 of the Criminal Justice (Miscellaneous Provisions) Act 1997, as amended by S.6 of the 2006 Act and if the images were located under such a search, he/she could then seize them under S.10 of the 1997 Act.

Alternatively, the member could apply to the District Court for a production order under the Criminal Justice Act 2011, as amended.[87] For such an order to be issued, a District Court Judge must be satisfied that the information supplied on oath by the member making the application for the order contains reasonable grounds for believing that the documents sought are relevant to the investigation of a relevant offence and that there are reasonable grounds for suspecting that the documents 'may constitute evidence of or relating to the commission of that

85 Criminal Justice Act 2006, s 7(1)
86 ibid
87 Criminal Justice Act 2011, s 15

offence'.[88] The Act does not offer any indication as to what might constitute "reasonable grounds". Section 15 of the Act refers to 'particular documents or documents of a particular description'.[89] In an application for a production order in relation to photographs, there is no requirement under S.15 that specific images must be stated in the order application. Thus, it would appear that a description such as "photographs taken at event X on date Y at Z Street, Galway" could fulfil the requirement under S.15 of the Act. The Act does not specify any required level of evidential value in respect of material sought under a S.15 production order. There is no requirement under S.15 that the material sought will be of "substantial value" either to an investigation or as evidence. Furthermore, it is not a requirement under S.15 that only specified documents, for example specified, individual photographic images, would be covered by a S.15 order. Section 15 only requires that the documents or "some" of the documents sought "may" constitute evidence. Such an investigative or evidential value level is extremely low. Coupled with the wide document description permitted on an order application, S.15 of the Act could facilitate An Garda Síochána by granting it access to photographic images which most likely would be of no investigative or evidential value to it and for An Garda Síochána to just undertake fishing expeditions at the expense of photographers. It is arguable that the provisions of the Act are overly broad and could adversely impact on photographers' rights and their ability to practice as photographers without being looked upon by members of the public as evidence gatherers on behalf of An Garda Síochána.[90] A court order granted under S.15 may also grant powers of entry to An Garda Síochána.[91] Under Section 15 of the Act, an order under S.15 also empowers a member of An Garda

88 ibid s 15(2)
Note: Section 2 of the Criminal Justice Act 2011 defines a "document" as including 'information recorded in any form and any thing on or in which information is recorded and from which information can be extracted'.

89 ibid

90 Note: See (1): Dave Molloy, 'Photography Agency: Gardaí Used Warrant to Seize Pictures of Water Protests' *Irish Examiner* (Cork, 16 February 2015) <www.irishexaminer.com/breakingnews/ireland/photography-agency-gardai-used-warrant-to-seize-pictures-of-water-protests-662466.html> accessed 08 June 2018
(2): Sue Murphy, '"They Were Looking for Material Which We Had Not Put Out Into the Public Domain in Relation to a Protest": The Photocall Editor Discussed a Warrant Issued by Gardaí for Photos' *Newstalk 106–108FM* (Dublin, 18 February 2015) <www.newstalk.com/They-were-looking-for-material-which-we-had-not-put-out-into-the-public-domain-in-relation-to-a-protest> accessed 06 June 2018
(3): National Union of Journalists, *NUJ Condemns Garda Order Against Photocall Ireland* (17 February 2015) <www.nuj.org.uk/news/nuj-condemns-garda-order-against-photocall-ireland/> accessed 06 June 2018
(4) Alan O'Keeffe, 'Regency Murder Trial to Continue After Judges Give Green Light to Key Prosecution Evidence' *Irish Independent* (Dublin, 02 February, 2018) <www.independent.ie/irish-news/courts/regency-murder-trial-to-continue-after-judges-give-green-light-to-key-prosecution-evidence-36560506.html> accessed 15 June 2018

91 Criminal Justice Act 2011, s 15(5)

Síochána to make a copy of a required original document and to take away such a copy.[92] The decision to take away an original document sought or a copy of it is at the discretion of the member of An Garda Síochána. However, the member may only accede to a S.15(8)(a) request from the person affected by the order for the latter to retain the original document if the undertakings and provisions specified in S.15(8)(b) of the Act are met.[93] Any documents taken away by a member of An Garda Síochána pursuant to a S.15 order may be retained as evidence in any criminal proceedings.[94] The Act does not impose any limitation on the persistence of such a retention. If such a seizure and removal occurred in respect of a photographer's images, he/she could apply to the District Court for their return.[95] However, such a request may or may not be granted by the Court.

The competing interests relating to the obtaining, retention and preservation of evidence for use in court proceedings have been addressed by the courts. This issue was central to the 1887 Irish Exchequer Division court case of *Dillon v O'Brien and Davis*.[96] In more recent times, it featured in the 2001 Irish Supreme Court case of *Braddish v DPP*,[97] in which Hardiman J stated that members of An Garda Síochána are obliged to search for and to preserve all evidence having a relevance to the matter of guilt or innocence of an accused.[98] In the 2007 Irish High Court case of *O'Sullivan and Others v DPP*,[99] Feeney J held that this obligation was not an absolute obligation, as such an obligation may be impacted by any one of a range of factors, such as a competing obligation to return property held as evidence to its owner.[100]

Any search for, and seizure of, a photographer's cameras and image storage devices by a member of An Garda Síochána must be in accordance with, and as prescribed for, in law. Of relevance to this point is the 2010 ECtHR case of *Sanoma Uitgevers BV v Netherlands*,[101] which concerned a production order in respect of photographic images of an illegal streetcar race. Under Article 96a of the Netherlands' Code of Criminal Procedure, the decision on whether or not material sought by the police was to be handed over was a matter for the public prosecutor rather than for an independent judge.[102] In *Sanoma*, the Grand Chamber held that the public prosecutor as a party to proceedings could not

92 ibid s 15(7) and s 15(8)
93 ibid s 15(8)(b)
94 ibid s 15(9)
95 ibid s 15(14)
96 *Dillon v O'Brien and Davis* [1887] 20 LRIR 300, 317
97 *Braddish v DPP* [2001] IESC 45
98 ibid
99 *O'Sullivan and Others v DPP* [2007] IEHC 137
100 ibid
101 *Sanoma Uitgevers BV v Netherlands* (App No 38224/03) (ECHR, 14 September 2010)
102 ibid para 93

be classed as being objective and impartial.[103] Consequently, it held that the law was deficient and the applicant's Art. 10 right had been violated.[104]

If An Garda Síochána were to seize or seek a production order for a photographer's camera memory cards, computer hard drives and/or library of photographs for evidential examination and use in a criminal investigation or trial, the latter's ability to undertake any photographic work could potentially grind to a halt and he/she most likely would have to seek a court order to have the seized equipment and/or photographic images returned. Also, if a photographer were to either destroy or refuse to hand over images being sought under a production order, it is a possible that he/she could face any one of a number of charges including attempting to pervert the course of justice, contempt of court, withholding information[105] and concealing facts disclosed by documents.[106]

5.2.5) Stop, search and seizure powers of United Kingdom's police

In the United Kingdom, members of the police may stop and search people in accordance with their powers under a range of statutes, in particular the Police and Criminal Evidence Act 1984 (PACE), as amended.[107] However, S.1 of the Act does not give a police constable

> the power to search a person or vehicle or anything in or on a vehicle unless he has reasonable grounds for suspecting that he will find stolen or prohibited articles, any article to which subsection (8A) below applies or any firework to which subsection (8B) below applies.[108]

Section 8 of the Act provides for the issuing of warrants by justices of the peace to authorise the police to enter and search premises for material which is likely to be of relevance to the investigation of an indictable offence which has been committed.[109] A constable may seize and retain anything for which a search has been authorised under S.8.[110] However, for a S.8 warrant to be issued, such

103 ibid
104 ibid para 100
105 Criminal Justice Act 2011, s 19(1)
Note: The very similarly worded offence of withholding information under Section 9(1)(b) of the Offences Against the State (Amendment) Act 1998 was held by Baker J, at para 112, in the 2017 Irish High Court case of *Sweeney v Ireland* [2017] IEHC 702 to offend the constitutional right to remain silent.
106 ibid s 17
107 Police and Criminal Evidence Act 1984, s 1
108 ibid s 1(3)
Note: Section 1(8A) refers to offences under S.139 of the Criminal Justice Act 1988, as amended (namely, the offence of having article with blade or point in public place).
109 Police and Criminal Evidence Act 1984, s 8
110 ibid s 8(2)

material may not include items subject to legal privilege, excluded material or special procedure material.[111] "Excluded material" is defined by S.11 of the Act as including, among other things, 'journalistic material which a person holds in confidence and which consists of documents or of records other than documents'.[112] "Special procedure material" is defined by the Act as including, among other types of material, 'journalistic material, other than excluded material'.[113] For the purposes of the Act, material is only journalistic material if 'it in the possession of a person who acquired or created it for the purposes of journalism'.[114] A photographer's photo library could consist of both journalistic and non-journalistic material. Depending upon the type of photographic material being sought, a police constable who is investigating an indictable offence and reasonably believes that a photographer has images which would be of evidential value to his/her investigation could seek to obtain either a S.8 search warrant or a S.9 search warrant (as mentioned later) in order to get possession of such images. It is noted that S.15 and S.16 of the Act do provide some safeguards in respect of the issuance and execution of search warrants.[115]

Under S.9(1) of the Act, a police constable may seek to obtain access to special procedure material or excluded material, which includes journalistic material, for the purposes of a criminal investigation by applying to the court for a production/access order under, and in accordance, with the detailed provisions of Schedule 1 of the Act.[116] If a judge is satisfied that one of the two sets of access conditions specified in Schedule 1 has been fulfilled, he/she may grant the requested production/access order in accordance with paragraph 4 of Schedule 1 of the Act.[117] For a judge to grant such an order he/she must be satisfied that, among other specified requirements, 'there are reasonable grounds for believing that an indictable offence has been committed', that the material sought is 'likely to be of substantial value (whether by itself or together with other material) to the investigation in connection with which the application is made' and that the material 'is likely to be relevant evidence'.[118] Should a production/access order not be complied with, a court may issue a search warrant to the police.[119] Under S.19 of the Act, a police constable who is lawfully on any premises may seize anything found on the premises if he/she has reasonable grounds to believe that it is evidence relating to an offence or that it is necessary to seize it so as to prevent such evidence from 'being concealed, lost,

111 ibid s 8(1)
112 ibid s 11(1)(c)
113 ibid s 14(1)(b)
114 ibid s 13
115 ibid ss 15–16
116 ibid s 9(1)
117 ibid sch 1, para 1
118 ibid sch 1, para 2
119 ibid sch 1, para 12

altered or destroyed'.[120] A police constable's power of seizure extends to computerised information.[121] However, it does not extend to any item which the constable has reasonable grounds for believing is subject to legal privilege.[122] The police also has the power to retain anything seized under either S.19 or S.20[123] or Schedule 1[124] of the Act. However, nothing seized for use as evidence in a trial, for forensic examination or the investigation of an offence may be retained if a photograph or copy would suffice.[125] The police have been using the previously mentioned seizure and retention powers against photographers and television news film crews to obtain their still images and film footage, particularly of riots and other public order disturbances. A recent example is the case of *BSkyB & Others v Chelmsford Crown Court*,[126] which concerned a production order that the police had obtained from Chelmsford Crown Court in respect of television camera footage of Dale Farm in Essex from which a group of travellers had been evicted from an illegal encampment. In allowing the appeal in *BskyB*, Eady J stated that the production orders sought did not relate to any specific indictable offence and that police had sought the orders so as to engage in a fishing exercise to search for evidence of any possible offences that might have been committed.[127] Eady J also stated that 'There is a burden to be discharged and disclosure orders against the media, intrusive as they are, can never be granted as a formality'.[128]

In contrast to the decision in *BSkyB*, in a case involving freelance photographer Jason Parkinson, who was also a party to the *BskyB* case, Greater Manchester Police succeeded in getting a production order against him to obtain his video footage of a 2010 Unite Against Fascism (UAF) counter-protest to an English Defence League demonstration.[129] Parkinson stated that unlike the "Dale Farm" case, the Greater Manchester Police did eventually disclose a specific offence in respect of which his video footage was being sought as evidence (a perversion of the course of justice charge against a police officer). He also stated that due to the disclosure of this information by the police, he had to comply with the production order or else he would have faced a contempt of court charge.[130]

While the police has the power through PACE to seek to obtain journalists' and photographers' materials, it has similar powers under the Terrorism

120 ibid s 19(3)
121 ibid s 20
122 ibid s 19(6)
123 ibid s 22
124 ibid sch 1, para 13
125 ibid s 22(4)
126 *BSkyB & Others v Chelmsford Crown Court* [2012] EWHC 1295 (Admin)
127 ibid para 6
128 ibid para 31
129 Jason Parkinson, *Seven Months Just to Force the Police to Obey the Law* (14 May 2013) <www.jasonnparkinson.com/2013/05/14/seven-months-just-to-force-the-police-to-obey-the-law> accessed 08 June 2018
130 ibid

Act 2000, as amended. Under Schedule 5 of the Act, a police constable may apply to either a Circuit or a District judge for an access order in respect of either excluded material or special procedure material for the purposes of a terrorism investigation.[131] Such an application must refer to 'particular material or material of a particular description, which consists of or includes excluded material or special procedure material'.[132] However, for a judge of either court to grant such an order he/she must be satisfied:

(a) that the material to which the application relates consists of or includes excluded material or special procedure material,
(b) that it does not include items subject to legal privilege, and
(c) that the conditions in sub-paragraphs (2) and (3) are satisfied in respect of that material.[133]

The conditions to be satisfied, as referred to in (c) earlier, are that:

(a) the order is sought for the purposes of a terrorist investigation, and
(b) there are reasonable grounds for believing that the material is likely to be of substantial value, whether by itself or together with other material, to a terrorist investigation.[134]

Furthermore, in respect of the condition (b) earlier, there must be reasonable grounds for believing

> that it is in the public interest that the material should be produced or that access to it should be given having regard –
>
> (a) to the benefit likely to accrue to a terrorist investigation if the material is obtained, and
> (b) to the circumstances under which the person concerned has any of the material in his possession, custody or power.[135]

The 2012 Belfast Recorder's Court case of *BBC v PSNI*[136] concerned an application by the Police Service of Northern Ireland (PSNI) for a production order under Schedule 5, Paragraph 5 of the Terrorism Act 2000 to require the *BBC* to produce all of its journalistic material including broadcasted, non-broadcasted

131 Terrorism Act 2000, sch 5, part 1, s 5
Note: Under Sch 5, Part 1, S.4 of the Act the terms "excluded material" and "special procedure material" are given the same meaning as that respectively contained in S.11 and S.14 of PACE.
132 ibid s 5(2)
133 ibid s 6(1)
134 ibid s 6(2)
135 ibid s 6(3)
136 *BBC v PSNI* [2012] NICty 1

and unedited footage of an incident at Londonderry City Cemetery.[137] One could describe such a wide-sweeping application as a "fishing expedition". In *BBC*, Burgess J refused to grant the requested order as the evidence presented to the Court did not demonstrate that the required material would be of "substantial benefit" to the police investigation.[138] However, Burgess J also stated that had that condition been satisfied, he would have granted the requested order.[139]

In December 2012, *BBC* reported that McFarland J, the Recorder for Belfast, ordered photojournalists *Press Eye* and *Photopress* to hand over their images of the 12th July riots in Ardoyne, Belfast to the PSNI, but that footage taken by cameras for *BBC*, *UTV* and *Sky* would not have to be handed over. The latter had successfully argued that as their cameras were behind police lines and PSNI cameras during the riot, their photographs would not have offered anything of greater value than what was contained in the images photographed by the PSNI.[140] That point is actually debatable. However, as the photojournalists had been in front of the police lines, McFarland J held that they would have had an unobstructed view of the riot and their images could be of substantial value to the police investigation.[141] It would appear from the *BBC*'s report on the case that as no evidence of possible attacks on journalists as a result of their being perceived as evidence gatherers for the police had been presented to the court, McFarland J was not influenced by such an assertion.[142] However, attacks on press photographers in Northern Ireland are not unknown.[143]

In addition to the previously mentioned powers of the police under the Terrorism Act 2000, as amended, the Act also provides the police with other powers to either prevent photographers from actually taking photographs in public places and/or to seize photographs and camera equipment from photographers.[144] Sections 43, 44 and 45 of the Act have been used by the police to

137 ibid para 1
138 ibid para 18
139 ibid para 19
140 —— 'Press Photographers Must Hand Over Ardoyne Riot Pictures' (*BBC News*, 05 December 2012) <www.bbc.co.uk/news/uk-northern-ireland-20616107> accessed 08 June 2018
141 ibid
142 ibid
143 Note: See: —— 'Pipe Bomb Attack on Northern Ireland Photographer Mark Pearce's Home' *Belfast Telegraph* (Belfast, 14 December 2012) <www.belfasttelegraph.co.uk/news/northern-ireland/pipe-bomb-attack-on-northern-ireland-photographer-mark-pearces-home-29005170.html> accessed 09 June 2018
144 Note: Schedule 7 of the Terrorism Act 2000, as amended, grants an examining officer (a police constable, an immigration officer or a designated customs officer) at designated ports or within specified border areas the power to stop, detain and search a specified class of individuals. An examining officer also has the power to examine goods either given to him in accordance with the Schedule or as a result of a search and to seize goods. The question of whether the power of an examining officer to question a person under Sch. 7, Para. 2(1) of the Act was repugnant to Art. 10 of the Convention was one

stop and search people taking photographs in public places. Section 43 of the Act permits a constable to:

> stop and search a person whom he reasonably suspects to be a terrorist to discover whether he has in his possession anything which may constitute evidence that he is a terrorist.[145]

Section 43(4) of the Act also grants a constable seizure powers in respect of anything discovered during a search of a person under S.43(1) or S.43(2) of the Act which he/she reasonably suspects may constitute evidence that the person is a terrorist.[146] The Metropolitan Police's "*Photography Advice*" makes specific mention of police officers' powers under S.43 of the Act in respect of their interaction with photographers in public places. In particular, it states that members of the public do not require a permit to take photographs in public places and that police officers have no power to stop people taking photographs of incidents or members of the police in public places. It also states that under S.43 of the 2000 Act, police officers have the power to view digital images contained on a camera in the possession of a person, who has been stopped and searched under S.43. The *Advice* goes on to state that police officers do not have the power to delete digital images or destroy film at any point during a search. Furthermore, it states that a police officer does not have the power to stop members of the media from recording individuals who are distressed or bereaved if requested to do so by such individuals.[147] Such advice guidelines can be extremely useful. In Ireland, interactions of a confrontational and/or negative nature between members of An Garda Síochána and photographers do not occur often. So as to reduce the possibility of members of An Garda Síochána unlawfully attempting to prevent photographers from taking photographs in public places, it would be beneficial if it were to publish a "photography advice" guideline for its members. Any such guideline should also be made available to members of the public.

---

of the central issues in the 2014 judicial review case of *David Miranda v The Secretary of State for the Home Department and The Commissioner of the Police of the Metropolis* [2014] EWHC 255 (Admin). In *Miranda*, Laws LJ held that Sch.7 of the Act did not breach Art. 10. In the Court of Appeal case of *David Miranda v The Secretary of State for the Home Department and The Commissioner of the Police of the Metropolis* [2016] EWCA Civ 6, the Master of the Rolls held, at para 118, that the exercise of the stop power granted under Sch. 7, Para. 2(1) of the Act as exercised against the appellant was lawful. However, he also held that the power to stop an individual was incompatible with Art. 10 in relation to journalistic material, because it was not subject to safeguards against its arbitrary use.

145 Terrorism Act 2000, s 43(1)

146 ibid s 43(4)

147 Metropolitan Police, *Photography Advice* <www.met.police.uk/advice/advice-and-information/ph/photography-advice/> accessed 9 June 2018

Section 44 of the Act, now repealed, dealt with the authorisation element of stop and searches. It did not require a police officer to hold a "reasonable suspicion" prior to stopping and searching someone.[148] In the 2010 ECtHR case of *Gillan and Quinton v United Kingdom*,[149] the Court held that S.44 of the Act was in breach of the applicant's right to a private life under Article 8. Following *Gillan*, the stop and search powers under Sections 44–47(1) of the Act were repealed by S.2 of The Terrorism Act 2000 (Remedial Order 2011).[150] Section 3 of the Remedial Order inserted a new S.47A in the 2000 Act dealing with the authorisation element of stop and searches in specified areas or places and it includes a requirement for a "reasonable suspicion" to be held.[151] Subsequently, the Protection of Freedoms Act 2012 repealed S.44–S.47 of the 2000 Act[152] and new powers to stop and search were inserted in the 2000 Act by the 2012 Act.[153] Section 58 of The Terrorism Act 2000 deals with the collection and recording of information which could be used for terrorist purposes and it includes "photographic record" under its definition of "recording".[154] Section 39 of the Counter-Terrorism Act 2008[155] amended S.58 of the 2000 Act. Also, S.76 of the 2008 Act inserted a new S.58(A) in the Act concerning information relating to members of the armed forces, the intelligence services and the police and it states:

> A person commits an offence who (a) elicits or attempts to elicit information about an individual who is or has been (i) a member of Her Majesty's forces, (ii) a member of any of the intelligence services, or (iii) a constable, which is of a kind likely to be useful to a person committing or preparing an act of terrorism, or (b) publishes or communicates any such information.[156]

Section 58(A) is extremely broad in its scope and it could have major implications for photographers, particularly press photographers and publishers who wish to photograph and/or publish images of police constables or members of the armed forces lawfully undertaking their duties in public places.[157] However,

148 Terrorism Act 2000, s 44
149 *Gillan and Quinton v United Kingdom* (2010) 50 EHRR 45, para 87
150 The Terrorism Act 2000 (Remedial Order 2011), SI 2011/631, s 2
151 ibid s 3
152 Protection of Freedoms Act 2012, s 59
153 ibid ss 60–61
154 Terrorism Act 2000, s 58(A)
155 Counter-Terrorism Act 2008, s 76(1)
156 Terrorism Act 2000, s 58(A)
157 Note: See: Richard Alleyne, 'Police Apologise For Gay Jibe Against Photographer: A Schoolboy Photographer Has Been Paid Thousands of Pounds in Compensation by the Police After they Wrongfully Arrested Him Claiming He Was "Running Around Being Stupid and Gay"' *The Telegraph* (London, 12 December 2011) <www.telegraph.co.uk/news/8951188/Police-apologise-for-gay-jibe-against-photographer.html> accessed 09 June 2018

under S.58(A)(2) of the 2000 Act, it is a defence for persons charged with an offence under this section to prove that they had a reasonable excuse for their action.[158] Photographers could avail of this defence.

5.3) Restrictions resulting from the individual's right to a fair trial

The right to a fair trial is guaranteed by both the Constitution of Ireland and the European Convention. Article 34.1 of the Constitution provides for public or open justice:

> Justice shall be administered in courts established by law by judges appointed in the manner provided by this Constitution, and, save in such special and limited cases as may be prescribed by law, shall be administered in public.[159]

The norm, therefore, is that both the public and the media, as the "eyes and ears" of the public, will be admitted to court and the media will be entitled to accurately report on proceedings on behalf of the public. In relation to the trial of people charged with criminal offences, Article 38.1 of the Constitution states: 'No person shall be tried on any criminal charge save in due course of law.'[160] In addition, Art. 6(1) of the ECHR states:

> In the determination of his civil rights and obligations or of any criminal charge against him, everyone is entitled to a fair and public hearing within a reasonable time by an independent and impartial tribunal established by law.[161]

The guarantee of justice in public under Art. 34.1 of the Constitution is not absolute and it may be restricted. The inclusion of the words "special and limited cases" in Art. 34.1 in relation to the administration of justice provides the basis under which members of the media and/or the public may be excluded from court proceedings and/or court reporting restrictions may be imposed. Such exclusions and restrictions may be imposed, in accordance with prescribed laws, in order to safeguard the administration of justice, to protect the right to a fair trial and to ensure that the presumption of innocence is respected and maintained during a trial. They may also be imposed for a variety of other reasons, such as in family law cases. The issue of balancing the right to a fair trial with the competing right of freedom of expression and particularly the right of the

158 ibid s 58(A)(2)
159 Constitution of Ireland (*Art. 34.1*) (on The Courts)
160 ibid (*Art. 38.1*) (on Trial of Offences)
161 European Convention on Human Rights Act 2003, sch 1, art 6(1)

press to report on court proceedings has featured in a number of court cases. The 1994 Irish Supreme Court case of *D v Director of Public Prosecutions*[162] concerned an applicant who had been tried twice on a charge of indecent assault and in both instances the jury had been discharged and a retrial ordered. The second trial had been halted due to prejudicial reporting of it. Subsequent to the discharge of the jury in that trial, the *Sunday Tribune* published an article which included an interview with the complainant. Neither the complainant nor the applicant was named in the article, which included a rear-view drawing or photograph of a young girl with a child in her arms.[163] The applicant obtained a High Court order prohibiting another retrial and that order was appealed.[164] While the appeal was allowed, Finlay J, in dissention, raised the important test, which is for the applicant to prove, of whether the published article and the accompanying drawing/photograph would influence a jury member's opinion of the accused's guilt or innocence and thus create a "real and substantial risk" of an unfair trial resulting from such an external influence.[165] In dealing with the hierarchy of constitutional rights relevant to this case, Denham J, who upheld the appeal, stated that the right to a fair trial was superior to the right to prosecute.[166]

The "real and substantial risk" test elaborated in *D* was applied shortly after in the High Court case of *Magee v O'Dea*,[167] in which the plaintiff was the subject of an extradition warrant to the United Kingdom in relation to the murder of a British army sergeant. The plaintiff claimed that he would not receive a fair trial in the United Kingdom due to previously published newspaper articles, which included sensational headlines, photographs of the plaintiff and the articles identified him as the murderer. In allowing the plaintiff's appeal, Flood J balanced the weight to be given to the various factors that pointed towards the "probability of a serious risk of an unfair trial" with the "fade factor" in the mind of individuals who may have seen the newspapers' articles and who may be potential jurors in the proposed trial of the applicant in England.[168]

The test in *D* was subsequently developed into a two-stage test by Denham J in the 1998 Irish Supreme Court case of *The Irish Times Ltd. v Ireland*[169] concerning a ban on media reporting of a major drugs trial. In *The Irish Times*,

162 *D v Director of Public Prosecutions* [1994] 2 IR 465
163 ibid 465 and 469
164 ibid 465
165 ibid 474
166 ibid
Note: In the more recent 2017 Irish Supreme Court case of *Sunday Newspapers Limited and Others V Gilchrist and Rogers* O'Donnell J stated, at para 36, that the Constitution does not rank the rights and obligations which it provides.
167 *Magee v O'Dea* [1994] 1 IR 500
168 ibid 513
169 *The Irish Times Ltd. v Ireland* [1998] 1 IR 359

Denham J stated that if a trial judge determines that by holding a trial in public there would be a real risk that an accused would not receive a fair trial, then the trial judge should determine whether such a risk may be prevented by making an appropriate ruling, such as a reporting restriction.[170] That two stage test was, in turn, further developed by Clarke J in the 2006 High Court case of *Independent Newspapers and Others v Anderson and Condell*[171] in which the doctrine of proportionality was added to the test.

The competing right of freedom of expression and the right to fair court procedures have been considered by the ECtHR. For example, *Egeland and Hanseid v Norway*[172] resulted from the conviction of two Norwegian journalists following the publication of a photograph, in contravention of Norwegian law, of a convicted triple murderer leaving a court building in a distraught state.[173] The Court held that as there was an absence of a European consensus on the prohibition of photography at court buildings and the publication of such photographs states should be granted a wide margin of appreciation.[174] The Court ranked the need to protect the convicted prisoner's privacy rights with equal status to the state's duty to safeguard due process. The Court went on to hold that the interest in restricting publication outweighed the need to inform the public of an issue of public concern.[175]

5.4) Restrictions on court reporting

Article 34.1 of the Constitution of Ireland states: 'Justice shall be administered in courts established by law by judges appointed in the manner provided by this Constitution, and, save in such special and limited cases as may be prescribed by law, shall be administered in public.'[176] In accordance with Article 34.1, statute law gives the courts the powers in certain circumstances to hold court proceedings *in camera* whereby members of the public, including the media in some instances,[177] may be excluded from the proceedings and to issue publication prohibition orders in relation to such cases. A number of statutes give courts the power to clear members of the public from a courtroom during particular parts of a court case and to issue orders

170 ibid 399–400
171 *Independent Newspapers and Others v Anderson and Condell* [2006] IEHC 62, para 7.9
172 *Egeland and Hanseid v Norway* (2010) 50 EHRR 2
173 ibid para 19
174 ibid paras 54–55
Note: While it is not an offence in Ireland to photograph a party to a court proceeding within the precincts of a court building and to publish such a photograph, in England both activities constitute an offence under Section 41 of the Criminal Justice Act 1925, as amended.
175 ibid para 63
176 Constitution of Ireland (*Art. 34.1*) (On The Courts)
177 Note: For example, see: *Sunday Newspapers Limited and Others V Gilchrist and Rogers* [2017] IESC 18

which either restrict or prohibit the reporting of court proceedings. Other statutes make court reporting prohibition orders mandatory in respect of certain matters. On the previously mentioned constitutional requirement that justice be administered in public, Denham J stated in the 1998 Irish Supreme Court case of *The Irish Times Ltd. v Ireland*[178] that as it is not realistic for all people to attend all court proceedings, they are informed of such proceedings through the press. Any restriction on the reporting of court proceedings by the press must be viewed as a restriction on the public's right of access to the administration of justice.[179] In the 2015 English High Court Family Law Division case of *Ekaterina Fields v Richard Fields*,[180] Holman J made an interesting pragmatic comment on the restricting by the courts of what accredited journalists may report in respect of court proceedings. In *Fields* he stated:

> To permit the presence of accredited journalists, but then tightly to restrict what they can report, creates a mere illusion of transparency.[181]

The Courts (Supplemental Provisions) Act 1961, as amended, sets out a number of areas where cases could be heard in private, either because of the urgency or sensitivities involved. Section 45(1) of the Act states:

> Justice may be administered otherwise than in public in any of the following cases:
>
> (a) applications of an urgent nature for relief by way of habeas corpus, bail, prohibition or injunction;
> (b) matrimonial causes and matters;
> (c) lunacy and minor matters;
> (d) proceedings involving the disclosure of a secret manufacturing process;[182]

The previously mentioned types of cases are in addition to any others prescribed by Acts of the Oireachtas.[183]

Section 45 of the 1961 Act, in so far as it relates to matrimonial causes and matters and minor matters, was amended by the Civil Liability and Courts Act 2004.[184] This was the first relaxation of the "in camera" rule relating to such

178 *The Irish Times Ltd. v Ireland* [1998] 1 IR 359
179 ibid 398
180 *Ekaterina Fields v Richard Fields* [2015] EWHC 1670 (Fam)
181 ibid para 3
182 Courts (Supplemental Provisions) Act 1961, s 45(1)
183 ibid s 45(2)
184 Civil Liability and Courts Act 2004, s 40(2)
Note: Section 40(2) of the Civil Liability and Courts Act 2004 was repealed by S.2 of the Courts and Civil Law (Miscellaneous Provisions) Act 2013.

proceedings. In amending S.40 of the 2004 Act, the Courts and Civil Law (Miscellaneous Provisions) Act 2013 relaxed the *in camera* rule in respect of family law and childcare proceedings so as to permit the presence of accredited members of the press at such proceedings, but with provisions to maintain the existing anonymity restrictions in respect of such court proceedings.[185] Attendance by bona fide representatives of the press at court proceedings in accordance with S.3A(a) of the 2013 Act is not an absolute right and it may be restricted or prohibited by a court.[186] In deciding whether or not to make such a restriction order, a court must take into consideration a range of issues, duties and needs, mainly concerned with protecting the parties and particularly children, as specified in S.3(A)(c) and S.3(A)(d) of the Act. In relation to the reporting of such court proceedings, S.6 of the 2013 Act inserted a new S.40A in the 2004 Act, which is applicable to everybody and not just to members of the media. It makes it an offence for any person or corporate body to publish or broadcast any information which is likely to result in members of the public being able to identify the parties to proceedings to which a relevant enactment relates or any child to whom those proceedings relate.[187] In such cases where the identity of the parties is to be protected, photographs may not be published. As held by Birmingham J in the case stated to the Irish High Court in 2012 *Health Service Executive v L.N. and Others*,[188] an intention to breach the in-camera rule is not a prerequisite for a finding by a court of a breach of the rule.

Considering in turn the issues specified in S.45(1) of the 1961 Act, as amended, the urgency of habeas corpus applications to challenge the legality of holding a person in depravation of his/her liberty is clear. In respect of applications for bail, the Bail Act 1997, as amended, allows for the holding of bail applications otherwise than in public. Under Section 4 of the Act, bona fide representatives of the press may attend and report on the proceedings. An offence is committed if any published report of such proceedings includes any evidence of a criminal record of any person applying for bail.[189] Injunction applications, for example to prevent an imminent publication, may also be made to the courts at short notice. The easing of reporting restrictions in respect of family law cases as introduced through the Courts and Civil Law (Miscellaneous Provisions) Act 2013, while maintaining anonymity restrictions, permits the public to gain an insight to such proceedings.

185 Courts and Civil Law (Miscellaneous Provisions) Act 2013, s 5
Note: Section 5 of the Act was commenced on 10 January 2014 by the Courts and Civil Law 2013 (Sections 3 to 12) (Commencement) Order 2014, SI 2014/5

186 Civil Liability and Courts Act 2004, s 3(A)(b) as inserted by Section 5 of the Courts and Civil Law (Miscellaneous Provisions) Act 2013

187 Courts and Civil Law (Miscellaneous Provisions) Act 2013, s 6

188 *Health Service Executive v L.N. and Others* [2012] IEHC 611, para 41

189 Bail Act 1997, s 4

The grouped heading "Lunacy and Minors" in the Courts (Supplemental Provisions) Act 1961 is, to say the least, unfortunate. It possibly resulted from the reference in the Act to the Lunacy Regulation (Ireland) Act 1871, which in turn makes reference to 'the solicitor for lunatics and minors'.[190] While S.9(4)(a) of the 1961 Act did make provision for the President of the High Court or such other Judge of the High Court as may be assigned by him under S.9 of the Act to substitute the expression "ward of court" or another similar expression for the word "lunatic",[191] one would have to wonder why the Oireachtas did not do so itself when it was debating and approving the Bill that became the 1961 Act. Under Order 67 of the Rules of the Superior Courts, any court hearing instituted under the Lunacy Regulation (Ireland) Act 1871 is to be held *in camera*.[192] The Mental Health Act 2001, as amended, provides a patient with the right to appeal to the Circuit Court against a decision of a tribunal affirming an order made in relation to him on the grounds that he does suffer from a mental disorder. Section 19(8) of the Act specifies the classes of people which the Court may permit to be present or exclude from such a hearing[193] and the Act prohibits the publication of any matter likely to lead members of the public to identify such a patient.[194]

Notwithstanding the previously mentioned, legislative provisions concerning the attendance of bona fide members of the press at, and their reporting on, court proceedings concerning the welfare of children under the Courts and Civil Law (Miscellaneous Provisions) Act 2013, there are separate legislative provisions that apply to family law and child law civil cases as well as criminal proceedings either against a child or in which a child is a witness. For example, where an application is made to a court for a declaration of parentage under S.35 of the Status of Children Act 1987, as amended, the court may, under S.36 of the Act, direct that the whole or part of such an application is to be heard otherwise than in public.[195] The Children Act 2001, as amended, defines a "child" as a person under 18 years of age.[196] Section 252 of the Act provides for the anonymity of a child who is either the subject of court proceedings or

190 Lunacy Regulation (Ireland) Act 1871, s 2
191 Courts (Supplemental Provisions) Act 1961, s 9(4)(a)
192 RSC Ord 67, r 38(3)
193 Mental Health Act 2001, ss 19(1) and 19(8)
194 ibid s 19(9)
195 Status of Children Act 1987, s 36(4)
Note (1): In the 2013 Irish High Court case of *M.R. & Anor v An tÁrd Chláraitheoir & Ors* [2013] IEHC 91, following an application by three newspapers, Abbott J, at paras 120–122, lifted a blanket reporting restriction on the proceedings. However, in doing so he imposed explicit reporting restrictions on the newspapers including a prohibition on contemporaneous social media reporting.
Note (2): *M.R. and Anor* was decided prior to the commencement of the Courts and Civil Law (Miscellaneous Provisions) Act 2013.
196 Children Act 2001, s 3(1)

a witness in such proceedings.[197] However, a court may dispense with such a requirement if it is satisfied to do so in the interests of the child. If a court makes such a decision, it must give its reason for doing so in an open court.[198] Section 139 of the Criminal Justice Act 2006 amended the 2001 Act by substituting the existing S.93 in the 2001 Act with a new S.93. This new S.93 deals with proceedings before a court concerning a child and it prohibits the publication of specified types of material, including photographs, which might result in the identification of such a child.[199] In specified instances, such as to avoid injustice to a child, a court may dispense with such a restriction. If it does so, it must explain in open court its reasons for making that decision.[200] The 2001 Act specifies the classes of people (includes bona fide representatives of the press) that are permitted to attend court proceedings held under it.[201] Any decision or order made by the Court in such proceedings is to be announced in public.[202] Where a child is a witness in proceedings for an offence, a court may exclude all persons except those classes of people specified in the Act, which includes bona fide representatives of the Press.[203]

Aside from the previously mentioned statutory provisions, many other statutes, particularly those concerning criminal offences and specifically certain sexual offences,[204] contain provisions which may result in either the restricting or

197 ibid s 252(1)
198 ibid s 252(2) and s 252(3)
199 Children Act 2001, s 93 as inserted by Criminal Justice Act 2006, s 139
200 ibid
201 Children Act 2001, s94(1)
202 ibid s 94(2)
203 ibid s 257(1)
204 Note (1): The Criminal Law (Rape) (Amendment) Act 1990 amended the Criminal Law (Rape) Act 1981. Sections 6, 7 and 8 of the 1981 Act respectively deal with the exclusion of the public from court proceedings under the Act, the anonymity of a complainant of a "sexual assault offence" and the pre-conviction anonymity of a person accused of a "rape offence". Section 17(2)(c) of the 1990 Act substituted the words "sexual assault offence" for "rape offence" in S.7(1) of the 1981 Act. This amendment was not made to S.8 of the 1981 Act. The definition of a "sexual assault offence" under S.12 of the 1990 Act includes a "rape offence" and also a range of specified sexual assault offences. Consequently a person accused of a sexual assault offence does not have a right to pre-conviction anonymity.
Note (2): Section 30 of the Criminal Law (Sexual Offences) Act 2017 (on the anonymity of a person charged under the Punishment of Incest Act 1908 and of a person to whom the offence relates).
Note (3): Criminal Law (Sexual Offences) Act 2006, as amended, S.6 (on the application of S.7 and S.8 of the Act of 1981 to the offence of defilement under the 2006 Act).
Note (4): In the United Kingdom, the right of pre-conviction anonymity of a person accused of a rape offence was removed by S.158(5) of the Criminal Justice Act 1988.
Note (5): See: Conor Gallagher, 'Untangling the Vexed Question of Anonymity in Sex Cases' *The Irish Times* (Dublin, 03 March 2014) <www.irishtimes.com/news/crime-and-law/untangling-the-vexed-question-of-anonymity-in-sex-cases-1.1708235> accessed 23 June 2018

prohibiting of court reporting. Some statutes, such as the Official Secrets Act 1963, provide for part(s) of a hearing to be held in camera on the ground that the publication of any evidence or statement to be given or made during any part of the hearing would be prejudicial, in this instance to the safety or preservation of the state.[205] Court proceedings under the Proceeds of Crime Act 1996, as amended,[206] may be held otherwise than in public.[207] Also, the court may impose reporting restrictions in relation to specified information relating to such court cases.[208] The Refugee Act 1996 provides for the protection of the identity of an asylum applicant and no matter likely to lead to the applicant's identity may be published without the consent of the applicant and the Minister.[209] To do so is an offence.[210] Section 11 of the Criminal Law (Human Trafficking) Act 2008, as amended, deals with the anonymity of victims of human trafficking and it specifically makes it an offence to publish a photograph of an alleged victim.[211] Section 11(5) of the Act states that "publishes" means publishing to any person and the Internet is specified as a means of publication.[212] When hearing a retrial application,[213] a court may order the exclusion of members of the public or any person other than bona fide representatives of the press from the court, if it deems it necessary in the interests of justice.[214] It may also prohibit the publication or broadcasting of any matter which is likely to identify the person, who is the subject of the retrial application or anybody else connected with the retrial for which such an application order is being sought.[215] Under Section 212 of the Companies Act 2014, as amended, which concerns

Note (6): See: Jimmy Woulfe, 'Man Cleared of Sex Assault: Anonymity Should be a Right' *Irish Examiner* (Cork, 03 May 2013) <www.irishexaminer.com/ireland/man-cleared-of-sex-assault-anonymity-should-be-a-right-230214.html> accessed 23 June 2018

205 Official Secrets Act 1963, s 12
Note: Through the use of the word "shall" in S.12 of the Act, it would appear that a court would not have any discretion over the making or not of an *in-camera* order. However, under Section 12 of the Act, the verdict and sentence (if any) in such an *in-camera* court case shall be announced in public.

206 Note: Section 8 of the Proceeds of Crime Act 1996 was amended by S.9 of the Proceeds of Crime (Amendment) Act 2005.

207 Proceeds of Crime Act 1996, s 8(3)

208 ibid s 8(4)

209 Refugee Act 1996, s 19(2)

210 ibid s 19(3)

211 Criminal Law (Human Trafficking) Act 2008, s 11(1)

212 ibid s 11(5)

213 Note: Sections 8 and 9 of the Criminal Procedure Act 2010 respectively concern applications by the Director of Public Prosecutions for a retrial order where new and compelling evidence becomes available and where a previous acquittal was tainted.

214 Criminal Procedure Act 2010, s 12(2)

215 ibid s 12(3)

"protection for minorities", a court may order that proceedings held under S.212 are to be held in camera.[216]

In civil cases involving a person with a medical condition, a court may make a publication prohibition order under the Civil Law (Miscellaneous Provisions) Act 2008.[217] While an application for such a court order may be brought at any stage during court proceedings,[218] S.27(3) of the Act specifies the conditions (including the likelihood of the applicant being subject to undue stress as a result of his/her identification) that the court must be satisfied exist for it to make such an order.[219]

5.5) Court reporting and contempt of court

Although there is no statutory prohibition on the use of photographic or sound recording equipment to record court proceedings in Ireland, in effect such activity is not permitted. The Rules of Court deal with the topic of the recording of court proceedings in the superior, circuit and district courts. Under Rule 8 of Order 123, as amended, of the Rules of the Superior Courts, unless permitted by the Court, no person except the Courts Service or a person authorised by it may make a recording of a court proceeding other than by a written or shorthand note.[220] Rule 7 of Order 67A of the Circuit Court Rules contains a similarly worded prohibition.[221] Section 2 of the District Court (Recording of Proceedings) Rules 2013[222] amended the District Court Rules 1997[223] by inserting a new Order 12B in the 1997 Rules.[224] Rule 4 of Order 12B contains a similarly worded provision to that of the previously mentioned Rule 7 of Order 67A of the Circuit Court Rules.[225] The unapproved recording of court proceedings occurs infrequently.[226] Unlike in Ireland where there is no statutory prohibition on the taking and/or publication of photographs of court

216 Companies Act 2014, s 212(9)
Note (1): Section 212 of the Act on "Protection for minorities" concerns the protection of the interests of a member of a company.
Note (2): Sections 556, 788(9), 789(7) and 795(7) of the Act also contain provisions for the hearing of court proceedings otherwise than in public. It is noted that the Act uses both of the terms "otherwise than in public" and "*in camera*".

217 Civil Law (Miscellaneous Provisions) Act 2008, s27(1)

218 ibid s 27(2)

219 ibid s 27(3)

220 RSC Ord 123, r 8

221 RCC Ord 67A, r 7

222 District Court (Recording of Proceedings) Rules 2013, SI 2013/99, s 2

223 District Court Rules 1997, SI 1997/93

224 RDC Ord 12B, r 2

225 ibid r 4

226 Note: For example, see: (1) Gerry Hand, 'Murdered Man's Brother Jailed for Contempt of Court' *Irish Examiner* (Cork, 20 July 2015) <www.irishexaminer.com/ireland/murdered-mans brother-jailed-for-contempt-of-court-343423.html> accessed 10 June 2018

proceedings or parties to court proceedings either within or while entering or leaving a court building or its precincts, to do such in either England or Wales is an offence under the Criminal Justice Act 1925, as amended.[227] The Crime and Courts Act 2013, as amended, permits the Lord Chancellor to make an order to permit the filming and broadcasting of specified court proceedings below the level of the Supreme Court.[228] The provisions of the Court of Appeal (Recording and Broadcasting) Order 2013 specify the types of Court of Appeal proceedings which may be filmed and broadcast to the public and the conditions under which approved filming and broadcasting may be undertaken.[229] Rather than the current situation in Ireland of not having a statutory provision, which either permits or prohibits the taking of photographs in a court, but, in effect, having such a prohibition in place as a consequence of the courts' non-granting of permission to take photographs in the courts through their powers under the Rules of Court, it would be preferable that this issue would be put on a statutory footing. One would have to question, however, the actual benefit to be derived from legislating for the permitting of the taking of still photographs during court cases and their subsequent publication and their potential disruption of, and impact on, the fair administration of justice, the court cases themselves and the parties, witnesses, jurors and others involved in court cases. The photographing and/or publication of photographs of parties to court cases, their relatives and/or witnesses while they are either entering or leaving a court building is a related, but different, issue and is a common daily occurrence. Such practice is sometimes criticised by the courts.[230] The impact of this activity by press photographers on the individuals being photographed will vary from one person to another. The primary issue here is the need to balance the competing right of press photographers to exercise their right to create and publish photographs of any parties to, or witnesses in, court proceedings, who are not the subject of statutory or court-imposed identification reporting restrictions or prohibitions, with the individual's right to not feel unduly harassed or stressed

(2) Gordan Deegan, 'Man in Custody After Filming His Uncle in Witness Box: Two Men Involved in Court Incident Had Been Previously of 2010 Manslaughter' *The Irish Times* (Dublin, 25 October 2018) <www.irishtimes.com/news/crime-and-law/courts/district-court/man-in-custody-after-filming-his-uncle-in-witness-box-1.2842778> accessed 15 June 2018

(3) Gordan Deegan, 'Suspended Sentence for "Snapchat" Photo of Judge: Eoin McDonnell Took Picture of Judge Fiona Lydon at Ennis District Court' *The Irish Times* (Dublin, 28 March 2018) <www.irishtimes.com/news/crime-and-law/courts/district-court/suspended-sentence-for-snapchat-photo-of-judge-1.3443351> accessed 15 June 2018

227 Criminal Justice Act 1925, s 41

228 Crime and Courts Act 2013, s 32

229 The Court of Appeal (Recording and Broadcasting) Order 2013, SI 2013/2786
Note: See also The Crown Court (Recording) Order 2016, SI 2016/612

230 Note: For example, see: —— 'Lillis Sentenced for Cawley Manslaughter' (*RTÉ News*, 8 February 2010) <www.rte.ie/news/2010/0205/127249-cawleyc/> accessed 10 June 2018

by photographers while they walk in a public thoroughfare to or from a court building. It would be appropriate if "rules of engagement" relating to the photographing of such individuals were to be statutorily specified. The onus for marshalling the behaviour of photographers outside courts cannot be left to media outlets, as many published court photographs are, or may be, obtained from non-staff photographers and/or are published on online news sites, which are not subject to press ethical codes of practice. In respect of the photographing of defendants in criminal cases entering or leaving court buildings, there should be a statutory prohibition on the publication of such images which show them wearing handcuffs. Such images have the potential to influence a viewer's opinion that a handcuffed defendant featured in a published photograph is a dangerous individual and/or guilty of a serious criminal offence, when such may not be the case. Such a defendant could end up being acquitted of any charges against him, yet the published image would remain in existence in either printed publication archives, on the Internet or both.

The media's reporting of court cases and the publication of articles on individuals and other matters either directly associated or not with court cases can result in organs of the media being held in contempt of court. Occasionally, where media outlets have been held to be in contempt of court, the publication of photographs has been a central issue. Unlike the United Kingdom, which has a Contempt of Court statute,[231] Ireland currently does not. The Contempt of Court Bill 2017[232] provides for both criminal and civil contempt of court. The Bill defines criminal contempt as 'behaviour calculated to prejudice the due course of justice' and it includes, among other matters, 'contempt in the face of the court, scandalising the court, words written or spoken or acts calculated to prejudice the due course of justice'.[233] Civil contempt is defined as 'a disobedience to an order of the court by a party to the proceedings, whether by actions or failures to act'.[234] The Bill provides that the use of recording equipment (audio or visual) to record court proceedings and/or the publication of such a recording without the permission of a court would constitute a contempt of court.[235] A publication would amount to a contempt of court if it creates a substantial risk of prejudicing the fairness of court proceedings.[236] The Bill makes specific mention of the matter of revealing sources of information upon which

231 Contempt of Court Act 1981

232 Contempt of Court Bill 2017 <https://data.oireachtas.ie/ie/oireachtas/bill/2017/117/eng/initiated/b11717d.pdf> accessed 11 June 2018

233 ibid s 2

Note: See also: *Director of Public Prosecutions v Independent News and Media Plc and Others* [2017] IECA 333 – Edwards J, at para 22, on the meaning at common law of the word "calculated" in respect of the publication of material and the risk of an unfair trial.

234 ibid s 3

235 ibid s 4

236 ibid s 5

a publication is based and it provides that a refusal to reveal such sources shall not constitute a contempt of court unless 'disclosure is necessary in the interests of justice or national security or for the prevention of crime'. It would be for the presiding judge in each case to determine whether such a disclosure is necessary.[237] Under S.6 of the Bill, a court would have the power to order, in specified circumstances, the removal of information published on the Internet relating to court proceedings.[238] In addition to active court proceedings, the Bill also covers pending and imminent proceedings and it states that civil proceedings would be imminent once a trial date has been set,[239] while criminal proceedings

> which are before the District Court but which may be tried on indictment shall be considered to be imminently before the Circuit Court until such point as the District Court accepts jurisdiction, and the defendant elects for summary disposal, if applicable.[240]

The Bill provides a defence of innocent publication or distribution.[241] It also provides that the publication in good faith of a fair and accurate contemporaneous report of a court proceeding held in public shall not constitute a contempt of court.[242]

Under the United Kingdom's Contempt of Court Act 1981, as amended, 'conduct may be treated as a contempt of court as tending to interfere with the course of justice in particular legal proceedings regardless of the intent to do so'.[243] This strict liability rule applies to publications, which include 'any speech, writing, programme included in a cable programme service or other communication in whatever form, which is addressed to the public at large or any section of the public'.[244] However, it only applies to a publication which 'creates a substantial risk that the course of justice in the proceedings in question will be seriously impeded or prejudiced.'[245] Also, such strict liability applies to publications 'only if the proceedings in question are active within the meaning of the section at the time of the publication'.[246] Schedule 1 of the Act specifies

237 ibid
238 ibid s 6
239 ibid s 5(7)
240 ibid s 5(8)
Note: In the 2003 Irish High Court case of *Director of Public Prosecutions v Independent Newspapers and Others* [2003] 2 IR 367, Kelly J (at 394–385) refused to extend the law on contempt of court to include publications relating to "imminent" court proceedings.
241 ibid s 7
242 ibid s 9
243 Contempt of Court Act 1981, s 1
244 ibid s 2(1)
245 ibid s 2(2)
246 ibid s 2(3)

the times at which proceedings become active and at which they cease to be active.[247] The Act does offer a defence of innocent publication or distribution to a charge of contempt of court; however, the burden of proof lies on a person seeking to use such a defence.[248] One is not guilty of contempt of court under the previously mentioned strict liability rule in respect of 'a fair and accurate report of legal proceedings held in public, published contemporaneously and in good faith'.[249] Where a court believes that the reporting of contemporaneous or of pending or imminent proceedings may prejudice the administration of justice, it may order 'that the publication of any report of the proceedings, or any part of the proceedings, be postponed for such period as the court thinks necessary for that purpose'.[250] Although the Act stipulates the commencement and concluding points of active proceedings,[251] it offers neither a definition of nor timeline parameters in respect of what it refers to as "pending" and "imminent" proceedings. Also, under S.11 of the Act, a court may prohibit the publication of matters, which it has exempted from disclosure to the public during court proceedings.[252]

At present, two types of contempt of court exist in Ireland – civil contempt and criminal contempt. In the Irish 1973 Supreme Court case of *Keegan v De Búrca*,[253] Ó Dálaigh CJ stated that civil contempt relates to a disobedience of a court order and its purpose is to compel a party to comply with a court order. On criminal contempt, Ó Dálaigh stated that it was a common law misdemeanour and that its objective was to punish the offender.[254] Unless they breach a court order, criminal contempt rather than civil contempt is the form of contempt of greater relevance to members of the media. In the 1981 Irish Supreme Court case of *The State (DPP) v Walsh and Conneely*,[255] O'Higgins CJ classified criminal contempt into three categories, namely: *Contempt in the Face of the Court* (obstructive conduct or conduct prejudicial to the course of justice committing during a court proceeding), *Constructive Contempt* (a contempt committed outside of a court where a pending proceeding may be interfered with or prejudiced by something that is said or done by somebody) and *Scandalising the Court* (an allegation, without foundation, of corruption or malpractice on the part of a court, which has the potential to erode public confidence in the court and consequently interfere with the administration of justice).[256] The distinction between civil and criminal contempt of court is not as rigid nowadays

247 ibid sch 1
248 ibid s 3
249 ibid s 4(1)
250 ibid ss 4(2) and 4(3)
251 ibid sch 1
252 ibid s 11
253 *Keegan v de Búrca* [1973] 1 IR 223
254 ibid 227
255 *The State (DPP) v Walsh and Conneely* [1981] 1 IR 412
256 ibid 421

as it was historically and it is becoming blurred. This development was central to the 2014 Irish Supreme Court case of *Laois County Council v Hanrahan*.[257] In *Hanrahan*, Fennelly J outlined the court's rationale for, and approach to, civil contempt and he also highlighted the High Court's blurring of the distinction between civil and criminal contempt of court.[258]

5.5.1) Journalists and contempt in the face of the court

In contrast to the legal position in Ireland, in the United Kingdom journalists including press photographers, have a qualified statutory right to refuse to disclose their sources of information to a court. Except in specified instances, such a refusal is not a contempt of court.[259] In Ireland, journalists have been held in contempt in the face of the court by refusing to answer questions during proceedings regarding their sources of information. For example, in the Irish Supreme Court case of *Keegan v De Búrca*,[260] the Court held that the defendant had been in criminal contempt in the face of the court by refusing to answer a judge's question during a civil action.[261] While journalists have claimed to have a privilege over their sources, the courts have been slow to recognise its existence. Following the 1996 ECtHR case of *Goodwin v United Kingdom*,[262] in which the Court recognised the protection of journalistic sources as one of the basic requirements for freedom of the press,[263] the Irish courts have recognised the existence of such a privilege. However, neither the Irish courts nor the ECtHR recognise it as being an absolute privilege. The ECtHR's decision in *Goodwin* was reiterated and accepted by Fennelly J in the 2009 Irish Supreme Court case of *Mahon v Keena*.[264] While allowing the appellants' claim of confidentiality of journalistic sources, Fennelly J stated that only an overriding public interest requirement could justify a court to compel a journalist to reveal his sources.[265] In the 2012 Irish High Court case of *Cornec v Morrice & Others*.[266] In Cornec, Hogan J stated that, strictly speaking, there is no such thing as journalistic privilege, but that the right of freedom of expression under the Constitution would be meaningless 'if the law could not (or would not) protect the general right of journalists to protect their sources'.[267] Hogan J went on to hold that such a right is not absolute and that a public interest may override

257 *Laois County Council v Hanrahan* [2014] IESC 36
258 ibid paras 59–61
259 Contempt of Court Act 1981, s 10
260 *Keegan v de Búrca* [1973] 1 IR 223
261 ibid 230
262 *Goodwin v United Kingdom* (1996) 22 EHRR 123
263 ibid paras 39–40
264 *Mahon v Keena* [2009] IESC 64
265 ibid paras 92 and 100
266 *Cornec v Morrice & Others* [2012] IEHC 376
267 ibid para 43

it.[268] As a consequence of the Supreme Court's consideration of the decision in *Goodwin* while it reached its decision in *Mahon v Keena* and also of the High Court's decision in *Cornec v Morrice*, it would appear that the Irish courts are now placing a greater weight on the protection of journalists' sources of information. Such protection would apply equally to photographers. The Irish courts are also prepared to offer similar protection to "bloggers" (as occurred in *Cornec*) – a recently new class of individuals operating in the field of journalism.

5.5.2) Journalists and constructive contempt

Breach of the *sub-judice* (literally "under the judge") rule is a form of constructive contempt of court. Journalists and photographers could find themselves in constructive contempt of court by, for example, prejudicing an accused's right to a fair trial by publishing articles and/or photographs relating to court proceedings or the publication of matters discussed during a court case, including where the judge has asked the jury to temporarily leave the court for the duration of such a discussion. Publicity both prior to and during court cases has been an issue in a number of court cases, such as the 1994 Irish High Court case of *Magee v O'Dea*, as previously discussed,[269] and in the 2000 Irish Court of Criminal Appeal case of *Director of Public Prosecutions v Davis.*[270] The latter case concerned the publication of photographs of the applicant held in restraints.[271] Since *Davis*, new court buildings, such as the Courts of Criminal Justice in Dublin, have been designed so as to prevent press photographers from being in a position to photograph an accused person either entering or leaving the court.

5.5.3) Journalists and scandalising the court contempt

Although contempt of court cases concerning journalists scandalising the court are rare nowadays, it was a central issue in the Irish Supreme Court in the 1970s case of *In Re Kennedy and McCann.*[272] Following the publication of the United Kingdom's Law Commission's *Report on Contempt of Court: Scandalising*

268 ibid para 44
Note: More recently in the 2018 Irish High Court case of *Kean v Independent Star Ltd.* 2018 [IEHC] 206, Barr J, at para 16, upheld the principle of journalistic privilege.

269 *Magee v O'Dea* [1994] 1 IR 500, 512–513

270 *Director of Public Prosecutions v Davis* [2000] 10 JIC 2303

271 ibid

272 *In Re Kennedy and McCann* [1976] IR 382
Note: See also: Owen Bowcott, 'Peter Hain Contempt Charge Dropped' *The Guardian* (London, 17 May 2012) <www.guardian.co.uk/politics/2012/may/17/peter-hain-contempt-case-dropped> accessed 11 June 2018

the Court,[273] the Crime and Courts Act 2013 abolished the offence of scandalising the judiciary in England and Wales.[274] As previously noted, the Contempt of Court Bill 2017, in Ireland, proposes to place "scandalising the court" on a statutory footing as an element of criminal contempt of court.

5.6) Miscellaneous statutory restrictions

In addition to the previously mentioned statutory restrictions and prohibitions on photographers and photograph publishers, a number of other miscellaneous statutes contain provisions may either directly or indirectly restrict the creation, publication and/or sale of photographs. The following are examples. The Casual Trading Act 1995, as amended, concerns casual trading in publicly owned areas administered by local authorities and through powers granted under both this Act[275] and in accordance with the Local Government Act 2001,[276] as amended, local authorities implement bye-laws covering casual trading in such places. Prosecutions of photographers under casual trading and street statutes are extremely rare in Ireland or the United Kingdom.[277]

The responsibility for the management of Irish controlled airspace, the safety regulation of Irish civil aviation and the oversight of civil aviation security lie with the Irish Aviation Authority (IAA).[278] Under the Irish Aviation Act 1993, as amended, both the Authority and the Minster for Transport, Energy and Communications have the legal power to make orders and regulations.[279] Among other matters, such orders and regulations may designate areas as flight prohibited,[280] restricted[281] or danger[282] areas. For example, a minimum flying height restriction may be imposed within a specified geographical area or an area may be designated for use by only military aircraft. Consequently, orders and regulations made by the IAA may therefore indirectly either restrict or prohibit photographers in undertaking aerial photography using aircraft within Irish controlled airspace. As an alternative to using piloted helicopters or aeroplanes for aerial photography, in recent years some photographers have taken to using remotely piloted, small, unmanned aircraft systems, or "drones" as they are more commonly known, with cameras fitted underneath. The use of drones in Ireland is

273 Law Commission, *Report on Contempt of Court: Scandalising the Court* (Law Com No 335) (London 2012) <www.lawcom.gov.uk/wp-content/uploads/2015/06/lc335_scandalising_the_court.pdf> accessed 11 June 2018
274 Crime and Courts Act 2013, s 33
275 Casual Trading Act 1995, s 6
276 Local Government Act 2001, s 199
277 Note: For examples, see: (1) *Belfast Corporation v Reilly* [1960] NI 171 and (2) *M'Pherson v Copeland* (1956) JC 11
278 Irish Aviation Authority Act 1993, s 14
279 ibid s 5, s 58(1) and s 59
280 ibid s 60(1)(h)
281 ibid s 60(1)(i)(1)
282 ibid s 60(1)(i)(2)

governed by the Irish Aviation Authority Small Unmanned Aircraft (Drones) and Rockets Order 2015.[283] All drones subject to the Order must be registered with the IAA.[284] Those which weigh over 25 kilogrammes are also subject to the Irish Aviation Authority (Nationality and Registration of Aircraft) Order 2015[285] and must be registered in a like manner to manned aircraft.[286] Section 7 of the Small Unmanned Aircraft (Drones) and Rockets Order specifies the parameters under which a drone with a mass of less than 25 kilogrammes may be flown without a special permission from the IAA, such as for example the maximum flight heights over ground or water, the minimum flight distance from a person or a group of more than 12 people, a structure, a vehicle or a vessel not under the control of the drone operator, the drone's maximum flight distance from its operator and flying within controlled or restricted airspaces.[287] A person in charge of a drone weighing between 4 kilogrammes and 25 kilogrammes must not permit it to be flown unless he has undertaken a safety-training course acceptable to the IAA.[288] Also, a person may not permit a drone weighing between 25 kilogrammes and 150 kilogrammes to be flown without the permission of the IAA.[289] Although permission from the IAA is not required if one wishes to fly a drone for commercial purposes, such as commercial photography, a specific operating permit from the IAA is required if one wishes to operate a drone outside the limits prescribed in the 2015 Order. In the United Kingdom, regulations in respect of the operation of unmanned aircraft systems (drones) are implemented by the Civil Aviation Authority.[290]

The Wildlife Act 1976,[291] as amended, details the specific species of wild birds and animals (including land and marine based mammals) and flora which are protected from being disturbed. Under the Wildlife Acts 1976–2012, it an offence, in certain circumstances, to disturb protected wild birds, wild animals and flora. In relation to wild birds, subject to the exceptions specified in S.22(5) of the 1976 Act, S.22(4)(e) of the 1976 Act states that any person who 'wilfully disturbs a protected wild bird on or near a nest containing eggs or unflown

283 Irish Aviation Authority Small Unmanned Aircraft (Drones) and Rockets Order 2015, SI 2015/563

284 ibid s 7(1)

285 Irish Aviation Authority (Nationality and Registration of Aircraft) Order 2015, SI 2015/107

286 Irish Aviation Authority, *Drone Registration* <www.iaa.ie/general-aviation/drones/drone-registration> accessed 11 June 2018

287 Irish Aviation Authority Small Unmanned Aircraft (Drones) and Rockets Order 2015, SI 2015/563, s 7(5)

288 ibid s 7(6)

289 ibid s 7(8)

290 Civil Aviation Authority, *Unmanned Aircraft: Requirements for Operating in Airspace* <www.caa.co.uk/Commercial-Industry/Aircraft/Unmanned-aircraft/Unmanned-Aircraft/> accessed 11 June 2018

291 Wildlife Act 1976

young shall be guilty of an offence'.[292] Section 23 of the 1976 Act deals with the protection of wild animals and under S.23(5)(d) any person who 'wilfully interferes with or destroys the breeding place of any protected wild animal, shall be guilty of an offence'.[293] With regard to protected flora, under S.21(3)(c) of the 1976 Act and subject to the exceptions specified in S.21(5), it is an offence for anyone to 'wilfully alter, damage, destroy or interfere with the habitat or environment of any species of flora to which an order under this section for the time being applies'.[294] The Wildlife (Amendment) Act 2000[295] introduced a number of amendments to the 1976 Act, which are of benefit to photographers wishing to legally photograph protected wildlife. Section 22(9) of the 1976 Act was amended by S.30 of the 2000 Act by the insertion of a new S.22(9)(f) under which 'the Minister may grant a licence to a person 'to take or make photographic, video or other pictures of a protected wild bird of a species specified in the licence on or near a nest containing eggs or unflown young'.[296] Also, Section 31 of the 2000 Act amended S.23(6) of the 1976 Act by the insertion of a new S.23(6)(b) under which the Minister may grant a licence to a person 'to take or make photographic, video or other pictures of a protected wild animal of a species so specified on or near the breeding place of such an animal'.[297] Photography of any protected wild birds or wild animals may be undertaken legally following the acquisition of a photography licence from the National Parks and Wildlife Service's Wildlife Licensing Unit.[298]

Occasionally, firms wish to reproduce banknotes in their advertising and promotional materials. The photography and reproduction of banknotes for such usage is restricted by law. The European Central Bank is the copyright holder to the Euro banknotes and it permits their reproduction for advertising purposes. Any such reproduction must be in accordance with the reproduction rules[299] stipulated by the Bank. The copyright in previously issued Irish Pound banknotes vests in the Central Bank of Ireland.[300] Its prior approval is required in respect of any proposed reproductions. The reproduction of British Pound Sterling banknotes is governed by the Forgery and Counterfeiting Act 1981,

292 ibid s 22(4)(e)
293 ibid s 23(5)(d)
294 ibid s 21(3)(c)
295 Wildlife (Amendment) Act 2000
296 Wildlife Act 1976, s 22(9)(f)
297 ibid s 23(6)(b)
298 National Parks and Wildlife Service, *Licence to Photograph or Film a Protected Wild Animal or Bird* <www.npws.ie/licences/disturbance/photograph-or-film-protected-wild-animal-or-bird> accessed 11 June 2018
299 European Central Bank, Decision of the European Central Bank of 20 March 2003 on the denominations, specifications, reproduction, exchange and withdrawal of euro banknotes, art 2, s 3 *(ECB/2003/4) (2003/206/EC)*, Official Journal of the European Union, [2003] OJ L78/16 <www.ecb.int/ecb/legal/pdf/l_07820030325en00160019.pdf> accessed 11 June 2018
300 Copyright and Related Rights Act 2000, s 200

as amended.[301] The Bank of England owns the copyright to its banknotes. It permits the reproduction of its banknotes under a licence from it, but not novelty banknotes.[302]

5.7) Restrictions on ground of public morality

The Constitution guarantees freedom of expression. However, that right is subject to subject to the protection of public morality.[303] Consequently, the state has the legal power to introduce legislative measures on public morality grounds, which could result in restricting photographers' and photograph publishers' freedom of expression rights. Also, a number of common law restrictions exist. The following are examples.

5.7.1) (1) Censorship of publications and (2) pornography

The Censorship of Publications Acts 1929–1967, as amended, govern the censorship of books and periodical publications. The 1946 Act, as amended, repealed and replaced much of the 1929 Act. It also established the Censorship of Publications Board, which must examine any book or periodical publication referred to it by either an officer of Customs and Excise or any other person in order to determine its suitability for sale or distribution within Ireland.[304] The 1946 Act defines a "book" as 'every printed publication which is not a periodical publication and, save where the context otherwise requires, includes every edition of a book'.[305] It defines a "periodical publication" as

> a newspaper, magazine, journal or other printed publication which is published periodically or in parts or numbers, other than a publication published in parts or numbers at intervals which ordinarily exceed three months, and, save where the context otherwise requires, includes every edition and every issue of a periodical publication.[306]

Although Censorship of Publication Acts were enacted prior to the invention of the Internet, it is feasible that a court could give a wide interpretation of the meaning of the words "printed publication" so as to bring online publications of books and periodicals within the scope of the Acts. It is an offence for anybody to sell, offer, advertise or keep for sale or to distribute any prohibited

301 Forgery and Counterfeiting Act 1981, s 18(1)
302 Bank of England, *Reproducing Banknotes: Guidelines* <www.bankofengland.co.uk/banknotes/Pages/reproducing_banknotes.aspx> accessed 11 June 2018
303 Constitution of Ireland *(Art. 40.6.1º(i))* (on Personal Rights)
304 Censorship of Publications Act 1946, s 6 and s 9
305 Censorship of Publications Act 1946, s 1
306 ibid

book or periodical publication.[307] While neither the 1929 nor the 1946 Act define the word "obscene", both Acts state, that the word "indecent" includes 'suggestive of, or inciting to, sexual immorality or unnatural vice or likely in any other similar way to corrupt or deprave'.[308] Section 18 of the 1929 Act is relevant to photograph publishers, as it makes it an offence to 'sell or offer, expose, or keep for sale, or import for sale any indecent picture'.[309]

Special statutory protection is afforded to children and specific statutory offences relating to child pornography have been enacted. The Child Trafficking and Pornography Act 1998, as amended, defines a 'child' as 'a person under the age of 18 years'.[310] Section 2(1) of the Act, as amended, contains a detailed definition of "child pornography" and states that it includes, among other things, specified types of visual representations of children.[311] A "visual representation" is defined by S.2(1) as including, among other matters, a photographic representation and it states that a photographic representation 'includes the negative as well as the positive version'.[312] Under a new Section 5 of the Act, as inserted by S.12 of the Criminal Law (Sexual Offences) Act 2017, it is an offence for anybody to knowingly produce, distribute, sell, transmit, disseminate, print or publish child pornography.[313] Knowingly possessing child pornography is an offence under S.6 of the Act, as inserted by S.14 of the 2017 Act.[314] Section 6(4) of the Act offers a defence to a person accused of a S.6(1) offence and it is for an accused to prove that 'he or she possessed the child pornography concerned for the purposes of bona fide research'.[315] It could be extremely difficult for an accused, particularly a photographer, to succeed in proving such a defence. For comparative purposes, in the United Kingdom the publication of obscene material comes within the scope of the Obscene Publications Act 1959, as amended. Under the 1959 Act, it is an offence for a person, whether for gain or not, to either publish or to possess for publication an obscene article.[316] The Act defines an "article" as 'any description of article containing or embodying matter to be read or looked at or both, any sound record, and any film or other record of a picture or pictures'.[317] An article is obscene if its effect tends to 'deprave or corrupt persons who are likely . . . to read, see or hear the matter contained or

307 Censorship of Publications Act 1946, s 14(1) and s 14(2)
308 Censorship of Publications Act 1929, s 1 and Censorship of Publications Act 1946, s 1
309 Censorship of Publications Act 1929, s 18(1)
310 Child Trafficking and Pornography Act 1998, s 2(1). Note: Section 2(1) of the 1998 Act was amended by S.9 of the Criminal Law (Sexual Offences) Act 2017.
311 ibid
312 ibid
313 ibid s 5(1)
314 ibid s 6(1)
315 ibid s 6(4)
316 Obscene Publications Act 1959, s 2
317 ibid s 1(2)

embodied in it'.[318] The Obscene Publications Act 1964 amended the 1959 Act and made it an offence for one to possess negatives for the purpose of the production of obscene material.[319] The possession of extreme pornographic images is an offence under the Criminal Justice and Immigration Act 2008, as amended.[320] The Act states that an extreme pornographic image consists of an image which is both pornographic and of an extreme image.[321] Section 63(3) of the Act states that an image is "pornographic" 'if it is of such a nature that it must reasonably be assumed to have been produced solely or principally for the purpose of sexual arousal'.[322] In relation to the possession of an extreme image in England or Wales, S.63(5A) of the Act, as inserted by the Criminal Justice and Courts Act 2015,[323] states that an "extreme image" is one which:

(a) falls within subsection (7) or (7A), and
(b) is grossly offensive, disgusting or otherwise of an obscene character.[324]

For the purposes of the S.63 offence of possession of extreme pornographic images, Section 63(8) defines an "image" as '(a) a moving or still image (produced by any means) or (b) data (stored by any means) which is capable of conversion into an image within paragraph (a)'.[325] Section 63(7) of the Act specifies the types of acts portrayed in images, such as bestiality, that fall within Section 63 of the Act.[326] Section 63(7A) of the 2008 Act deals with the possession of pornographic images of rape and assault by penetration.[327] A number of defences against a charge of possession of extremely pornographic images are offered by S.65(2) of the 2008 Act including that the accused had a legitimate reason for possessing the images.[328] Under S.62 of the Coroners and Justice Act 2009, the possession of a prohibited image of a child is an offence.[329] A prohibited image is an image which: '(a) is pornographic, (b) falls within subsection (6), and (c) is grossly offensive, disgusting or otherwise of an obscene character'.[330] An image falls within Section 62(6) of the act if it '(a) is an image which focuses solely or principally on a child's genitals or anal region, or

318 ibid s 1(1)
319 Obscene Publications Act 1964, s 2
320 Criminal Justice and Immigration Act 2008, s 63(1)
321 ibid s 63(2)
322 ibid s 63(3)
323 Criminal Justice and Courts Act 2015, s 37(2)
324 Criminal Justice and Immigration Act 2008, s 63(6)
325 ibid s 63(8)
326 ibid s 63(7)
327 ibid s 63(7A)
328 Criminal Justice and Immigration Act 2008, s 65(2)
329 Coroners and Justice Act 2009, s 62
330 ibid s 62(2)

(b) portrays any of the acts mentioned in subsection (7)'.[331] The Act classifies an image as being a pornographic image 'if it is of such a nature that it must reasonably be assumed to have been produced solely or principally for the purpose of sexual arousal'.[332] A number of defences to a charge of an offence under S.62 of the Act are provided under S.64 of the Act. These defences are similar to those offered under the previously mentioned S.65(2) of the 2008 Act.[333] The previous legislative provisions are of general application and in both Ireland and the UK there have been a number of convictions under the respective Acts.

5.7.2) Prohibition of incitement to hatred

In Ireland, incitement to hatred is an offence under the Prohibition of Incitement to Hatred Act 1989, as amended.[334] The Act defines "hatred" as:

> hatred against a group of persons in the State or elsewhere on account of their race, colour, nationality, religion, ethnic or national origins, membership of the travelling community or sexual orientation.[335]

Although "hatred" is defined as being hatred against a group of persons, there have been convictions in respect of incitement to hatred against individuals.[336] "Written material" is defined as 'any sign or other visual representation'.[337] Thus, a photograph would come within the meaning of "written material". The preparation or possession of material likely to stir up hatred is an offence.[338] The broadcasting of material likely to stir up hatred is an offence under S.3(1) of the Act[339] and the wording of Principle 5 of the Broadcasting Authority of Ireland's *Code of Programme Standards* is in keeping with S.3(1).[340] Prosecutions under the 1989 Act have been infrequent. In 2011, the first prosecution taken under the Act in respect of online incitement to hatred was dismissed as the

331 ibid s 62(6)
Note: Section 62(7) of the Act specifies a number of acts the portrayal of which in images is prohibited, for example, 'the performance by a person of an act of intercourse or oral sex with or in the presence of a child'.

332 ibid s 62(3)

333 ibid s 64(1)

334 Prohibition of Incitement to Hatred Act 1989, s 2(1)

335 ibid s 1

336 Note: For example, see: —— 'Bus Driver Convicted Under Incitement to Hatred Act' (*RTÉ News*, 14 September 2000) <www.rte.ie/news/2000/0914/8916-hatred/> accessed 11 June 2018

337 Prohibition of Incitement to Hatred Act 1989, s 1

338 ibid s 4(1)

339 ibid s 3(1)

340 Broadcasting Authority of Ireland, *Code of Programme Standards*, Principle 5 <www.bai.ie/en/codes-standards/#al-block-4> accessed 11 June 2018

Killarney District Court did not regard a once-off publication as being an incitement to hatred.[341] The Communications Regulation (Amendment) Act 2007[342] inserted a new S.13(1) in the Post Office (Amendment) Act 1951, under which it is an offence to use a telephone to send a message, that is either grossly offensive, indecent, obscene or menacing.[343] It has been suggested that S.13(1) of the Act does not take account of the use of modern telecommunications and computer equipment to publish online materials, including photographs, which are designed to incite hatred.[344] The Report of the Internet Content Governance Advisory Group recommended that S.13 of the 2007 Act should be amended in order to include electronic communications within its meaning.[345] Any amendment to S.13 of the Act should also expressly include the sending of messages, including photographs, which are designed to incite hatred.

In the United Kingdom, the provisions of the Public Order Act 1986, as amended, which deal with incitement to hatred,[346] are broadly similar to those contained in Ireland's Prohibition of Incitement to Hatred Act 1989, which includes incitement on religious grounds. The 1986 Act was amended by the Racial and Religious Hatred Act 2006, which inserted a new Part 3A in the Act dealing with "hatred against persons on religious grounds".[347] "Religious

341 See (1): John O'Mahony, 'Man Cleared of Online Hatred Against Travellers' *Irish Examiner* (Cork, 01 October 2011) <www.irishexaminer.com/ireland/man-cleared-of-online-hatred-against-travellers-169325.html> accessed 12 June 2018
(2): Law Reform Commission, *Report on Harmful Communications and Digital Safety* (LRC 116–2016) (Dublin 2016) <https://publications.lawreform.ie/Portal/External/en-GB/RecordView/Index/37669> accessed 12 June 2018
(3): Law Reform Commission, *Issues Paper on Cyber-Crime Affecting Personal Safety, Privacy and Reputation Including Cyber-Bullying* (LRC IP 6–2014) (Dublin 2014) <www.lawreform.ie/_fileupload/Issues%20Papers/ip6Cybercrime.pdf> accessed 12 June 2018

342 Communications Regulation (Amendment) Act 2007, s 4 and sch 1 part 2

343 Post Office (Amendment) Act 1951, s 13(1)
Note: Section 43 of the United Kingdom's Telecommunications Act 1984, as amended, contains a similar provision.

344 See: Houses of the Oireachtas Joint Committee on Transport and Communications, *Report: Addressing the Growth of Social Media and Tackling Cyberbullying* (31TC 007) (Dublin, July 2013) 34 <https://webarchive.oireachtas.ie/parliament/media/report-on-social-media-july-2013-website.pdf> accessed 12 June 2018

345 Department of Communications, Climate Action and Environment, *Report of the Internet Content Governance Advisory Group*, 3(3)(1) (Dublin May 2014) <www.dccae.gov.ie/en-ie/communications/publications/Documents/70/InternetContentGovernanceAdvisoryGroupReport.pdf> accessed 12 June 2018
Note: Section 2(2) of the European Communities (Electronic Communications Networks and Services) (Privacy and Electronic Communications) Regulations 2011, SI 2011/336 defines "communication" as 'any information exchanged or conveyed between a finite number of parties by means of a publicly available electronic communications service, but does not include any information conveyed as part of a broadcasting service to the public over the electronic communications network except to the extent that the information can be related to the identifiable subscriber or user receiving the information'.

346 Public Order Act 1986, part 3

347 Racial and Religious Hatred Act 2006, sch

hatred" is defined by the Act as 'hatred against a group of persons defined by reference to religious belief or lack of religious belief'.[348] Under Part 3A, a person is guilty of an offence if he/she intends to stir up religious hatred through the use of threatening words or behaviour or written material;[349] the publication or distribution of threatening written material;[350] the public performance of a play involving the use of threatening words or behaviour;[351] the distribution, showing or playing of a recording or the broadcasting or inclusion in a programme of threatening visual images or sounds.[352] Also, it is an offence to possess either written material or a recording of visual images or sounds that is or are threatening with a view to having it or them displayed, published, distributed or included in a broadcasted programme with the intention to stir up religious hatred.[353] This new Part 3A of the Act also offers a statutory protection of the right of freedom of expression in relation to religions and belief systems.[354] As is the case under S.5 of the Irish Prohibition of Incitement to Hatred Act 1989, Part 3A of the Act does not apply to the fair and accurate reporting of either parliamentary proceedings or of publicly heard judicial proceedings.[355] Any proposed reform of the Irish Prohibition of Incitement to Hatred Act 1989 should consider the inclusion of a provision covering incitement to hatred against "individuals".

5.7.3) Outraging public decency

Outraging public decency is a common law offence and in the 2013 Irish High Court case of *Douglas v Director of Public Prosecutions and Others*,[356] Hogan J stated that the offence comprises 'the performance of an act which is (i) lewd, obscene and disgusting; (ii) an outrage to public decency and (iii) in public'.[357] The 2007 English Court of Appeal case of *R v Hamilton*[358] concerned an appellant who had been convicted of a number of offences including the common law offence of outraging public decency following his taking of video footage up the skirts of adult women and a young teenage girl in a supermarket using a concealed camera.[359] In *Hamilton*, Thomas LJ held that for one to be convicted of the offence of outraging public decency it is necessary to prove that the act complained of must be of a lewd, obscene or disgusting nature to

348 Public Order Act 1986, s 29(A)
349 ibid s 29(B)(1)
350 ibid s 29(C)(1)
351 ibid s 29(D)(1)
352 ibid s 29(E)(1) and s 29(F)(1)
353 ibid s 29(G)(1)
354 ibid s 29(J)
355 ibid s 29(K)
356 *Douglas v Director of Public Prosecutions and Others* [2013] IEHC 343
357 ibid para 54
358 *R v Hamilton* [2007] EWCA Crim 2062
359 ibid paras 1–5

the extent that it would outrage public decency; it must have been undertaken in a public place or a place which members of the public could see the act being undertaken and the act must have been capable of being seen by at least two people who were present irrespective of the fact that they may not have seen the act being undertaken.[360] Therefore, if the act were only capable of being seen by one person, the public element of the offence would not be satisfied. It would be appropriate to either repeal this common law offence or put it on a clearly defined statutory footing.

5.7.4) Restrictions on contents of advertising materials and of postal packets

Frequently, photographs are integral elements of advertising materials such as advertisements, printed promotional materials and displays. On a public morality basis, a number of statutes prescribe offences in respect of advertising materials and practices including the use of photographs. The Statute Law Revision Act 2007,[361] as amended, retained the Indecent Advertisements Act 1889, as amended. Worded in keeping with the time period of the late 1800s, the Act prescribes penalties for the offence of public distribution or display of pictures or printed or written matter of an indecent or obscene nature.[362] The Censorship of Publications Act 1929, as amended, amended the 1889 Act and among such amendments it amended Section 3 of the 1889 Act so as to prohibit the advertising of, among other things, contraceptives.[363] In turn, Section 17(1) was subsequently amended by the Health (Family Planning) Act 1979 in order to remove the prohibition on the advertising of contraceptives.[364] However, the 1979 Act provides that any advertisements relating to contraceptives must be in accordance with, and as permitted, under regulations pertaining to such advertisements.[365]

Section 7 of the Criminal Justice (Public Order) Act 1994, as amended, makes it an offence for any person in a public place:

> to distribute or display any writing, sign or visible representation which is threatening, abusive, insulting or obscene with intent to provoke a breach

360 ibid paras 30–31
361 Statute Law Revision Act 2007, sch 1, part 4
362 Indecent Advertisements Act 1889, s 3
363 Censorship of Publications Act 1929, s 17(1)
364 Health (Family Planning) Act 1979, s 12(2)
365 ibid s 7(1)
Note: The Health (Family Planning) Regulations 1980, SI 1980/248, s 8 and the Health (Family Planning) Regulations 1992, SI 1992/312, s 6(1) deal with the advertising and display of contraceptives

of the peace or being reckless as to whether a breach of the peace may be occasioned.[366]

As the contents of a "sign" may or may not include a photograph and as a "visible representation" could be taken to include a photograph, it is conceivable that photographs would come within the scope of S.7 of the Act. Under the Communications Regulation (Postal Services) Act 2011, as amended, it is an offence to send by post any postal packet which 'encloses any article or thing whatsoever which is indecent, obscene, grossly offensive or menacing'.[367] Thus, it would be an offence for a photographer to send any indecent or obscene photographic images to a publisher for publication or to anyone else or for a publisher to distribute such printed materials via a postal service provider. It is noted, that the Act does not define what actually constitutes "indecent, obscene, grossly offensive or menacing" articles.

5.8) Ethical restrictions

While an individual may determine his/her own moral standards, the state may legislate on the standard of public morals, which it requires to be observed and upheld within the state. Ethical standards are the behavioural standards set by groups within society, which must be observed and upheld by the members of such groups. In the business environment, ethical codes of behavioural standards are referred to variously as codes of standards and practice or as codes of conduct. While commercial and industry sector codes of standards and practice are primarily self-developed and self-regulated, such codes may also be required by specific sectors as a consequence of legislative provisions. For example, the Defamation Act 2009 requires the Press Council to adopt and implement a code of standards to which its members must adhere[368] and the Broadcasting Act 2009, as amended, requires the Broadcasting Authority of Ireland to implement codes of standards and practice to be observed by broadcasters.[369]

Primarily due to publicity surrounding court cases concerning sexual assaults on children and the possession of child pornography, the taking and publication of photographs of children have, in recent years, been brought into sharp focus in the minds of members of the public. Schools and virtually all organisations which have a direct involvement with children, such as sports organisations, have written policies in place in respect of the photographing and publication of photographs of children within their care.[370] In some instances, photographers and publishers of photographs may also have to abide by the code of practice

366 Criminal Justice (Public Order) Act 1994, s 7(1)
367 Communications Regulation (Postal Services) Act 2011, s 55(1)(b)
368 Defamation Act 2009, sch 2, para 10
369 Broadcasting Act 2009, s 42
370 Note: for example, see: GAA, *Code of Behaviour (Underage)*, 51 <http://res.cloudinary.com/dvrbaruzq/image/upload/uspspssby7jneiyjgd0b.pdf> accessed 13 June 2018

of either a public or a private body. Examples of the codes of standards and practice of public bodies are the National Museum of Ireland's "*Image Safe Handbook*",[371] which covers the photography of children and young people at the Museum's sites, and The Arts Council's "*Guidelines for taking and using images of children and young people in the arts sector*".[372] An example of a code of behaviour of a private body which may be relevant to some photographers is the Dóchas "*Code of Conduct on Images and Messages*".[373] Depending upon the type(s) of photographic work undertaken by them, their membership of photographer associations and whether or not they work in the media and advertising sectors, photographers may be required either directly or indirectly to adhere to a number of codes of standards and behavioural practice. Many of those codes are also applicable to photograph publishers. The codes of standards and practice of the Press Council of Ireland, the Advertising Standards Authority of Ireland, the National Union of Journalists, the Irish Professional Photographers Association and the Broadcasting Authority of Ireland are of primary relevance and are discussed later. For comparative purposes, the codes of IMPRESS (UK), the Independent Press Standards Organisation (UK) and the Advertising Standards Authority (UK) are also discussed.

5.8.1) Press regulation in Ireland

Pursuant to the provisions of S.44 of Defamation Act 2009, the Press Council of Ireland was given legal recognition as the Press Council for the purposes of the Act.[374] The Press Council of Ireland is independent of both the government and the media and it is responsible for overseeing the principles contained in the code of practice for its members and for upholding the freedom of the press.[375] Newspapers, magazines and digital publications that are members of the Press Council agree to abide by its *Code of Practice*. Anybody who feels that they have been wronged or damaged by material published by one of the member publications and who has not received satisfaction from an alleged offender may file a complaint with the Office of the Press Ombudsman and seek a resolution through either conciliation or a determination by the Ombudsman. Complaints made to the Ombudsman may be referred by him to the Press

371 National Museum of Ireland, *Image Safe Handbook* <www.museum.ie/NationalMuseumIreland/media/Corporate-Information/Policies%20and%20Guidelines/IMAGE_SAFE_HANDBOOK.pdf> accessed 13 June 2018

372 The Arts Council, *Guidelines for Taking and Using Images of Children and Young People in the Arts Sector* <www.artscouncil.ie/uploadedFiles/Guidelines.pdf> accessed 13 June 2018

373 Dóchas, *Code of Conduct on Images and Messages* <https://dochas.ie/sites/default/files/Images_and_Messages_0.pdf> accessed 13 June 2018
Note: Dóchas is an Irish association of non-governmental development organisations.

374 Defamation Act 2009 (Press Council) Order 2010, SI 2010/163

375 Press Council of Ireland, *About Us* <www.presscouncil.ie/about-us> accessed 13 June 2018

Council for a decision or the Council may decide on an appeal to a decision made by the Ombudsman. Some complaints to the Ombudsman have concerned photographs published as elements of news stories by Press Council member organisations.[376] In many instances, the published photographs were not the dominant element of those complaints. The contents of the Press Council's *Code of Practice* are in keeping with the principles of the Constitution of Ireland, the ECHR, decisions of the courts and with statute law. The Code embraces 10 principles, namely truth and accuracy, distinguishing fact and comment, fairness and honesty, respect for rights, privacy, protection of sources, court reporting, prejudice, children and publication of the decision of the Press Ombudsman/Press Council. The Code's principles dealing with fairness and honesty and privacy make specific mention of the acquisition of photographs, while the principle dealing with court reporting makes specific mention of the use of "images". The Code permits that the principles dealing with fairness and honesty and privacy need not be abided by if justified on public-interest grounds. In relation to stories dealing with children, the Code places an onus on editors to justify the public interest, if any, in such stories being published.[377]

5.8.2) Press regulation in the United Kingdom

As a consequence of the recommendations contained within the *Report of the Leveson Inquiry into the Culture, Practices and Ethics of the Press*,[378] a Royal Charter on self-regulation of the press was granted in 2013.[379] The Charter specified the criteria to be met by a body seeking recognition as a press regulatory body.[380] The Press Recognition Panel was established to approve applicants as recognised, independent, press regulatory bodies.[381] It has recognised IMPRESS as an approved press regulator.[382] A number of print media organisations opposed to the proposals resulting from the Report of the Leveson Inquiry established the Independent Press Standards Organisation (IPSO) following the demise of the Press Complaints Commission, which had been heavily criticised – particularly during the Leveson

376 Note: To view decisions of the Press Ombudsman and of the Press Council, see: <www.presscouncil.ie/Decided-by-the-Press-Ombudsman> and <www.presscouncil.ie/press-council-of-ireland-1/appeals-and-referrals> accessed 15 June 2018

377 Press Council of Ireland, *Code of Practice* <www.presscouncil.ie/press-council-of-ireland-1/code-of-practice-> accessed 13 June 2018

378 Her Majesty's Stationary Office, *Leveson Inquiry – Report into the Culture, Practices and Ethics of the Press* (29 November 2012) <www.official-documents.gov.uk/document/hc1213/hc07/0780/0780.asp> accessed 13 June 2018

379 Department for Digital, Culture, Media and Sport, *Final Royal Charter on Self-Regulation of the Press* (London, 30 October 2013) <www.gov.uk/government/publications/leveson-report-cross-party-royal-charter> accessed 13 June 2018

380 ibid sch 3

381 Press Recognition Panel <http://pressrecognitionpanel.org.uk> accessed 13 June 2018

382 Press Recognition Panel, *PRP Board Recognises IMPRESS* <https://pressrecognitionpanel.org.uk/impress-2/> accessed 13 June 2018

Inquiry. IPSO has not and does not intend to seek recognition from the Press Recognition Panel.[383] It would appear that many of the larger publishers are outside of the press recognition system, as they have not joined IMPRESS,[384] that some publishers have not joined either IMPRESS or IPSO[385] and that the membership of IMPRESS is predominantly composed of small publishers.[386] Under Section 34 of the Crime and Courts Act 2013 and subject to S.34(3), exemplary damages may not be awarded in a relevant claim against a defendant who at the material time was a member of an approved press regulator.[387]

IMPRESS

At the time of writing, IMPRESS[388] was the only press regulator approved by the Press Recognition Panel. It operates a code of practice for its members – *The IMPRESS Standards Code*.[389] IMPRESS states that in relation to complaints concerning publications or acts committed after the 24 July 2017 it would apply the *IMPRESS Standards Code* and that the *Editors' Code of Practice* (the code of practice of the former Press Complaints Commission) would be applied in respect of complaints concerning publications or acts committed prior to that date.[390] The IMPRESS *Standards Code* contains specific provisions in relation to the acquisition and publication of photographs, namely in respect of matters pertaining to children and to harassment.[391] The Code also makes provision for public-interest exceptions to the Code.[392]

Independent Press Standards Organisation

The Independent Press Standards Organisation (IPSO) operates as a press regulator although it is not officially recognised by the Press Recognition Panel. It has

383 ibid

384 Press Recognition Panel, *Annual Report on the Recognition System 2017* <https://pressrecognitionpanel.org.uk/annual-report-on-the-recognition-system-2017/> accessed 13 June 2018

385 ibid

386 IMPRESS, *Regulated Publications* <www.impress.press/complaints/regulated-publishers.html> accessed 13 June 2018

387 Crime and Courts Act 2013, s 34(2)
Note: Section 42 of the Act states that a relevant claim is a civil claim for either libel, slander, breach of confidence, misuse of private information, malicious falsehood or harassment.

388 IMPRESS, *About Us* <www.impress.press/about-us/> accessed 14 June 2018

389 IMPRESS, *The IMPRESS Standards Code* <www.impress.press/downloads/file/code/the-impress-standards-code.pdf> accessed 13 June 2018

390 ibid

391 ibid clause 3 and clause 5

392 ibid

a code of practice – *The Editors' Code of Practice*.[393] As is the case with the Press Council of Ireland's *Code of Practice*, a number of clauses in the IPSO Code place specific restrictions on both the manner in which photographs are acquired and on the publication of photographs, namely Clauses 2, 3, 6 and 10, which respectively deal with matters concerning privacy, harassment, young children and clandestine devices and subterfuge.[394] The Code provides for the making of exceptions to its provisions on "public interest" grounds and it specifies in detail what constitutes public-interest grounds.[395] Should a person believe that they have been wronged or damaged by material published by an IPSO member publications and that they have not received satisfaction from an alleged offender, they may make a complaint to IPSO and seek a determination.[396] Some of the complaints determined by IPSO have concerned photographs published by its members.[397]

5.8.3) National Union of Journalists

Although a greater proportion of National Union of Journalists (NUJ) members are working journalists, many of its members are photographers.[398] The NUJ is headquartered in London and its branch in Dublin serves its Irish members.[399] The NUJ's *Code of Conduct* applies to all of its members including photographers. It makes specific reference to the photography of children and stipulates that the consent of an appropriate adult is normally a requirement when a child is being photographed for a story in respect of his or her welfare.[400] The NUJ does not operate a press regulator–style function through which members of the public or others may lodge complaints in respect of material published by NUJ members which they believe has wronged or damaged them.

5.8.4) The Irish Professional Photographers' and Videographers' Association

The Irish Professional Photographers' and Videographers Association (IPPVA) is the representative organisation for professional photographers working in

393 Independent Press Standards Organisation, *Editors' Code of Practice* <www.ipso.co.uk/editors-code-of-practice/> accessed 14 June 2018

394 ibid

395 ibid

396 Independent Press Standards Organisation, *Make a Complaint* <www.ipso.co.uk/IPSO/makeacomplaint/makingacomplaint.html> accessed 14 June 2018

397 Independent Press Standards Organisation, *Rulings* <www.ipso.co.uk/rulings-and-resolution-statements/> accessed 14 June 2018

398 National Union of Journalists, *About, Welcome to the NUJ* <www.nuj.org.uk/about/> accessed 14 June 2018

399 National Union of Journalists, *Contacts* <www.nuj.org.uk/contacts/> accessed 14 June 2018

400 National Union of Journalists, *NUJ Code of Conduct* <www.nuj.org.uk/about/nuj-code/> accessed 14 June 2018

Ireland. The Association publishes two codes – "*Code of Ethics*" and "*Best Business Practices*". Its *Code of Ethics*[401] essentially requires its members to be courteous and helpful to clients and fellow photographers and to respect the internal working rules of the Association. It does not place any requirements or restrictions on its members as regards the manner or circumstances under which they either create or publish photographs as a consequence of the need to protect and enforce the rights of others (non-members of the Association). The IPPVA's *Best Business Practices*[402] primarily deals with a mixture of standard best business practices, taxation and other legal requirements which would be applicable to any type of business operating in Ireland. This Code requires that IPPVA members do not break any laws and specifically the CRRA, as amended, by copying another photographer's work without written permission or pass-off another's photographer's work as their own. Save for the requirement that members do not breach a client's right to confidentiality, the IPPVA's *Best Business Practices* do not place any other restrictions or requirements on its members for the purpose of the protection and respect of the legal rights of other, non-photographer parties.

5.8.5) Regulation of advertising and marketing communications standards

The production and publication of advertisements and marketing communication materials in Ireland and the United Kingdom is subject to the codes of standards implemented respectively by the Advertising Standards Authority of Ireland and the United Kingdom's Advertising Standards Authority. In addition, broadcasted advertisements and marketing communication materials are subject to conformity with the codes of standards of either the Broadcasting Authority of Ireland or Ofcom.

5.8.5.1) Advertising Standards Authority of Ireland

The Advertising Standards Authority of Ireland (ASAI) is an independent, self-regulating body which was established and is financed by Ireland's advertising industry. Through the commitment and support of advertisers, advertising agencies and the media, it promotes and enforces a code of standards in relation to marketing communications, which comprises advertisements, promotional marketing and direct marketing activities.[403] The Authority's *Code of Standards*

401 Irish Professional Photographers' and Videographers' Association, *IPPVA Code of Ethics* <www.irishphotographers.com/downloads.php?section=ethics> accessed 14 June 2018

402 Irish Professional Photographers' and Videographers' Association, *IPPVA Best Business Practices* <www.irishphotographers.com/downloads.php?section=bestpractice> accessed 14 June 2018

403 Advertising Standards Authority of Ireland, *About ASAI* <www.asai.ie/about-us/> accessed 14 June 2018

for Advertising and Marketing Communications in Ireland[404] is extremely detailed. The scope of the Code covers marketing communications materials published through a variety of specified types of market communications media including for example, newspapers, magazines, promotional brochures, television and radio broadcasts and online.[405] The Code specifies the types of marketing communications materials, such as press releases and other public relations materials, which do not come within the scope of the Code.[406] The General Rules of the Code state that responsibility for observance of the Code is placed upon advertisers themselves and that others involved in the preparation and publication of marketing communications, such as service providers, are also obliged to abide by the Code.[407] Photographers supplying photographic services for use in marketing communications would therefore come within the scope of the Code. In addition to its General Rules, the Code contains standards applicable to a number of specific product and business sectors, such as alcoholic drinks,[408] gambling[409] and the health and beauty sector.[410] Noting that children lack maturity, knowledge and life experience and with the safety of children being kept to the fore, the Code specifies the standards which must be abided by advertisers when they are either directly or indirectly addressing their marketing communications to children or when children are featured in their marketing communications.[411] The Code makes both indirect and direct references to the use of photographs in marketing communications and a direct requirement under Clause 3(27) to obtain model, product and property releases.[412] Clause 3(28) provides for a number of exceptions to this Clause 3(27) requirement, such as crowd scenes.[413] Although there is no statutory requirement that a signed model, property or product release must be obtained prior to the use of a photographic portrayal of a person or their property in a marketing communications material, this stipulation within the Code is the nearest there is to such. In respect of the Health and Beauty Sector, the Code makes a direct reference to the use of photographs in marketing communications.[414] The Code

404 Advertising Standards Authority of Ireland, *Code of Standards for Advertising and Marketing Communications in Ireland* (7th edn) <www.asai.ie/asaicode/> accessed 14 June 2018
405 ibid clause 2(2)
406 ibid clause 2(3)
407 ibid clause 3(1)
408 ibid
409 ibid clause 10
410 ibid clause 11
411 ibid clause 7
412 Note: Throughout the Code, the terms “photographs”, “image”, “images”, “imagery”, “depict”, “depicted”, “depiction”, “portray”, “portrayal” and “portrayed” are variously used. However, the term “photographs” is only used in Clause 11(7(b) of the Code.
413 ibid clause 3(28)
414 ibid clause 11(7)(b)

requires that marketing communications must not be misleading.[415] Any person or body may make a complaint to the ASAI that either a marketing communication or online behavioural advertising may be in breach of the Code.[416] The ASAI regularly publishes complaints bulletins which detail the complaints received by it and its determinations on them.[417]

5.8.5.2) Broadcasting Authority of Ireland

Established by the Broadcasting Act 2009,[418] the Broadcasting Authority of Ireland (BAI) is the regulator of broadcasting in Ireland.[419] In accordance with the requirements of the 2009 Act,[420] the Authority operates and regularly updates a range of broadcasting codes and standards[421] by which broadcasters and their advertisers must abide. Such codes and standards include, among others, the General Commercial Communications Code; the Code of Fairness, Objectivity and Impartiality; the Code of Programme Standards and the Children's Commercial Communications Code. Of particular relevance is Clause 2 of the General Commercial Communications Code, which includes advertisements within its definition of a commercial communication.[422] The BAI Codes and Standards neither make any specific reference to, or place any specific responsibilities upon, still photographers. However, throughout the General Commercial Communications Code specific mention is made of "images".[423] Where a still photograph (an image) is featured in either a broadcasted programme or an advertisement, there is an onus on the programme or advertisement

415 ibid clause 4(1)

416 Advertising Standards Authority of Ireland, *Make a Complaint* <www.asai.ie/make-a-complaint/> accessed 14 June 2018
Note: Online behavioural advertising (targeted advertisements based on collected web viewer browser data) is governed by Clause 18 of the Code.

417 Advertising Standards Authority of Ireland, *Complaints Bulletins* <www.asai.ie/complaints-bulletins/> accessed 14 June 2018

418 Broadcasting Act 2009, s 6

419 Broadcasting Authority of Ireland, *About Us* <www.bai.ie/en/about-us/#al-block-1> accessed 14 June 2018

420 Broadcasting Act 2009, s 42

421 Broadcasting Authority of Ireland, *Codes and Standards* <www.bai.ie/en/codes-standards/> accessed 14 June 2018

422 Broadcasting Authority of Ireland, *General Commercial Communications Code*, clause 2 <www.bai.ie/en/codes-standards/#al-block-2> accessed 14 June 2018

423 Broadcasting Authority of Ireland, *General Commercial Communications Code* <www.bai.ie/en/codes-standards/#al-block-2> accessed 14 June 2018
Note: In addition to the references made in the General Commercial Communications Code on the use of images in broadcasted programmes and advertisements, such references are made throughout the Children's Commercial Communications Code; Code of Programme Standards; BAI Right of Reply Scheme; the BAI Rules on Advertising and Teleshopping (Daily and Hourly Limits) and the ODAS Code of Conduct for media service providers of on-demand audio-visual media services.

maker to ensure that such a photograph meets the requirements of the BAI's codes of practice and standards. Any viewer of a broadcasted programme or advertisement may make a complaint directly to its broadcaster if dissatisfied with the manner in which a broadcaster is complying with the BAI Codes. Complaints may also be referred to the BAI under its Complaints Referral Procedure.[424]

5.8.5.3) Advertising Standards Authority (United Kingdom) and Ofcom

In the United Kingdom, the Advertising Standards Authority (ASA) is the independent regulator of advertising across all media.[425] While the scope of the ASAI's *Code of Standards for Advertising and Marketing Communications in Ireland*, as previously mentioned, includes the medium of broadcast, the ASA differs from the ASAI in that it is the regulatory authority for both non-broadcast and broadcast advertising.[426] It self-regulates non-broadcast advertising and it co-regulates broadcast advertising. The ASA's dual regulatory role is a consequence of its contract with the Office of Communications (Ofcom),[427] under which it regulates television and radio advertising. Ofcom separately implements *The Ofcom Broadcasting Code*, which regulates the contents of programmes broadcasted by its licensed broadcasters.[428] Two codes of advertising standards written by the Committee of Advertising Practice[429] are regulated by the ASA,

424 Broadcasting Authority of Ireland, *How to Make a Complaint* <www.bai.ie/en/viewers-listeners/complaints/> accessed 14 June 2018

425 Advertising Standards Authority, *About the ASA and CAP* <www.asa.org.uk/about-asa-and-cap/about-regulation/about-the-asa-and-cap.html> accessed 14 June 2018

426 Advertising Standards Authority, *About Regulation* <www.asa.org.uk/about-asa-and-cap/about-regulation.html> accessed 14 June 2018

427 Note (1): Ofcom (the Office of Communications) is the United Kingdom's communications regulator and it regulates, among other matters, the television and radio media. Ofcom, *About Ofcom: What Is Ofcom?* <http://ask.ofcom.org.uk/help/ofcom/ofcomdef> accessed 14 June 2018

Note (2): Ofcom was established by the Communications Act 2003, as amended, and under Sections 3(2)(e) and 3(2)(f) of the Act, Ofcom is obliged to implement standards in respect of television and radio services to protect the public from offensive and harmful material, unfair treatment in programmes and unwarranted infringements of privacy.

Note (3): Ofcom transferred the regulation of broadcast advertising content to the ASA on 17 May 2004.

—— 'Ofcom Simplifies Advertising Regulation With "One-Stop-Shop" for Consumer Complaints' *Ofcom* (17 May 2004) <http://media.ofcom.org.uk/news/2004/ofcom-simplifies-advertising-regulation-with-one-stop-shop-for-consumer-complaints/> accessed 14 June 2018

428 Ofcom, *The Ofcom Broadcasting Code (With the Cross-Promotion Code and the On-Demand Programme Services Rules)* <www.ofcom.org.uk/__data/assets/pdf_file/0005/100103/broadcast-code-april-2017.pdf> accessed 14 June 2018

429 Committee of Advertising Practice, *About CAP* <www.asa.org.uk/about-asa-and-cap/about-regulation/about-the-asa-and-cap.html> accessed 14 June 2018

namely *The CAP Code: The UK Code of Non-broadcast Advertising, Sales Promotion and Direct Marketing & Sales Promotion*[430] and *The BCAP Code: The UK Code of Broadcast Advertising.*[431] The scope and contents of these two Codes are broadly similar to those of the codes of the ASAI and the BAI.

5.8.5.4) Sanctions for breaches of advertising and marketing communications codes of practice

Both the ASAI and the ASA have powers to sanction advertisers which they deem to be in breach of their respective codes of practice. They may, for example, request an advertiser to remove or amend an offending advertisement or marketing communications material. They may also request media members of their respective associations to refuse to continue publishing the offending material. However, they do not have any legal power to enforce financial sanctions on offenders and thus their sanctioning powers may be somewhat limited. Where a broadcasted advertisement breaches a BAI Code, Section 55 of the Broadcasting Authority Act 2009 provides for the imposition of a financial sanction on the offending broadcaster in cases of serious or repeated breaches.[432] In the United Kingdom, the ASA may refer a complaint regarding a code-offending, broadcasted advertisement to Ofcom, which has the legal power to impose a variety of sanctions upon a code-breaching broadcaster licensed by it. Among the sanctions available to Ofcom, it may issue a direction to a broadcaster to not re-broadcast an offending programme or advertisement or it may impose a financial penalty on the broadcaster.[433]

430 Advertising Standards Authority, *The CAP Code: The UK Code of Non-Broadcast Advertising and Direct Marketing & Sales Promotion* <www.asa.org.uk/uploads/assets/uploaded/243f1a5f-15f9-4cf8-9702519a67f9d770.pdf> accessed 14 June 2018

431 Advertising Standards Authority, *The BCAP Code: The UK Code of Broadcast Advertising* <www.asa.org.uk/uploads/assets/uploaded/d34f6bcf-d281-4eba-bcf0fa76297f5779.pdf> accessed 14 June 2018

432 Broadcasting Authority Act 2009, s 55
Note: Section 52 of the Act defines a "breach" as 'a serious or repeated failure by a broadcaster to comply with a requirement referred to in section 53(1)'. The requirements specified in Section 53(1) of the Act include a 'breach of a broadcasting code or rule'.

433 Ofcom, *Procedures for the Consideration of Statutory Sanctions in Breaches of Broadcast Licences*, para 1.14 <www.ofcom.org.uk/__data/assets/pdf_file/0030/71967/Procedures_for_consideration.pdf> accessed 14 June 2018
Note: The power under which Ofcom may impose a sanction on an offending broadcaster will depend upon the type of broadcasting licence held by the broadcaster. Ofcom is granted such power under a number of statutory and other provisions, such as Section 40(1) of the Broadcasting Act 1990, as amended, and Section 236(6) of the Communications Act 2003, as amended, and Clause 94(1) of *An Agreement Between Her Majesty's Secretary of State for Culture, Media and Sport and the British Broadcasting Corporation* (28 June 2006), as amended. <www.gov.uk/government/publications/agreement-between-her-majestys-secretary-of-state-for-culture-media-and-sport-and-the-bbc> accessed 14 June 2018

5.9) Brief conclusions

This chapter examined the range of restrictions which may be imposed on either the taking or the publication of photographs in the interests of protecting public order, the security and defence of the state and the administration of justice. It also discussed a miscellaneous range of statutory provisions under which restrictions may be imposed on photographers and photograph publishers. In addition, certain classes of photographers, principally press photographers and those involved in the production of images for use in advertisements and marketing communications materials, may have restrictions imposed on them as a consequence of ethical codes of behaviour. While ethical codes of behaviour contain restrictions on the activities of photographers and photograph publishers, in practical terms they do not constitute a major interference with the legal rights of photographers and photograph publishers who act responsibly towards others. A number of issues raised in the chapter which would benefit from the implementation of legislative changes are recommended in Chapter 6.

References

Books

Carolan E and O'Neill A, *Media Law in Ireland* (Bloomsbury Professional 2010)
Dodd M and Hanna M, *McNae's Essential Law for Journalists* (24th edn, Oxford University Press 2018)
Hogan G and Gerry Whyte G, *J.M. Kelly: The Irish Constitution* (4th edn, Lexis Nexis 2003)
McGonagle M, *Media Law* (2nd edn, Thompson Round Hall 2003)
McIntyre T, McMullan S and Ó Toghda S, *Criminal Law* (Round Hall 2012)
Michalos C, *The Law of Photography and Digital Images* (Sweet and Maxwell 2004)
Murphy Y and McGuinness D, *Journalists and the Law* (3rd edn, Round Hall 2011)
Orange G, *Police Powers in Ireland* (Bloomsbury 2014)
Quinn F, *Law for Journalists* (2nd edn, Pearson Longman 2009)
Warby M, Moreham N, Christie I and Tugendhat M, *Tugendhat and Christie, The Law of Privacy and the Media* (2nd edn, Oxford University Press 2011
Ward J, Daly M and Murphy B, *The Garda Síochána Guide* (7th edn, Blackhall 2008)

Newspaper articles and other online articles and press releases

—— 'Bus Driver Convicted Under Incitement to Hatred Act' *RTÉ News* (14 September 2000) <www.rte.ie/news/2000/0914/8916-hatred/> accessed 11 June 2018
—— 'First Prosecution for Flying Drones Sees Security Guard Fined £1,800' *ITV News* (15 September 2015) <www.itv.com/news/2015-09-15/first-prosecution-for-flying-drones-sees-security-guard-fined-1-800/> accessed 19 June 2018
—— 'High Court Fines Media €65K Over Contempt' *Irish Examiner* (Cork, 14 January 2009) <www.irishexaminer.com/ireland/icrime/high-court-fines-media-65k-over-contempt-81885.html> accessed 05 June 2018

—— 'Intimidation of Media at Polling Station "Affront to Democracy"' *National Union of Journalists* (Dublin, 26 February 2016) <www.nuj.org.uk/news/intimidation-of-media-at-polling-station-affront-to-democracy/> accessed 06 June 2018

—— 'Lillis Sentenced for Cawley Manslaughter' *RTÉ News* (08 February 2010) <www.rte.ie/news/2010/0205/127249-cawleyc/> accessed 10 June 2018

—— 'The Journalist's Right to Protect Sources: European Court of Human Rights Begs to Differ on Irish Times Case' *The Irish Times* (Dublin, 25 October 2014) <www.irishtimes.com/business/media-and-marketing/the-journalist-s-right-to-protect-sources-european-court-of-human-rights-begs-to-differ-on-irish-times-case-1.1976187>

—— 'Newspapers Found in "Technical Contempt of Court" in Ennis Case' *Irish Examiner* (Cork, 29 April 2011) <www.irishexaminer.com/breakingnews/ireland/newspapers-found-in-technical-contempt-of-court-in-ennis-case-503184.html> accessed 11 June 2018

—— 'NUJ Condemns Garda Order Against Photocall Ireland' *National Union of Journalists* (17 February 2015) <www.nuj.org.uk/news/nuj-condemns-garda-order-against-photocall-ireland/>

—— 'Ofcom Simplifies Advertising Regulation With "One-stop-shop" for Consumer Complaints' *Ofcom* (17 May 2004) <http://media.ofcom.org.uk/news/2004/ofcom-simplifies-advertising-regulation-with-one-stop-shop-for-consumer-complaints/>

—— 'Pipe Bomb Attack on Northern Ireland Photographer Mark Pearce's Home' *Belfast Telegraph* (Belfast, 14 December 2012) <www.belfasttelegraph.co.uk/news/northern-ireland/pipe-bomb-attack-on-northern-ireland-photographer-mark-pearces-home-29005170.html>

—— 'Press Photographers Must Hand Over Ardoyne Riot Pictures' *BBC News* (05 December 2012) <www.bbc.co.uk/news/uk-northern-ireland-20616107>

—— 'Special Constable David Baddiel Guilty of Possessing Extreme Pornography' *ITV News* (27 August 2015) <www.itv.com/news/london/2015-08-27/special-constable-david-baddiel-guilty-of-possessing-extreme-pornography/>

Akkoc R, 'Teenager Fined After Taking Selfie in Court' *The Telegraph* (London, 03 July 2014) <www.telegraph.co.uk/news/uknews/crime/10943704/Teenager-fined-after-taking-selfie-in-court.html>

Alleyne R, 'Police Apologise for Gay Jibe Against Photographer: A Schoolboy Photographer Has Been Paid Thousands of Pounds in Compensation By the Police After They Wrongfully Arrested Him Claiming He Was "Running Around Being Stupid and Gay"' *The Telegraph* (London, 12 December 2011)

Bowcott O, 'Peter Hain Contempt Charge Dropped' *The Guardian* (London, 17 May 2012) <www.guardian.co.uk/politics/2012/may/17/peter-hain-contempt-case-dropped>

Brady C, 'Garda Practice of Leaking Is Nasty and Vindictive' *The Irish Times* (Dublin, 11 February 2013) <www.irishtimes.com/debate/garda-practice-of-leaking-is-nasty-and-vindictive-1.1251417>

Cusack J and Ryan P, 'Minister to Review Law Allowing GSOC Snoop on Journalists: "More Garda Time Is Now Devoted to Trawling Journalists Phone Records than Investigating Any Single Case of Rape or Murder"' *Irish Independent* (Dublin, 17 January 2016) <www.independent.ie/irish-news/news/minister-to-review-law-allowing-gsoc-snoop-on-journalists-34370816.html>

Deegan G, 'Man in Custody After Filming His Uncle in Witness Box: Two Men Involved in Court Incident Had Been Previously of 2010 Manslaughter' *The Irish Times* (Dublin, 25 October 2018) <www.irishtimes.com/news/crime-and-law/courts/district-court/man-in-custody-after-filming-his-uncle-in-witness-box-1.2842778>

—— 'Suspended Sentence for "Snapchat" Photo of Judge: Eoin McDonnell Took Picture of Judge Fiona Lydon at Ennis District Court' *The Irish Times* (Dublin, 28 March 2018) <www.irishtimes.com/news/crime-and-law/courts/district-court/suspended-sentence-for-snapchat-photo-of-judge-1.3443351>

Doyle K, Phelan S and Murphy S, 'Investigation Launched Into GSOC Assess of Journalists' Phone Records' *Irish Independent* (Dublin, 19 January 2016) <www.independent.ie/irish-news/investigation-launched-into-gsoc-access-of-journalists-phone-records-34377459.html>

Gallagher C, 'Untangling the Vexed Question of Anonymity in Sex Cases' *The Irish Times* (Dublin, 03 March 2014) <www.irishtimes.com/news/crime-and-law/untangling-the-vexed-question-of-anonymity-in-sex-cases-1.1708235>

Griffin D, 'Garda Stops Journalists Photographing "Slab" Murphy at Polling Station: Associate of Murphy's Tells Photographers Not to Take Pictures Outside Co Louth School' *The Irish Times* (Dublin, 26 February 2016) <www.irishtimes.com/news/politics/garda-stops-journalists-photographing-slab-murphy-at-polling-station-1.2549485>

Hand G, 'Murdered Man's Brother Jailed for Contempt of Court' *Irish Examiner* (Cork, 20 July 2015) <www.irishexaminer.com/ireland/murdered-mans-brother-jailed-for-contempt-of-court-343423.html>

Healy A, 'Child Rape Videos Found After Car Theft' *Irish Examiner* (Cork, 26 March 2013) <www.irishexaminer.com/archives/2013/0326/world/child-rape-videos-found-after-car-theft-226484.html>

Lally C, '"Journalists" Texts Form Part of Garda Leak Inquiry: Messages and Call Details Accessed From Phone of Officer Who Is Under Investigation' *The Irish Times* (Dublin, 25 July 2015) <www.irishtimes.com/news/crime-and-law/journalists-texts-form-part-of-garda-leak-inquiry-1.2296482>

Lillington K, 'Journalists, This GSOC Story Isn't All About You, You Know: The Media Didn't Bother to Scrutinise What Was Happening When It Was About Everyone Else – This Story Is Still About Everyone Else' *The Irish Times* (Dublin, 21 January 2016) <www.irishtimes.com/business/technology/journalists-this-gsoc-story-isn-t-all-about-you-you-know-1.2504162>

McDonald H, 'Irish Journalists Accuse Police of "Stasi-like" Monitoring: Garda Síochána Alleged to Be Monitoring Phone Calls and Threatening Reporters With Arrest in Attempt to Reveal Sources' *The Guardian* (London, 11 May 2012) <www.guardian.co.uk/media/2012/may/11/irish-journalists-police-monitoring>

McLaughlin G, 'Garda Admits Passing Information to Criminals Known as "The Child" and "The Pharmacy"' *Irish Independent* (Dublin, 30 May, 2018) <www.independent.ie/irish-news/courts/garda-admits-passing-information-to-criminals-known-as-the-child-and-the-pharmacy-36960048.html>

Molloy D, 'Photography Agency: Gardaí Used Warrant to Seize Pictures of Water Protests' *Irish Examiner* (Cork, 16 February 2015) <www.irishexaminer.com/breakingnews/ireland/photography-agency-gardai-used-warrant-to-seize-pictures-of-water-protests-662466.html>

Murphy S, '"They Were Looking for Material Which We Had Not Put Out Into the Public Domain in Relation to a Protest": The Photocall Editor Discussed a Warrant

Issued By Gardaí for Photos' *Newstalk 106–108FM* (Dublin, 18 February 2015) <www.newstalk.com/They-were-looking-for-material-which-we-had-not-put-out-into-the-public-domain-in-relation-to-a-protest>

National Union of Journalists, 'NUJ Condemns Garda Order Against Photocall Ireland' (17 February 2015) <www.nuj.org.uk/news/nuj-condemns-garda-order-against-photocall-ireland/> accessed 06 June 2018

O'Keeffe A, 'Regency Murder Trial to Continue After Judges Give Green Light to Key Prosecution Evidence' *Irish Independent* (Dublin, 02 February, 2018) <www.independent.ie/irish-news/courts/regency-murder-trial-to-continue-after-judges-give-green-light-to-key-prosecution-evidence-36560506.html> accessed 15 June 2018

O'Mahony J, 'Man Cleared of Online Hatred Against Travellers' *Irish Examiner* (Cork, 01 October 2011) <www.irishexaminer.com/ireland/man-cleared-of-online-hatred-against-travellers-169325.html> accessed 12 June 2018

O'Sullivan K, 'Property Owners and Drone Users Vie for Rights to the Sky' *The Irish Times* (Dublin, 13 November 2015) <www.irishtimes.com/news/crime-and-law/who-owns-the-sky-property-owners-or-drone-users-1.2425692> accessed 15 June 2018

Parkinson J, 'Seven Months Just to Force the Police to Obey the Law' (14 May 2013) <www.jasonnparkinson.com/2013/05/14/seven-months-just-to-force-the-police-to-obey-the-law> accessed 08 June 2018

Phelan A, 'Gardaí Assaulted Man Who Filmed Their Raid' *Evening Herald* (Dublin, 07 December 2009) <www.herald.ie/news/gardai-assaulted-man-who-filmed-their-raid-1966471.html> accessed 12 June 2018

Phelan S, 'Gardaí Criticised for Hampering Photographers' *Irish Independent* (Dublin, 27 February 2016) <www.independent.ie/irish-news/news/garda-criticised-for-hampering-photographers-34490957.html> accessed 06 June 2018

Press Recognition Panel, 'PRP Board Recognises IMPRESS' <https://pressrecognitionpanel.org.uk/impress-2/> accessed 13 June 2018

Signal Magazine, 'Military Police at Government Buildings' (Dublin, 19 May 2005), vol Summer 2005, 49–51 <www.raco.ie/attachments/082_4_1_militarypolice.pdf> accessed 06 June 2018

Woulfe J, 'Man Cleared of Sex Assault: Anonymity Should Be a Right' *Irish Examiner* (Cork, 03 May 2013) <www.irishexaminer.com/ireland/man-cleared-of-sex-assault-anonymity-should-be-a-right-230214.html> accessed 23 June 2018

Official reports and publications

Bank of England, *Reproducing Banknotes: Guidelines* <www.bankofengland.co.uk/banknotes/Pages/reproducing_banknotes.aspx> accessed 11 June 2018

Civil Aviation Authority, *Unmanned Aircraft: Requirements for Operating in Airspace* <www.caa.co.uk/Commercial-Industry/Aircraft/Unmanned-aircraft/Unmanned-Aircraft/>

Council of Europe, Committee of Ministers, *Recommendation No. R (2000) 7 of the Committee of Ministers to Member States on the Right of Journalists Not to Disclose their Sources of Information* (Strasbourg, 08 March 2000) <www.coe.int/en/web/freedom-expression/committee-of-ministers-adopted-texts/-/asset_publisher/aDXmrol0vvsU/content/recommendation-no-r-2000-7-of-the-committee-of-

ministers-to-member-states-on-the-right-of-journalists-not-to-disclose-their-sources-of-information?inheritRedirect=false&desktop=true> accessed 06 June 2018

Data Protection Commission, *Guidance on the Use of Drones* <www.dataprotection.ie/docs/Guidance-on-the-use-of-Drone-Aircraft/1510.htm> accessed 11 June 2018

Department of Communications, Climate Action and Environment, *Report of the Internet Content Governance Advisory Group* (Dublin, May 2014) <www.dccae.gov.ie/en-ie/communications/publications/Documents/70/InternetContentGovernanceAdvisoryGroupReport.pdf> accessed 12 June 2018

Department of Defence and Defence Forces, *Annual Report 2016* (Newbridge, 2016), 49 <www.military.ie/fileadmin/user_upload/images/Info_Centre/documents/Annual_Reports/Annual_Report_2016__English_.pdf> accessed 06 June 2018

Department for Digital, Culture, Media and Sport, *Final Royal Charter on Self-regulation of the Press* (London, 30 October 2013) <www.gov.uk/government/publications/leveson-report-cross-party-royal-charter> accessed 13 June 2018

Department of Justice and Equality, *General Scheme Communications (Retention of Data) Bill 2017* (Dublin, 03 October 2017) <http://justice.ie/en/JELR/General_Scheme_-_Communications_(Retention_of_Data)_Bill.pdf/Files/General_Scheme_-_Communications_(Retention_of_Data)_Bill.pdf> accessed 08 June 2018

—— *Review of the Law on the Retention of and Access to Communications Data* (April 2017) (Dublin, 03 October 2017) <http://justice.ie/en/JELR/Review_of_the_Law_on_Retention_of_and_Access_to_Communications_Data.pdf/Files/Review_of_the_Law_on_Retention_of_and_Access_to_Communications_Data.pdf> accessed 08 June 2018

European Central Bank, *Decision of the European Central Bank of 20 March 2003 on the Denominations, Specifications, Reproduction, Exchange and Withdrawal of Euro Banknotes (ECB/2003/4) (2003/206/EC)*, Official Journal of the European Union, [2003] OJ L78/16 <www.ecb.int/ecb/legal/pdf/l_07820030325en00160019.pdf> accessed 11 June 2018

Her Majesty's Stationary Office, *Leveson Inquiry – Report into the Culture, Practices and Ethics of the Press* (29 November 2012) <www.official-documents.gov.uk/document/hc1213/hc07/0780/0780.asp> accessed 13 June 2018

Houses of the Oireachtas Joint Committee on Transport and Communications, *Report: Addressing the Growth of Social Media and Tackling Cyberbullying* (31TC 007) (Dublin, July 2013) <https://webarchive.oireachtas.ie/parliament/media/report-on-social-media-july-2013-website.pdf> accessed 12 June 2018

Independent Reviewer of Terrorism Legislation, *The Terrorism Acts in 2016: Report of the Independent Reviewer of Terrorism Legislation on the Operation of the Terrorism Acts 2000 and 2006* (January, 2018) <https://terrorismlegislationreviewer.independent.gov.uk/wp-content/uploads/2018/01/Terrorism-Acts-in-2016.pdf> accessed 26 June 2018

Interception of Communications Commissioner's Office, *IOCCO Inquiry Into the Use of Chapter 2 of Part 1 of the Regulation of Investigatory Powers Act (RIPA) to Identify Journalistic Sources* (February 2015) <http://webarchive.nationalarchives.gov.uk/20170914105829/www.iocco-uk.info/sections.asp?sectionID=1&type=top> accessed 07 June 2018

Irish Aviation Authority, *Drone Registration* <www.iaa.ie/general-aviation/drones/drone-registration> accessed 11 June 2018

Law Commission, *Report on Contempt of Court: Scandalising the Court* (Law Com No 335) (London 2012) <www.lawcom.gov.uk/wp-content/uploads/2015/06/lc335_scandalising_the_court.pdf> accessed 11 June 2018

Law Reform Commission, *Issues Paper on Cyber-Crime Affecting Personal Safety, Privacy and Reputation Including Cyber-Bullying* (LRC IP 6–2014) (Dublin 2014) <www.lawreform.ie/_fileupload/Issues%20Papers/ip6Cybercrime.pdf> accessed 12 June 2018

—— *Report on Contempt of Court* (LRC 46–1994) (Dublin 1994) <www.lawreform.ie/_fileupload/Reports/rContempt.pdf> accessed 14 June 2018

—— *Report on Harmful Communications and Digital Safety* (LRC 116–2016) (Dublin 2016) <https://publications.lawreform.ie/Portal/External/en-GB/RecordView/Index/37669> accessed 12 June 2018

—— *Report on Inchoate Offences* (LRC 99–2010) (Dublin 2010) <www.lawreform.ie/_fileupload/Reports/r99InchoateOffences.pdf> accessed 11 June 2018

Metropolitan Police, *Photography Advice* <www.met.police.uk/advice/advice-and-information/ph/photography-advice/> accessed 09 June 2018

National Parks and Wildlife Service, *Licence to Photograph or Film a Protected Wild Animal or Bird* <www.npws.ie/licences/disturbance/photograph-or-film-protected-wild-animal-or-bird> accessed 11 June 2018

Press Recognition Panel, *Annual Report on the Recognition System 2017* <https://pressrecognitionpanel.org.uk/annual-report-on-the-recognition-system-2017/> accessed 13 June 2018

United Kingdom Home Office, *Acquisition and Disclosure of Communications Data: Code of Practice* (March 2015) <https://assets.publishing.service.gov.uk/government/uploads/system/uploads/attachment_data/file/426248/Acquisition_and_Disclosure_of_Communications_Data_Code_of_Practice_March_2015.pdf> accessed 06 June 2018

Codes of behavioural standards

Advertising Standards Authority, *The BCAP Code: The UK Code of Broadcast Advertising* <www.asa.org.uk/uploads/assets/uploaded/d34f6bcf-d281-4eba-bcf0fa76297f5779.pdf> accessed 14 June 2018

—— *The CAP Code: The UK Code of Non-broadcast Advertising and Direct Marketing & Sales Promotion* <www.asa.org.uk/uploads/assets/uploaded/243f1a5f-15f9-4cf8-9702519a67f9d770.pdf> accessed 14 June 2018

Advertising Standards Authority of Ireland, *Code of Standards for Advertising and Marketing Communications in Ireland* (7th edn) <www.asai.ie/asaicode/> accessed 14 June 2018

Broadcasting Authority of Ireland, *Code of Programme Standards* <www.bai.ie/en/codes-standards/#al-block-4> accessed 11 June 2018

—— *Codes and Standards* <www.bai.ie/en/codes-standards/> accessed 14 June 2018

—— *General Commercial Communications Code* <www.bai.ie/en/codes-standards/#al-block-2> accessed 14 June 2018

Dóchas, *Code of Conduct on Images and Messages* <https://dochas.ie/sites/default/files/Images_and_Messages_0.pdf> accessed 13 June 2018

GAA, *Code of Behaviour (Underage)* <http://res.cloudinary.com/dvrbaruzq/image/upload/uspspssby7jneiyjgd0b.pdf> accessed 13 June 2018

Independent Press Standards Organisation, *Editors' Code of Practice* <www.ipso.co.uk/editors-code-of-practice/> accessed 14 June 2018

IMPRESS, *The IMPRESS Standards Code* <www.impress.press/downloads/file/code/the-impress-standards-code.pdf> accessed 13 June 2018

Irish Professional Photographers' & Videographers' Association, *IPPVA Best Business Practices* <www.irishphotographers.com/downloads.php?section=bestpractice> accessed 14 June 2018

—— *IPPVA Code of Ethics* <www.irishphotographers.com/downloads.php?section=ethics> accessed 14 June 2018

National Union of Journalists, *NUJ Code of Conduct* <www.nuj.org.uk/about/nuj-code/> accessed 14 June 2018

Ofcom, *The Ofcom Broadcasting Code (with the Cross-Promotion Code and the On-Demand Programme Services Rules)* <www.ofcom.org.uk/__data/assets/pdf_file/0005/100103/broadcast-code-april-2017.pdf> accessed 14 June 2018

—— *Procedures for the Consideration of Statutory Sanctions in Breaches of Broadcast Licences* <www.ofcom.org.uk/__data/assets/pdf_file/0030/71967/Procedures_for_consideration.pdf> accessed 14 June 2018

Press Council of Ireland, *Code of Practice* <www.presscouncil.ie/press-council-of-ireland-1/code-of-practice-> accessed 13 June 2018

Websites of interest

Advertising Standards Authority, *About the ASA* and CAP <www.asa.org.uk/about-asa-and-cap/about-regulation/about-the-asa-and-cap.html> accessed 14 June 2018

—— *About Regulation* <www.asa.org.uk/about-asa-and-cap/about-regulation.html> accessed 14 June 2018

Advertising Standards Authority of Ireland, *About ASAI* <www.asai.ie/about-us/> accessed 14 June 2018

—— *Complaints Bulletins* <www.asai.ie/complaints-bulletins/> accessed 14 June 2018

—— *Make a Complaint* <www.asai.ie/make-a-complaint/> accessed 14 June 2018

Broadcasting Authority of Ireland, *About Us* <www.bai.ie/en/about-us/#al-block-1> accessed 14 June 2018

—— *How to Make a Complaint* <www.bai.ie/en/viewers-listeners/complaints/> accessed 14 June 2018

Committee of Advertising Practice, *About CAP* <www.asa.org.uk/about-asa-and-cap/about-regulation/about-the-asa-and-cap.html> accessed 14 June 2018

Defence Forces Ireland, Naval Service, *The Fleet* <www.military.ie/naval-service/fleet/> accessed 21 June 2018

IMPRESS, *About Us* <www.impress.press/about-us/> accessed 14 June 2018

—— *Regulated Publications* <www.impress.press/complaints/regulated-publishers.html> accessed 13 June 2018

Independent Press Standards Organisation, *Make a Complaint* <www.ipso.co.uk/IPSO/makeacomplaint/makingacomplaint.html> accessed 14 June 2018

—— *Rulings* <www.ipso.co.uk/rulings-and-resolution-statements/> accessed 14 June 2018

National Museum of Ireland, *Image Safe Handbook* <www.museum.ie/National-MuseumIreland/media/Corporate-Information/Policies%20and%20Guidelines/IMAGE_SAFE_HANDBOOK.pdf> accessed 13 June 2018

National Union of Journalists, *About, Welcome to the NUJ* <www.nuj.org.uk/about/> accessed 14 June 2018

—— *Contacts* <www.nuj.org.uk/contacts/> accessed 14 June 2018

Ofcom, *About Ofcom: What Is Ofcom?* <http://ask.ofcom.org.uk/help/ofcom/ofcomdef> accessed 14 June 2018

Press Council of Ireland, *About Us* <www.presscouncil.ie/about-us> accessed 13 June 2018

Press Recognition Panel <http://pressrecognitionpanel.org.uk> accessed 13 June 2018

The Arts Council, *Guidelines for Taking and Using Images of Children and Young People in the Arts Sector* <www.artscouncil.ie/uploadedFiles/Guidelines.pdf> accessed 13 June 2018

6 Overall conclusions and recommendations

6.1) Introduction

Overall, the legal rights of photographers and photograph publishers in Ireland to take and/or publish photographs are appropriate and, in the main, they are adequate. However, a number of weaknesses exist particularly in respect of the protection and enforcement of photographers' and photograph publishers' rights under copyright law. Recommendations to address these weaknesses are suggested later. Photographers' and photograph publishers' rights may be restricted in support of the private rights of individuals. However, the latter's rights are also subject to number of weaknesses and the author makes a number of recommendations in order to strengthen such rights. Legal restrictions may also be imposed on photographers and photograph publishers by the state in order to fulfil its legal duty to protect public order, the security and defence of the state and the administration of justice. The state may also impose restrictions on public morality grounds. In addition, voluntary non-binding codes of behaviour may result in the imposition of restrictions on specific categories of photographers and/or on photograph publishers. The author offers some recommendations in respect of these types of restrictions.

6.2) Photographers' and photograph publishers' rights under copyright law

In Ireland, photographers' rights under copyright law are broad in scope and, in general terms, the terms of protection offered to photographers are good. However, the exercise by photographers of these rights and their attainment of the protection afforded to them in their copyrighted works under copyright law is under attack by copyright infringers and vested interest groups. Under the Constitution of Ireland, the state has a duty to protect citizens' property rights from unjust attack. Copyright is a property right and the state needs to adopt a proactive approach to the enforcement of copyright infringement legislation. EU Directives concerning copyright refer to copyright holders' existing rights. These existing rights (the acts reserved to a copyright holder), which are legally recognised property rights, are being slowly eroded through an expansion of the types of permitted exceptions for the use of copyrighted works and also through the introduction of legislation dealing with orphaned works and extended collective licensing. At a national level, there has been little, if any, public debate on copyright and the use of copyrighted works. There has been absolutely no public call for legislation to permit the use of orphaned works. The latter has resulted from the calls at a European level from the vested interest groups covered by the Orphan Works Directive. If a similar erosion of existing rights in respect of other types of property, particularly real property, were to be proposed with an opt-out rather than an opt-in system being put in place, it is likely that there would be a great deal of public debate on, and opposition to, such a proposal. If both the Irish state and the European Union are really concerned about protecting the interests of copyright holders, an opt-in rather than an opt-out copyright licensing system covering the use and/or the commercial and/or non-commercial exploitation of both copyrighted works should be created and enforced. Such a new opt-in system could be a licence to use as opposed to the current system of exceptions to copyright holders' existing rights under the CRRA and the provisions of the Orphan Works and the Collective Management Directives. Also, both the EU and the Irish state should review the current permitted use exceptions in the legislation in respect of all copyrighted works with the view to converting them into licensed uses of works under which the copyright holder would be remunerated at market rates. The previously suggested reversal at both EU and national levels would greatly assist copyright holders to both protect their existing rights and to financially benefit from their creations.

One of their biggest problems facing professional photographers on a daily basis is the unauthorised use of their copyrighted works by third parties – particularly online. Also, the stripping-out of rights management information from photographers' published images' metadata files and the subsequent unauthorised reuse of such works is widespread and out of control. This is both a national and an international problem and online copyright infringement does not respect national borders. There is an urgent need to update and enforce national and EU copyright legislation to tackle these problems. A great deal of copyright infringement occurs on social media websites. Websites that promote and/or facilitate the display and sharing of copyright infringing photographs should be held legally accountable for the uploading to and display by users of their websites of copyright infringing photographs. Such websites should be legally required to offer and use a "nopin" meta tag in order to prevent the unauthorised copying of copyright protected images from websites to social media websites. The removal and/or alteration of rights management information from a photograph without its author's prior approval should be made a strict liability offence. The Copyright and Other Intellectual Property Law Provisions Bill 2018 currently before the Oireachtas proposes to rename the Controller of the Irish Patents Office as the Controller of Intellectual Property and the Irish Patents Office as the Intellectual Property Office of Ireland. The Oireachtas should give serious consideration to granting prosecutorial powers to this Office in respect of copyright infringement offences and thus assist copyright holders in tackling infringements of the copyright in their works. A cost-effective mechanism under which copyright holders may access the courts in order to enforce their rights under copyright is needed. Although the previously mentioned 2018 Bill does not propose to implement such a mechanism through the Small Claims Court, the Oireachtas should follow the lead from the United Kingdom and establish a low-cost specialist intellectual property court within the Irish Courts.

The forced transfer, via contract terms, of photographers' copyright and moral rights in images created by them for clients should be legally prohibited. The assignment of these rights should only be legally permitted on a completely voluntary basis and should not be a condition of obtaining a contract for photographic services.

The duration of the moral right against false attribution in photographs should be made of an equal duration to that of the other moral rights specified under the CRRA, namely the lifetime of the work's author and for 70 years after his/her death.

Where a website infringes the copyright in a photograph by illegally reproducing it, that website's domain name registrar (i.e. the person/organisation that registered the website's domain name) should be legally required to supply, upon a direct request, the website owner's full contact details to the image's copyright owner. A statutory measure should be introduced which would require all website owners and operators to publish a complete imprint (website owner's and operator's names, a valid postal address (non-post box) and a valid email address on their websites). At present, it can be extremely difficult to track-down the actual owner(s) and operator(s) of websites, who may or may not be the same person(s).

6.3) Legal restrictions on photographers resulting from the protection and enforcement of the personal rights of others

Right to privacy

There is no general statutory right to privacy either online or offline and the Data Protection Acts 1988–2018 have become surrogate privacy statutes. The number of Internet users is vast. A great part of the problem in relation to breaches of privacy online is the mindset of people using the Internet and social media platforms. They believe that they can do or say anything online as they please without any legal consequences. The courts have had to adapt existing common law and statutory legislation when considering cases concerning the breach of privacy online. The Oireachtas should consider the introduction of a general statutory right to privacy. If such a statutory right were to be created, it should include a public interest exemption for journalistic purposes.

Model, product and property releases

At present, model, product and property releases are not a legal requirement for the commercial publications of photographs. Release forms should be made a statutory requirement for the commercial publication, either offline or online, of images that easily enable the identification of any individual(s) featured in them. A similar legal requirement should pertain to the publication of photographs of products and privately owned properties. However, an exemption to a requirement for release forms should be specified in respect of photographs published for "journalistic purposes in the public interest". The possession of a signed model release form should be usable in a defence to a claim of either defamation or misrepresentation and if its wording covers the use in question, it should defeat such a claim. Due to the wide-ranging methods through which photographs are published, varying from printed newspaper and magazine advertisements through online publication to other uses such as on-vehicle promotional signage, it would impractical to create and impose standard, statutorily expressed wordings of such release forms. However, any such legislation could contain "model" wordings.

Personal image right and right of publicity

In view of the previous proposal concerning model releases, neither a personal image right nor a right of publicity should be created. Were a personal image right or a right of publicity to be made a statutory legal right, the publication of photographs featuring individuals for journalistic purposes in the public interest would, in effect, grind to a halt. For example, the publication of photographs featuring crowd scenes or street scenes would become an impossibility, as the obtaining of clearances from all of the individuals featured in such images would not be feasible. In any event, it is most likely that such clearances would not be forthcoming.

Right not to be harassed

Section 10(1) of the of the Non-Fatal Offences Against the Persons Act 1997, which concerns the harassment of individuals, makes use of the word "persistently" in relation to the following, watching, pestering, besetting or communicating with individuals. Consequently, the Section does not cover a once-off incidence. Any review of Section 10 of the Act should pay particular attention to the use of this word. Also, the existing offence of harassment should be widened to specifically take account of harassment via the Internet and social media sites. Statutorily defined offences concerning up-skirt and down-blouse photography and the disclosure or publication of private, sexual photographs of individual(s) without their consent with the intention of causing distress to the individual(s) featured in the images (colloquially termed "revenge porn") should be enacted. Also, the publication of images of individuals without their permission on pornographic websites or with captions of a highly sexual or pornographic nature on social media sites with the intention of causing distress to the individuals featured in the published images should be made an offence. An offence of stalking should be created in Ireland.

Voyeurism

It would also be appropriate for an offence of voyeurism to be introduced in Ireland rather than using the above-mentioned S.10 of the Act, the wording of which is not appropriate for the prosecution of cases of voyeurism. Depending upon the circumstances of each case, an act of voyeurism may or may not constitute a S.10 offence of harassment (as previously defined above) and for a S.10 offence of harassment to be established the activity complained of must, under S.10(1), be persistent – on more than one occasion.

The Internet and personal rights

To protect the personal rights of individuals, such as the right to privacy, the right to a good name and the right against harassment, consideration should be given at both national and EU levels to the introduction of a prima facie statutory liability and duty of care for website operators (including social media website operators) and search engines in relation of all material published on their websites and search engines. Also, there is a need for a review of the legal policy on the permitting of anonymous postings, including images, on the Internet and of the liability of websites that permit anonymous postings on their websites.

6.4) Legal restrictions on photographers and photograph publishers in support of public interests, through statutory provisions, on public morality grounds and under ethical codes of behaviour

In fulfilling its legal duty to protect public order, the security and defence of the state and the administration of justice, the state may impose legal restrictions on photographers and photograph publishers. Restrictions may also be imposed on them by the state on public morality grounds. In addition, certain classes of photographers, principally press photographers and those involved in the production of images for use in advertisements and marketing communications materials, may have restrictions imposed on them as a consequence of ethical codes of behaviour. However, these latter types of restrictions do not overly interfere with or cause a major impediment to the legal rights of photographers and photograph publishers, who act responsibly towards others. The author raised a number of issues in Chapter 5 which would benefit from the implementation of amendments to statutory law, as recommended later.

Interception of postal packets and communications

The Interception of Postal Packets and Telecommunications Messages (Regulation) Act 1993, as amended, and the Communications (Retention of Data) Act 2011 respectively provide for the authorisation to intercept either a postal packet or a telecommunications message and to obtain access to an individual's communications data. At present, an authorisation under the 1993 Act may be granted by the Minister for Justice, while an authorisation under the 2011 Act may be granted by a Chief Superintendent of An Garda Síochána. It would be more appropriate that such authorisations would not be respectively granted by a politician or a garda, but by a judge, who would be impartial and independent of any investigation for which an authorisation was being sought. Also, where a judge would be considering an application for access to a journalist's postal packets, telecommunications messages or communications data it should be a requirement for the party seeking such access to prove to the satisfaction of the judge that there is an overriding public interest in being granted such access for a specific and stated legal purpose and not as a fishing exercise.

Surveillance

In addition to the previously mentioned statutory provisions, the Criminal Justice (Surveillance) Act 2009, as amended, provides for a judge of the District Court to grant on an ex-parte basis and otherwise than in public an authorisation for surveillance to a superior officer of either An Garda Síochána, the Defence Forces or the Revenue Commissioners or a member of the Garda Síochána Ombudsman Commission other than its chairperson for specified purposes including the investigation or prevention of arrestable offences, the security of the State and revenue offences. Furthermore, Section 7 of the Act provides for the issuing of an authorisation (for a short-term duration as specified under S.7 of the Act) by a superior officer rather than a judge in the case of an application of an urgent nature. An overriding public interest test should apply in respect of the granting of an authorisation under this Act for the surveillance of a journalist and such an authorisation should only be granted by a senior judge.

Protection of journalists' sources of information

Journalists, including press photographers, should be granted a statutory right to refuse to either disclose or confirm their sources of information in court cases in order that they may protect both their sources and their rights of freedom of expression and of communication. The only exception to such a legal right should be where a High Court judge is satisfied on the evidence presented to him that an overriding public interest exists.

Production orders

Under Section 15 of the Criminal Justice Act 2011, a member of An Garda Síochána may apply to the District Court for a production order in respect of a photographer's images. Section 15(2)(a) of the Act just refers to 'particular documents or documents of a particular description'. There is no requirement under S.15 that specific images must be stated in the order application. The Act does not specify any required level of evidential value in respect of material sought under a S.15 production order. Under S.15(2)(c) of the Act, the material sought does not need to be of "substantial value" either to an investigation or as evidence. Furthermore, it is not a requirement under S.15(2)(c) that only specified documents, for example specific photographic images, would be covered by a S.15 order. Section15(2)(c) only requires that the documents or "some" of the documents sought "may" constitute evidence. Such an investigative or evidential value level is extremely low. Coupled with the wide document description permitted on an order application, S.15 of the Act would facilitate An Garda Síochána by granting it access to photographic images which most likely would be of no investigative or evidential value to it and for An Garda Síochána to just undertake fishing expeditions at the expense of photographers. The statutory provisions contained in Section 15 of the Act should be amended by requiring an applicant for a production order to specify the specific images being sought and the specific purpose for which they are being sought. Also, the use of production orders to facilitate fishing expeditions should be prohibited. Production orders should only be granted by a judge if he/she is satisfied that the specific images sought under the production order application are of a demonstrated, high investigative or evidential value.

Photography advice guidelines for members of An Garda Síochána

Interactions of a confrontational nature between members of An Garda Síochána and photographers do not occur often. However, so as to minimise the possibility of members of An Garda Síochána unlawfully attempting to either prevent photographers from taking photographs in public places or to seize cameras/film or to erase images stored on a photographer's camera, it would be beneficial if An Garda Síochána were to publish a "photography advice" guideline for its members. Such a guideline should also be made easily available for viewing by members of the public.

Photography at courts and contempt of court

The restriction on the taking of photographs within court buildings in Ireland is currently governed by the Rules of Court. Save for Section 10 of the Criminal Law Act 1976, which concerns the possession of photographs of the exterior or interior of prisons, Garda stations and courthouses by specified classes of individuals, such as a person in lawful custody, there is no legal prohibition on the taking of photographs outside court buildings. The Contempt of Court Bill 2017 proposes that the use of recording equipment (audio or visual) to record court proceedings and/or the publication of such a recording without the permission of a court would constitute a contempt of court. Ideally, the taking of photographs both inside and outside court buildings should be governed by clearly worded statutory provisions. Were such statutory provisions to be enacted by the Oireachtas, consideration should also be given to the issue of the taking and publication of photographs of defendants in criminal cases entering or leaving court buildings. Such provisions could also contain "rules of engagement" outside of court buildings between photographers and parties to criminal and civil court cases, so that they would not feel that they are being overly harassed by photographers while either entering or leaving court buildings. Also, there should be a statutory prohibition on the publication of images which show defendants in criminal cases wearing handcuffs, as a published image of a handcuffed defendant has the potential to influence a viewer's opinion that that individual is dangerous, aggressive and/or guilty of a serious criminal offence, whereas such may not be the reality.

Anonymity of a person accused of a sexual assault offence

At present, a person accused of a sexual assault offence does not have a right to pre-conviction anonymity, whereas a complainant of such an offence has a right of anonymity. The wording of S.8 of the Criminal Law (Rape) Act 1981, as amended, should be amended by substituting the words "sexual assault offence" for "rape offence" so as to afford a person accused of a sexual assault offence with a right to pre-conviction anonymity.

Incitement to hatred

Any proposed reform of the Prohibition of Incitement to Hatred Act 1989 should consider the inclusion of a provision covering incitement to hatred against "individuals" as opposed to the current position whereby "hatred" is defined by S.2 of the Act as being hatred against a "group" of persons. In addition, the Communications Regulation (Amendment) Act 2007 inserted a new S.13(1) in the Post Office (Amendment) Act 1951 concerning offences committed through the use of telephones. It has been suggested that S.13(1) of the Act does not take account of the use of modern telecommunications and computer equipment to publish online materials, including photographs, which are designed to incite hatred. Any amendment to S.13 should take account of the use of such technology.

Index

For Product Safety Concerns and Information please contact our EU
representative GPSR@taylorandfrancis.com
Taylor & Francis Verlag GmbH, Kaufingerstraße 24, 80331 München, Germany

www.ingramcontent.com/pod-product-compliance
Lightning Source LLC
LaVergne TN
LVHW052308200926
848481LV00002B/503
* 9 7 8 0 3 6 7 5 8 4 1 1 5 *